After starting his career as a schoolteacher, Ralph decided to change the direction of his life in order to explore the world of business and finance. Over the next two and a half decades, he was involved in a number of large property development and social care ventures throughout South Yorkshire. This activity was eventually overlapped with the trading of stocks, derivatives, and foreign exchange. During this time, he was on hand to witness three of the 'boom and bust' scenarios depicted in this book, through their formative phase, at their climax, and in their devastating aftermath. Ralph's decision to start writing *Bubbles, Crashes and Financial Disasters,* in fact emanated from these memories.

To Margo, Gabriella, Brett, and Nick.

Ralph Lyons

BUBBLES, CRASHES AND FINANCIAL DISASTERS

AUSTIN MACAULEY PUBLISHERS™

LONDON * CAMBRIDGE * NEW YORK * SHARJAH

A CIP catalogue record for this title is available from the British Library.

ISBN 9781035836116 (Paperback)
ISBN 9781035836123 (Hardback)
ISBN 9781035836130 (ePub e-book)

www.austinmacauley.com

First Published 2024
Austin Macauley Publishers Ltd®
1 Canada Square
Canary Wharf
London
E14 5AA

In particular, I would like to thank Richard Smith for his noteworthy role in this project. His unique ability to generate meaningful illustrations from flimsy ideas never ceased to amaze me.

Table of Contents

Introduction

Bubbles, Crashes and Financial Disasters

To those who believe they have an edge.

Over one particular weekend there had been a heavy storm, and when the manager opened the doors to the business on that grim Monday morning, his eyes were immediately drawn to a widening shaft of light connecting one part of the roof to the soaking-wet floor beneath his feet. Glancing at the grommet of blue sky at the top of the shaft, he hoped that good fortune was smiling down on him and that the storm had now passed. But his wishful thinking lasted only seconds before another menacing front of grey sky moved overhead, and rain started pouring in.

Still looking upwards, the manager was stirred from his thoughts when another member of his staff shook him by the arm and informed him that a sizeable part of the roof was sitting on top of a delivery van in the neighbour's car park. Clearly, something needed to be done to save the day.

After working from early morning into the late afternoon for two gruelling weeks, a young contractor by the name of Shaun completed the repair to the roof. Dave, the extremely grateful owner of the business, eventually handed the roofer £2,000 in the local public house, which had a pool table.

Now we had a deadly combination—booze, a big wad of cash—and a pool table.

Shaun's nervous twitch of excitement always tended to precede what would inevitably turn out to be an overwhelming urge, and it's very difficult to control human nature when a 'slam-dunk' opportunity seems to be in the offing. The two proponents were now circling the playing surface, staring defiantly at each other and tenderly caressing the base with their fingertips. An occasional ball would be plucked from the green and then elaborately glossed with overdoses of affection. The message was very simple – "I've got this."

The homely atmosphere of this lovely public house now set the scene for the most hare-brained gambling spree one could possibly imagine.

Shaun was not only good at his trade, he was a good pool player too, but he didn't know that Dave was much better and also liked to play for money. For over two hours, game after game followed, and when Shaun had handed back most of the £2,000—his wages for two whole weeks—Dave asked him to quit, but he refused point blank.

The anxiety was plain to see in Shaun's face, but there was bravado in his body language, and it was clear that he would not give up. For the next and final game, Dave offered to play him with just one hand. Predictably, Shaun hardly potted a ball, and the two thousand pounds ended up where it had started.

Realising what he had just done in a foolish rush of blood, Shaun slumped into a chair, speechless. He was now wishing in earnest that he had said no instead of accepting the challenge – but there is a happy ending to this true story. Dave handed back the £2,000 to this gullible young man and suggested, in a language I am unable to repeat in this text, that in a couple of hours of recklessness, he had simply thrown away a sum of money that had taken him two whole weeks to make.

Unlike this very generous outcome, speculation in games of chance or 'get rich quick schemes' tend to be very unforgiving, as you can lose your hard-earned stake or worse. However, it is possible to make a difference by having a carefully thought-out game plan, which is presided over by discipline, a good sense of timing and a keen eye. These precepts usually place speculators in a far better position to spot schemes where the odds are massively against them, thereby leaving hare-brained propositions to the bold and the credulous. In the long run, high probability strategies tend to produce fairly reliable results for disciplined, well-financed speculators.

On the other hand, ardent gamblers are often tempted to say yes to certain proposals purely out of impulse, as we have just seen with the young contractor. He was simply working in the dark, as he didn't know anything about his opponent, which soon revealed that this was not a good time to start potting balls for the money. With the odds stacked in such a way, it would have been far better if he had walked away before the game had started, as this would have re-established control over his emotions, as well as his finances.

Yes, all of this sounds simple enough, but when increasing numbers of people start to believe that an easy money-making opportunity is in the offing, the gambling ethos that stirred Shaun can become contagious. After all, when it comes to rationality, human nature all too often has a devilish tendency to conjure up certain distractions.

At various stages during the boom-and-bust cycles depicted in this book, we shall see how traditional values and beliefs were simply trampled in a rush to 'get rich quick.' In most of these events, this kind of impulsive behaviour took hold when masses of hapless souls made the fateful decision to follow the crowd, many of whom used borrowed money, whilst others used their savings and worldly possessions as collateral.

But there should also be a stark realisation that some of the biggest players around, such as the financial institutions and seasoned professional traders, were caught-up in the crashes that followed the boom. Those fortunate enough to turn a profit will probably have done so more by luck than good judgement, excellent timing, or because they had an edge, as they knew something that no one else did.

We shall see how unseemly behaviour claimed many gullible victims. Tragically, even those who chose to sit on the fence would have been unwittingly tangled in the wreckage because when an economy goes into recession, everyone is swept along by a rising tide of lost souls.

But what about those who were responsible for financial regulation?

With so many moving parts, bubbles are regarded by those in authority as intractable events that make an unwelcome appearance during the economic cycle. (*) But this powerful phenomenon deserves far more respect. Whenever large economic bubbles have manifested, they have all too often left in their wake financial hardship and widespread social suffering, followed by years of depression. When we consider that these incidents tend to reoccur every decade or so, it remains a mystery why those with regulatory powers do not seek enduring economic remedies instead of relying on what is usually belated intervention.

So, perhaps there is an acceptance now that the boom-and-bust scenario is simply a self-fulfilling prophecy, and this revolving door of economic events is randomly pushed by the unstoppable forces of human nature. However, there is another interesting standpoint. Some feel that large economic bubbles are non-organic as they are caused by large-scale feats of financial engineering – and this is certainly a possibility we shall explore.

As well as various boom and bust scenarios, we will also be taking a look at the financial disasters created by the likes of William Franklin Miller, Charles Ponzi, Bernard Madoff, and Nick Leeson, all of whom tried to shoot for the stars, but landed in big trouble.

The First Speculative Bubble?

There seems to be a very curious tendency for colourful historical events to reorganise themselves following years of enthusiastic coverage. All too often, the past thereby fades into legend.

Many contemporary historians now believe that some of the early accounts of Tulip Mania were based more on romantic myth or propaganda rather than hard facts. So, was this really the first speculative bubble ever recorded, or did self-interest or capricious interpretation turn the tulip craze into an over-inflated affair?

It is widely believed that large-scale trading of rare tulip bulbs originated in the 17th century Dutch Republic but, contrary to this belief, the seeds for Tulip Mania had been planted quite some time earlier in another part of the world.

However, when these beautiful flowers and their bulbs were eventually transported, on the wave, into the Dutch trading centre, people in the northern provinces of Europe quickly became smitten. The story has it that local merchants and parvenus soon recognised that the aesthetic value placed on tulips could provide an opportunity to make money. The craze for owning and trading the bulbs from this goddess of all flowers escalated rapidly, eventually sweeping through all reaches of the cosmopolitan Dutch society.

Although Tulip Mania has often been described as an early speculative bubble, let us pinch ourselves so we don't lose sight of the fact that we are talking about widespread speculation on a species of flower and its bulbs. It would seem far more comfortable to describe tulips as a delicate horticultural treasure rather than a speculative commodity. This was a view shared by many purists and botanists back in the day, but the 'get rich quick mob' disagreed. The gambling ethos at this time would seem even more remarkable when we compare tulips, for example, to more substantial commodities like gold, copper, silver, coffee or crude oil, all of which are now traded heavily in vibrant global markets.

A 'speculative bubble' today might also be referred to as a market bubble, a financial bubble, an economic bubble, or a market boom. These terms are frequently used interchangeably throughout the chapters that follow, as they describe the first phase of what is often referred to as 'the boom-and-bust scenario'. When taken at face value, the events in the 17th century Dutch Republic would appear to align with some of the terms that describe a modern-day bubble, with the exception of 'economic bubble' and 'financial bubble', which have much wider connotations than a fashionable trend in the tulip trade.

A common instrument used today in order to trade commodities like gold, copper, silver, coffee, or crude oil is a futures contract. However, during Tulip Mania, people were said to have used what were, essentially, very early versions of these contracts, in which the sums of money verbally agreed for the purchase of tulip bulbs would be paid at a pre-set future date. However, we need to place the efficacy of these contractual arrangements into their true light. In the latter stages of the tulip boom, many of those who owed money simply disappeared when their obligations fell due, and it is a popular view that this exacerbated the already delicate financial situation within the Dutch tulip market. However, there is probably a sense of irony in the fact that 'owing money' and 'disappearance' frequently go hand in glove in the financial episodes we shall look at throughout this book.

Following a crescendo of trading over several months, there was a rapid spike in the price of tulip bulbs, which suddenly stalled. This was a sign that the market was exhausted, and this left a great many speculators holding unwanted bulbs. It is perhaps worth noting, if only for the benefit of future chapters, that when a market spikes in price, it does not always signal that there is going to be a market crash. For example, whilst I was working on this book, oil prices spiked in excess of 20% on Monday 16th September 2019, following drone attacks during the previous Saturday on Saudi's Abqaiq processing site and the Khurais oil field. This is said to be the most sudden rise in three decades when the price of Brent Crude topped $70.13 a barrel at one point. However, this was simply an abrupt market reaction to an unexpected incident, and the price of Brent Crude soon returned to $58 a barrel.

In contrast to Brent Crude, it is significant that the price of tulip bulbs was in a prolonged upward trend when the spike occurred. This turned out to be a pre-exhaustion flurry (*) signalling that the price of tulip bulbs was about to tumble.

In contrast to most of the events described in this book, it is also important to recognise the fact that certain booms are not financially destructive as, in time, they are absorbed by the economic cycle. (*) For example, the boom in the use of the Internet during the 1990s has since had a profound impact on all of our lives. It sometimes goes unnoticed therefore when booms take place in the new forms of equipment, know-how and services that increasingly assist the social infrastructure of modern-day. It is quite easy to observe that, because of the constant updating of scores of household products, which are then filtered into our daily routine, mini booms are more or less designed to occur one after the other. In very important sectors such as housing, the car industry and the financial markets, booms may also occur – without attendant problems.

Chapter 1
Tulip Mania

After tulips were discovered in the Tien Shan Mountains of central Asia growing wild, they were first said to have been cultivated in the Ottoman Empire, where they were embraced by many as a status symbol. By the 15th century, Sultan Mehmed 2nd had so many flowers in his gardens that they were attended by almost 1000 gardeners and staff. Although the precise date is not known, tulip bulbs were shipped into Europe from Constantinople sometime around 1550, but carriage on a much smaller scale, possibly by curious botanists, might well have occurred before this time.

In recognition of the flower's vibrance, tulip cultivation developed rapidly throughout seven northern territories which, between 1581 and 1795, became known as the Dutch Republic. With ever-growing popularity, this beautiful flower was much celebrated in music, paintings, and festivals, as well as adorning many colourful decorative works and designs.

Under the influence of Napoleon, the country was annexed as a province of France between 1806 and 1810 and was called the Kingdom of Holland. After the defeat of Napoleon in 1815, a much expanded 'United Kingdom of the Netherlands' was created, encompassing Belgium and Luxembourg, with Monarchs from the House of Orange. Following a period of unrest, Belgium and Luxembourg managed to secure their independence from the Kingdom in 1839 and less than a decade later, it became a parliamentary democracy with a constitutional monarch.

It is officially known today as the Kingdom of the Netherlands, where the tulip is still lauded as the goddess of all flowers, and around nine billion bulbs are produced annually. In spring, tulips bloom across the entire nation and this lovely flower gives many areas of the Netherlands picture-postcard tranquillity.

In recognition of their beauty, the Dutch-born Carolus Clusius, a 16th-century botanist and passionate horticulturist, is reported to have written one of the first books on tulips in 1592. He became the director of a mesmerising tulip garden in Leiden, thereby creating extensive interest in these beautiful flowers.

As a result of their almost irresistible allure, there is said to have been widespread theft of flowers and bulbs from the gardens he had so lovingly cultivated. The era of the tulip in Holland had now dawned in what became known as the 'Golden Age', and this glorious period of Dutch history reached its zenith in the 17th century.

During this time, the Dutch gained independence from Spain after a grinding eighty-year war but, in spite of this, its provinces still managed to emerge as the principal trading centre of northern Europe, overtaking Flanders in this respect. As well as the tulip trade, this era saw rapid developments in industry and commerce, the fine arts, sciences, and culture, all of which fostered a vibrant cosmopolitan society. During the 17th and 18th centuries, the Dutch were looked upon as the wealthiest and most advanced nation in the whole of Europe. This period of the nation's prosperity was aptly described in Simon Schama's well-known book, 'An Embarrassment of Riches'.

During this epoch, however, pamphleteers were often employed to hand out material that was based on frivolous interpretation of current affairs, rather than actual facts, and the tulip era was a perfect set-up. Therefore, it would seem quite possible that the authors of some of these curious articles were the progenitors of many of the fanciful tales and tall stories that abound today.

A common theme in these stories was that the whole of Dutch society was so infatuated by this beautiful flower, and the bulbs from which it propagated, that an unstoppable bubble developed – and the term 'Tulip Mania' was thereby coined. There are yarns about speculators completely taking leave of their senses and exchanging farms and large estates for rare tulip bulbs. One poor soul is said to have been imprisoned after mistaking a tulip bulb for an onion, and then devouring it. It has even been reported that the collapse of the Tulip Trade precipitated devastating problems in the Dutch stock market (1) but, as we shall see later in this chapter, the following view seems far more plausible:

When the tulip bubble finally burst, the vestiges of Tulip Mania were quickly blown away by the economic might of the Dutch 'Golden Age'.

Therefore, in some of the modern accounts of the tulip era, it is hardly surprising that any number of colourful tales have been replicated but, in spite of this, history's integrity has not been totally lost. Three books in particular have delivered what are considered to be definitive statements. An early account of this period was provided by the British journalist Charles Mackay in *Extraordinary Popular Delusions and the Madness of Crowds* in 1841. Anne Goldgar's book of 2006, *Tulipmania*, provides a very well-documented contemporary view of this period; and Lorraine Boisseneault's book in 2017, *The Tulip Folly*, is equally acclaimed.

The introductory passage to this chapter would certainly embrace the idea that Tulip Mania was no more than an extravagant fad that provided the public with an ephemeral money-making opportunity – but is this view too harsh?

Let's pick-up the trail once again in 15th century Constantinople where, upon beholding the every-day scene, it was plain to see that the tulip was much loved by all in this part of the world. Tulips could be seen in vases, window boxes, small and large courtyard gardens, luxurious estates fastidiously attended by trusty servants and staff, botanical gardens in public areas, and also in decorative art and design. Indeed, tulips were a prominent feature of everyday Turkish life. In recognition of this, many of the wealthier families kept lavish tulip gardens as a sign of their status, and there was a widespread competition to own the most opulent flower display. This love of flowers was admirably described by a 17th-century traveller who also reported that 'Constantinople had eighty shops selling flower bulbs, which were supplied by three hundred growers'. (2)

The marketplace scene also reflected these sentiments. On display were many different species of flowers, plants and herbs, where collectors, traders, and merchants frantically but effortlessly tried to find common ground with buyers. Haggling over goods in the vibrant bazaar was a significant part of every-day life in Constantinople. Collectors at this time were not only concerned with tulips, but a plethora of things – antiquities, ornate objects, the exotic, rarities or, indeed, anything that caught the imagination. Dealers were always on hand to satisfy this curiosity, and they were aware that certain wealthy and middle-class people would compete for the ownership of rare tulip bulbs.

Sometimes the appeal of certain tulip specimens, and the rivalry for their ownership, was so strong that they changed hands for exorbitant sums. By 1725, the desire for this goddess of all flowers reached epic proportions when the decision had to be taken to cap prices. It is reported that one notable specimen was even given the name of the 'bankrupter'. (3)

It seems ironic that the 'Bankrupter' was highly sought after!

In spite of the omnipresence of tulips in this part of the world, it would not be safe to simply assume that the whole of Turkish society had been gripped by a wild speculative bubble at this time. Here, the love of tulips was a cultural construct where, apart from being smitten by the aesthetics of this beautiful flower, people simply wanted to be part of the vibrant trend, instead of envious onlookers.

The Dutch had started to receive shipments of tulip bulbs from Asia in the 16th century, and it wasn't long before similar sentiments permeated the whole of northern Europe (4) where tulips suddenly became the new news. Jehan Somer from Middleburg in the Dutch Republic, for one, had visited Constantinople in the 1590s, and his imagination had already been stretched beyond that of just an enthusiastic lover of flowers. He had been taken aback by the prices at which certain specimens were changing hands – and these same prices were carried, on the wave, into Dutch society.

Once again, tulips initially became the plaything of the rich who were willing and able to meet asking prices. This was nothing out of the ordinary as, elsewhere in Europe, most emerging prodigies were often able to command high prices – for a time at least. As another example, seashells were much lauded around this time, as were paintings or art, and it was quite normal for wealthy people to adorn their living quarters with these much sought-after collectibles. Indeed, this scene was reminiscent of the one that existed within the wealthier reaches of the Turkish population.

On a far more modest scale, however, certain people in the Dutch Republic had turned to collecting not only for the thrill of possession, but in the belief that it would enhance their social status. In the first half of the 17th century, in fact, around two-thirds of the population owned, on average, between five and eleven paintings of some kind. At this time, still-life paintings featuring tulips and shells were very popular, as well as portraits of certain tulips in full bloom. (5) No doubt, the popularity of this beautiful flower was on the increase in what was the formative part of the trend – as tulips had now started to adorn many aspects of the Dutch way of life.

At least in the beginning, connoisseurs and collectors participated as a hobby and for the love of what they did, with a willingness to meet current prices. Rarity defined a standard of beauty that led to the high prices that were often paid. (6) Naturally, merchants wanted to turn a profit on their trade but for those who held more puritanical values, there was no place in their lives for this kind of profiteering. In an attempt to highlight this, Jehan Somer corresponded with Carolus Clusius several times, who is said to have been extremely upset that the price of rare tulip bulbs was so high. Clusius simply believed that their real value was vested in the infectious beauty of the flowers they produced.

Indeed, both Clusius and Somer were driven by nothing more than honest enthusiasm for botanical matters, and their particular devotion to this lovely flower. The idea of tulip bulbs being used as a speculative commodity was alien to them. But these same feelings were not shared elsewhere in the wealthy cosmopolitan society of the day, and the nascent tulip trade eventually paved the way for speculation. Art and tulips became inextricably linked, and this was a time when certain shady individuals would represent themselves as connoisseurs of tulips and other things. More often than not, they were much lesser beings.

Those who grew and traded tulips were known as *'bloemisten'* and the province of Holland in particular was very active, but Amsterdam itself was the real focal point. At this time, in fact, the northern territories were regarded as the centre for collectibles, and this helped commercial enterprise to develop rapidly in this part of the Republic. In fact, it was the promising outlook in this region that drew increasing numbers from the general population, thereby setting the scene for the crude speculation that Clusius and Somer were referring to.

Quite often, commercial transactions between individuals during the tulip era were based on verbal agreements, which ultimately required a great deal of good faith. This was no doubt the ethos behind the transactions in the beginning. However, agreements by word of mouth left much of what had been agreed at the time, open debate later. With arrangements such as these, the potential for problems was enormous.

For most of the year, tulips spent their time outside in the garden, so when commercial transactions were negotiated, the bulbs were often in the ground. As a result, sales were agreed in the form of verbal futures contracts. This meant that an agreed price would be paid, at a future date, upon the delivery of the specified goods on that same date. The subjectivity surrounding the future outcome with tulip bulbs, and whether they would meet the purchaser's expectations, was not only flirting with wishful thinking, it was close to commercial folly. Who would decide if the product was in line with a verbal agreement made months earlier – the buyer or the seller? How could either party argue their case with any conviction, as the passage of time no doubt clouded the original terms of business?

This lack of transparency automatically created confusion and disputes. At the same time, it provided a contractual escape mechanism—an excuse—if the buyer decided that he wanted a way out. Of course, as tulip mania escalated, unseemly behaviour increased with it. Unfortunately, this was compounded by a number of other issues.

As we already know, many people had paintings, art and other collectibles which, as well as money, were used as fungibles during the tulip trade. The cash amount was the easy part, but when collectibles were being used to make up the balance of a transaction, or the whole of it, this now meant that the expectations of the tulip seller had to be met. Once again, this provided a great deal of leeway for sellers to perform some sort of manoeuvre, particularly if other purchasers appeared with more cash, or more appealing paintings or collectibles. But it became much worse.

Some tulip bulbs could change hands several times before they flowered, creating a price hike with each link in the chain. From its source, it has been reported that one bulb fetched f600 and tripled in price in just three weeks. (7) It is in relation to these commercial chains that we must consider the precarious contractual arrangements described earlier. By selling the same object to several different people in rapid succession—if there was a problem at any juncture in the chain—this had the potential to impact everyone else.

With so many possibilities for conflict already in the melting pot, it was hardly surprising that, amid the confusion, stolen goods often changed hands for large amounts of cash, as certain individuals would pay well over the odds for rare specimens.

As the fervour of tulip trading escalated, commercial brinkmanship often turned into outright deceit when opportunists stepped into the frame with very little intention of settling their commitments. They had entered the game looking to make a quick profit and it wasn't difficult in the euphoric atmosphere that existed at the height of tulip mania. The records show that Cornelius Guldewagen of Harlem was involved in a very large transaction for no less than 1,300 tulip bulbs in 1637. (8) This happened to be at the very peak of tulip mania, so was Guldewagen trying to off-load an impending liability? Or was he chasing an elusive profit at a very late stage?

Sometimes, gentlemanly behaviour gave way to less honourable tendencies!

It was during this phase that there was a quest for the sublime – a tulip that would transcend all others. Some, therefore, believed that there were ways in which man could use his craft in order to influence the process of nature. (9) In a bout of seminal lunacy, however, it was suggested that if two different bulbs were cut in half and stuck together, they could be grown as one flower – presumably, one that surpassed the beauty of all others. In spite of this, it is reported that Clusius did have some success growing tulip seeds. But, no doubt, this feat was devoted to botany and not to the propagation of commercial enterprise and speculation.

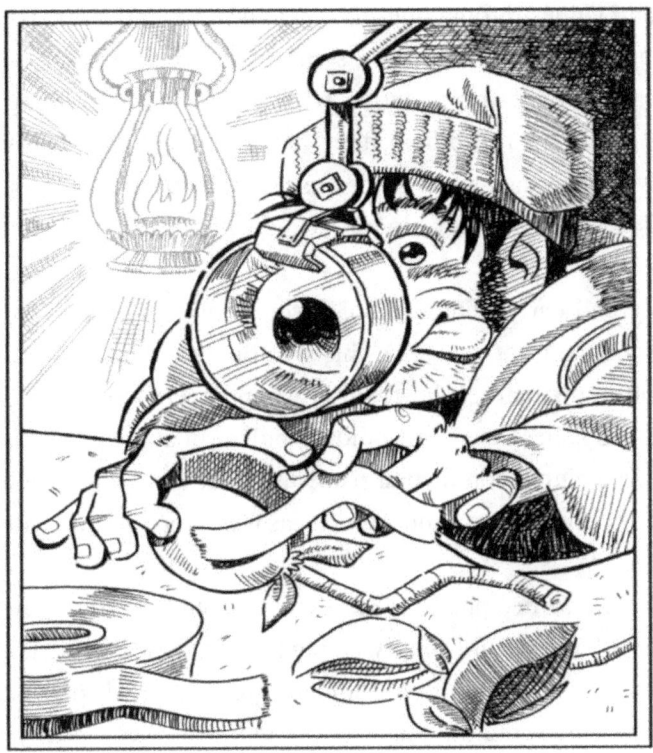

In this case, two halves would never make one!

It would be wrong to suggest that the whole of Dutch society was involved in tulip mania, but most of those involved were connected in some way or other, and the province of Holland was the centre of influence. (10) It is reported that, during the early part of tulip trading, wealthy people and connoisseurs set about their business with good intentions and gentlemanly conduct. At this time, the trading arrangements were often successful. But when this select club was infiltrated by the mob, and grew bigger, the self-control of its members, as well as ethical standards, suffered enormously. As a result of the very many disagreements between tulip buyers and sellers, some took their claims to court to seek redress, and this happened both before and after the end of tulip mania.

(11) Most of these affairs were not only complicated, they were also quite acrimonious when one party or the other felt that they had been cheated. Some dishonest speculators, in fact, fled the scene owing money.

Against this daunting backcloth, certain others within the trade itself now sensed that the market had been corrupted, not only by some of the high prices but by the people involved. After all, it was the people themselves who had influenced tulip values throughout this era, and some of the prices paid were far too extravagant. Irrespective of price, some speculators therefore woke up from their irrationality and came to terms with the fact that, although tulips had mesmerising beauty in full bloom, they had an ephemeral lifespan and value. The longevity of paintings, in which it was possible to portray the same theme— the aesthetics of tulips in full bloom—would have perhaps provided a better commercial option.

In January and early February 1637, some tulips bulbs saw a much larger increase in price than normal. (12) This was the pre-exhaustion flurry, and the bottom fell out of the market shortly after when buyers would no longer pay the asking price, and sellers were left holding bulbs. In any event, this now closed many of the convoluted contractual pathways. But these same pathways would never have led to common ground anyway, as they were littered with treacherous obstacles.

It is now time to decipher the messages woven into this rich tapestry and decide if Tulip Mania should simply be regarded as a well-known and colourful episode of Dutch history during the Golden Age – or a real speculative bubble.

There were bankruptcies, but 'Tulip Mania did not destroy the wealthy cosmopolitan economy of the time or even the livelihoods of most participants. (13) It might not have been a financial crisis, but it was a social and cultural one'. The disturbance it caused, in fact, lasted well after February 1637 when certain people still involved themselves in the trading of tulips, and residual disputes still found their way into court. However, discerning historians have now recognised that the crash that followed Tulip Mania was only in the price of bulbs, which caused sundry collateral damage.

In 1602, the Amsterdam Stock Exchange was established by the Dutch East India Company. One particular source indicates that the demise of Tulip Mania precipitated a crash in stock prices, but this is not mentioned in any of the other material that has been researched, and neither have any references to banking problems been found. (14) Nevertheless, market prices are usually sensitive to breaking news, so it is possible that the demise of Tulip Mania caused, at least, a wobble in stock prices. However, it is believed that any claims that there was a full-blown crash in the Amsterdam Stock Exchange, or beyond, are capricious.

It does seem, however, that the exuberance of the day did lead to tulip bulb consumption – with oil and vinegar. But there is very little information beyond this regarding the culinary excellence of such an unusual combination.

Reliable records indicating that houses and large estates were exchanged for rare bulbs have not been located, although it could have been possible at the height of the euphoria – yet, unlikely. In fact, this has often been a popular rumour during conversations about the Dutch tulip craze in more recent times. Certain notable transactions, however, did reach the equivalent price of some of the smaller abodes, and it has already been indicated that one bulb reached 600 guilders after changing hands three times.

In order to provide some idea of perspective, Rembrandt is said to have purchased a large home in the centre of Amsterdam in 1639 for 13,000 guilders and a farm was purchased for 1,060 guilders around this same time. Although tulip mania is known to have generated some fanciful tales, the notion that rare tulip bulbs were being exchanged for property at these sort of price levels might be stretching the imagination a little too far.

In 1623, the plague broke out in Amsterdam, killing over 16,000 local people, which was around 16% of the population. This outbreak lasted for around three years and, over the next decade, further bouts occurred. Following the very many deaths from the plague, it is said that a great deal of inheritance money was made available, and this fuelled tulip speculation to new levels.

"Yes, it's the castle I want – and your clothes."

A surfeit of money at this stage would have only exacerbated what was already a delicate situation, thereby accelerating the end of Tulip Mania.

In the two chapters that follow, we will understand why the bursting of the tulip bubble could never be compared to the economic crashes that followed the South Sea Bubble of 1720, or the Mississippi Scheme of the same era. In the aftermath of these events, shockwaves could be felt for years to come. In spite of this, Tulip Mania is still regarded as an excellent example of a speculative bubble, so let us try to figure out why. Let's start by comparing the events during the 17th century with certain circumstances we might encounter today.

It is a fairly common pass-time for gamblers from all over the nation to visit betting shops on a regular basis – many of whom also lose money on a regular basis. However, the cumulative effect of this sits neatly within the economic cycle and is not regarded as a financial disaster, nor a bubble, or worthy of special commentary. Again, the daily churning of the financial markets creates peaks and troughs of varying scale, and these price movements are everyday events in which money is won and lost, yet, this is more or less accepted as 'routine'.

In Tulip Mania, there were similar peaks and troughs in which money was won and lost on a regular basis but, instead of this being routine, people throughout the Dutch Republic and Europe paid special attention. As more people became involved, tulip speculation proliferated over quite a long period of time, and this attracted still more attention.

Gentlemen, I'm all in!

Ultimately, the heady enthusiasm developed into a gambling spree on rare tulip bulbs, and this created what may now be regarded as one of the earliest bubbles ever recorded – but hold on a moment! This was not followed by a devastating collapse in the Dutch Republic's economy, yet people everywhere have taken notice ever since.

Tulip Mania has probably continued to live on in people's minds simply because it was novel. This was a speculative bubble in which tulips were the delicate yet exquisite commodity, and this was prodigious in itself.

Central to the folly of tulip speculation was the fact that far too many people failed to relate the high market price of the bulbs to their real value. Since most speculators were oblivious to the importance of 'value', others saw this lack of awareness as an opportunity.

In reality, gullible people were paying a very high price to indulge in an improbable cause—even make-belief—and this is what made Tulip Mania amazing.

Innovative Ideas

During the early eighteenth century, the South Sea Company and John Law (1671–1729) dominated the headlines in Europe. Even though they were never connected in an official sense, both were inextricably linked contemporaries, frequently crossing each other's path in their illustrious search for wealth and primacy.

Law's intrepid spirit was based on an unshakable belief that his innovative ideas could bring untold riches and prosperity to his nation. But the mercurial Law had become a fugitive who was prepared to swear allegiance to almost any nation that might have the fortitude to embrace him. By the most remarkable quirk of fate, and auspicious timing, it was France who adopted this patriotic Scotsman as their messiah, soon reaping the benefit of his ingenuity and enviable commercial intellect.

Across the channel, England was dealing with a far more complex kettle of fish. There was a very uncertain political scene, enormous national debt, self-serving politicians, capricious royals – and then there was the South Sea Company and its directors, their furtive agents, emissaries and hangers-on.

As for the multitudes of restless souls in Paris and London, they were out to make money—plain and simple—so this was an era of heavy gambling in which recklessness and cupidity went hand in glove. It is hardly surprising, therefore, that there were speculative bubbles on both sides of the channel at this time.

At the turn of the 18th century, there had been a rapid increase in the formation of new 'joint stock companies' (*) and this became a prelude to the most remarkable period of speculation England had ever seen. This new and powerful trend carried many of its followers on a journey in which ethical and legal boundaries were flagrantly breached. Some of those involved simply regarded the bubble as a glorious opportunity to elevate their status, whilst the rich recognised that it could make them even richer. With the flock pre-occupied by wealth creation, gullibility became an unmistakeable feature of every-day life.

Indeed, this was a time when stock market gamblers were winning and losing staggering sums.

Meanwhile, over in Europe, the presence of the charming Edinburgh-born John Law had captured the imagination of the whole of French society. Notably, this included the Regent, the duke of Orleans, during the reign of young Louie XV. Law was appointed Controller General of French Finances by the duke and, believing that the wealth of any nation was dependent on trade, reminiscent of the South Sea Company, he had become the instigator of big, bold plans. As well as setting up the Mississippi Scheme, he was responsible for establishing Banque Generale, which was regarded as the first central bank of France. (1) Around 75% of its capital consisted of government bills and government-accepted notes, thereby denoting the state's involvement in an establishment that was falsely claimed to be private.

In both London and Paris, as always, the rumour mill was keen to serve and, throughout this era, it ground out many flagrant untruths. The likes of Daniel Defoe and Johnathan Swift were on hand to manipulate the sentiment of the nation, and over-enthusiastic speculators continued to step back from reality and harness themselves to hare-brained schemes. One was audaciously called *'A company for carrying out an undertaking of great advantage'*—but no one had a clue what it was—including the scoundrel who set-up the scam! At £2 a share, there were said to have been throngs of hopeful souls surrounding the company's office in Cornhill. The day after the funds from the first share subscription had been received, the founder simply fled London and headed for the continent.

In a similar fashion to Tulip Mania in the previous century, speculators had now fallen under the spell of self-delusion and, in both Paris and London, this was not a time to take leave of one's senses. In fact, bold talk of enterprising trading missions and the quest for untold riches had heralded Law's Mississippi Scheme in France. On the back of a similar ethos in England, the South Sea Bill was passed. By 1717, however, the rich rewards that had been envisaged failed to materialise – so the emphasis slowly but surely shifted. With rumour and lies, the share price of these two talisman organisations continued to climb and, with it, money poured into their coffers.

Any modicum of good faith that may have been intended at the outset of this 18th-century trend, was overtaken by brinkmanship and unseemly behaviour followed eventually, and inevitably, by insider-dealing, corruption and fraud.

The perpetrators were often those in high office or those who had assumed responsible positions within the proliferation of companies that were formed during this eventful period.

Indeed, the wildly over-optimistic mood of these two nations at this time had simply left the door wide open for opportunists and purveyors of folly to step in. However, the population in England had received an early warning of such perils by certain political figures, who repeatedly expressed their concerns about the unfettered speculation, but this had little or no effect. In a very sinister fashion, other members of parliament were not only playing both ends against the middle—much worse—they were taking bribes.

Chapter 2
The South Sea Bubble

One of the many business proposals during this era came from the directors of Puckles Machine Company who wanted to set-up an enterprise which would *'revolutionise the art of war by the production of square cannon fodder'.*

The nation was, indeed, riding a very high tide of optimism during the late 1700s. So much so that this was a time when hare-brained schemes could be turned into 'solid gold assets' – according to the villains who believed they could rip every page out of the rule book.

Towards the end of the first decade of the 18th century, England's national debt was estimated to be somewhere between 9 to 10 million pounds, a great deal of which had been incurred in order to support the efforts of the army and navy during the country's long-standing hostilities with France and Spain. (2) On the political front, this caused a great deal of concern and it was widely believed that the Whig Party's efforts to mitigate this enormous burden had been too sedentary. Therefore, with political change in the national interest, the Tories managed to wrest power from the Whig Party in 1710.

A very ambitious and daring era of commerce was now ushered in, with Robert Harley as the new Chancellor of the Exchequer. Harley was a man who did not believe that the ills of mankind could be resolved by war. This was a time, in fact, when the government's coffers had been ravaged by such conflict and, as a result of the puerile accounting of the Whig government, monetary control had become almost non-existent. The use of hazel-wood tally sticks was, perhaps, a good measure of the party's incompetence, as well as an unreliable method of keeping records. Sticks were notched on two sides and then split down the middle – the depositor retaining one strip and the treasury the other. (3)

Under this regime, the different government departments were able to arrange their own loans, and this led to terrible confusion as well as the misuse of funds. Once in office, Harley therefore decided to set-up the National Debt Investigation Committee, which was led by John Aislabie, two auditing officers and Harley himself. Its purpose was to unravel, and then scrutinise, the Whig management of the Exchequer.

The Chancellor found that the Exchequer had the paltry sum of 5,000 pounds in its kitty when he took office. England was literally at the fiscal brink with the national debt now confirmed by his Investigation Committee at nine million pounds. (4) The biggest worry was that the nation did not have any realistic strategy to pay it off. Harley immediately understood that only very drastic measures, or ground-breaking creativity, could avert an impending disaster. As always, funds were required in order to maintain the efficiency of England's 'military machine', as well as support national governance.

The monopoly of the Bank of England had been established in an Act of 1697, and this institution was dominated by powerful Whig politicians when Harley took office as Chancellor in 1710. One such figure was the influential

Robert Walpole, who was at the hub of the fierce opposition between the Whigs and the Tories. To counter this, Harley decided to seek counsel from John Blunt of the up-and-coming Sword Blade Company, which was also an unofficial bank. This company was well-known for its temerity, in fact, certain politicians felt that it was too ambitious for its own good and believed that its integrity was questionable. However, one way or another, this company was determined to cut its two biggest rivals down to size – the Bank of England and the East India company. These were two of England's largest private institutions, so this kind of competitive spirit impressed Harley, who was in need of a source of inspiration. This was a cue for the charismatic and single-minded Blunt, who was never afraid to proffer bold ideas.

Secretary Blunt was confident in the knowledge that he had very powerful colleagues at the Sword Blade Company. There was goldsmith Elias Turner as chairman, Jacob Sawbridge as his deputy, and the man whose family had held the Leominster seat in parliament for over 100 years, the privileged George Caswall. It was the acumen of this quartet, in fact, that would shortly be called upon to direct the operations of a truly titanic venture – into the south seas.

Meanwhile, Blunt suggested that the national lottery should be re-modelled in order to provide the financial respite that the exchequer needed. However, the Bank of England had been operating the state lottery on behalf of the Whig government and, by the time Harley took office, this had been far less than successful. Harley now played his master-card and asked Blunt if he would take charge of marketing to re-open this event. Blunt agreed straight away because he knew it was timely – a lottery would take advantage of the nation's gambling addiction. In London in particular, there was a propensity for its half a million inhabitants to speculate on almost anything and everything. Bouts of cock-fighting, bare-knuckle boxing and sword fighting could often be seen; not least of all, the buying and selling of shares was high on the agenda. So, after Blunt had changed the terms and conditions, and increased the prize money, lottery tickets were sold out in a matter of days. As a result, this became the first national lottery in England that was truly successful.

But, cunningly, this was Blunt's precursor to a more grandiose lottery, in which the prizes were bigger still. However, the tickets were now placed on offer at 100 pounds. (5) It was referred to as 'The Two Million Adventure', but there was a sting! The prize winners were to be paid out over a number of years in the form of fixed annuities of 6% – and the government would be able to hold the prize money in its coffers. Later, this turned out to be a regrettable decision as these annual payments severely burdened the government's finances. However, for some of the administrators of the lottery, the expenses and commissions were enormous and this had simply been an irresistible opportunity to make a quick buck. By a stroke of good fortune, or the very heavy purchase of tickets, a vast proportion of the winners came from the wealthier reaches of society; however, the two national lotteries are said to have raised 3.5 million and were held for several years thereafter. (6)

In the meantime, the 'stock-jobbers' (*) and 'monied men' continued to conduct their affairs in the tea-rooms, small offices and dens in and around Exchange Alley. This had been a tradition throughout the last decade of the seventeenth century, and still formed a significant part of everyday life. This area was a retreat where men could meet to drink an array of beverages in the privacy of select social gatherings, always convened to discuss the most pressing matter of the day – making money. Whispers floated gently through the meeting rooms like fumes from the tobacco whilst the value of certain shares hung precariously in the balance.

Pleased with the financial respite he had received from the proceeds of the national lottery, Harley decided that he should now seek measures which would enable him to clear the national debt of 9 million pounds. He had inherited this position because previous governments had been pleased to borrow money from almost any available source. At unavoidable financial cost, and the fateful cost of human endeavours, the wars that had been fought across Europe on a regular basis had left sovereign states with no choice but to defend their interests vigorously, or run the risk of them being usurped. Sources of funding often included goldsmiths, the ruling classes, institutions and the moneyed men of the day, who were usually opportunistic and hard-nosed businessmen. Harley, therefore, consulted the man of the moment, the shrewd John Blunt, who was always quick to offer help, provided there was a chance that he could also help himself. Once more, Blunt could feel the gusts of good fortune blowing his way, and also in the direction of the Sword Blade Company and his colleagues.

Indeed, benevolence was not something that was readily understood in the unforgiving streets of London, unless there was an opportunity—an opening – a prize—or even a morsel somewhere in the offing.

"Gentlemen, the Sword-Blade will now run the South Sea Company!"

Harley was very much in need of a streak of good luck, or some sort of ground-breaking idea. Influenced by whispers and popular opinions from the likes of Defoe, he looked towards Spain and its rich flow of goods from overseas trade. He therefore floated the idea of the South Sea Company, which would be an overseas trading enterprise similar to that of England's greatest rival, and Blunt was soon on board. On 2nd May 1711, Harley therefore announced the new company's formation, and said that it would not only be engaged in trade in the south seas, but its aim was also to take-over the floating portion of the national debt of £9 million. (7) Disguised by the grandeur of this noble affair, in fact, was the desire to create a rival to the Bank of England and the East India Company. Blunt, no doubt, had exerted his influence.

Harley's plan was simply to ask the government's creditors to exchange the money they were owed, for shares in the new company. By any stretch of the imagination, this was an ambitious proposition. In many cases, the creditors would actually be exchanging debentures (*) for shares with an artificial value. The shares were backed by a project that would have to negotiate very perilous waters before it could fulfil its promises. But the deal was cleverly gift-wrapped, and it would prove to have an irresistible allure for those who were inclined to have a punt, as the government's propaganda machine had done its work. The company would enjoy exclusive rights to trade in the south seas from early August 1711.

It was now necessary to attract the attention of the wider public, so the nascent South Sea Company was quick to float its grand ideas. Speculators were thereby captivated by visions of the enormous wealth and prosperity that would be generated by enterprising missions to the east coast of South America. In reality, such visions were merely delusions as there was a stubborn and treacherous obstacle. Most of the strategic ports in the south seas were controlled by Spain – with whom England was at war. In fact, misleading reports had purposely been placed in the public domain, indicating that the King of Spain, Philip V, was willing to allow access to important ports in Chili and Peru. It was suggested that Philip had extended this kind offer in the interests of free trade. Once again, this placed the South Sea Company firmly in the public's spotlight, and its share value thereby started to show promising signs. When people got wind of this, the nation's gambling ethos soon clicked into gear.

Of course, Philip had no intention of allowing English ships into the Spanish-controlled ports of South America. Harley was therefore desperate to negotiate peace with France and Spain, but his pleas to the House were fiercely resisted by Robert Walpole and the Whigs. They opposed the peace initiative in full knowledge that the south sea enterprise might founder as a result – and the Whig-dominated Bank of England would thereby maintain its primacy. (8)

Having located discrepancies in the army's accounts, both the duke of Marlborough and Walpole were now charged with corruption and sent to the tower. (9) The army's campaign against France was about to begin, and the commander of the allied forces in Flanders, the duke of Ormond, received a dispatch from his government in England. In one of the most ignoble days in the nation's history, the duke had received a restraining order which prevented his army from fighting. Despite diplomatic communications to confirm the dispatch, the French army still attacked the retreating allied forces. Later in 1711, Harley addressed his South Sea Company Directors but, in a bout of desperation, failed to disclose that he had abandoned his peace initiative.

Early in January 1712, the directors pressed Harley for a huge flotilla, attended by 4,000 soldiers, to carry goods and merchandise into the south seas. (10) By September that year, 1200 tons of cargo lay rotting in warehouses in and around London. Harley, now the Earl of Oxford, was a notable absentee at board meetings thereafter and, on 25th July 1714, Queen Anne was forced to dismiss Harley. Just seven days later, Queen Anne passed away and the Hanoverian, George 1st, became King of Great Britain. (11) This also brought a stark change in sentiment. The new King clearly favoured the Whigs to the Tories so, in an ironic twist of fate, Walpole was able to start a new political career, whilst Harley was now impeached for high treason. Sadly, Harley was never able to get rid of the national debt, in spite of his elaborate schemes.

In March of 2013, a peace deal was finally struck in Utrecht, and it was ignobly agreed that England would supply the colonies with slaves for a period of thirty years. (12) In addition, the King of Spain pompously offered to allow the English to send one vessel a year, with restrictions on the value and weight of its cargo, to trade with Mexico, Peru and Chili. In payment, the King demanded 25% of the profit, together with a 5% tax on the remainder. This was a huge source of annoyance to the South Sea Company's directors. In spite of this huge set-back, the propaganda machine swung into action, and the first ship sailed from England in 1717. As a direct result, the public's confidence in this corporation hardly wavered. Indeed, this was a time when impulsive members of the public were on the lookout for emerging prodigies, so an increasing number of joint stock companies were floated to satisfy their hunger.

During his speech in 1717, England's King George 1st reasserted his concerns about the national debt and therefore suggested that immediate steps should be taken to mitigate this lingering and most unwelcome burden.

"I order that the national debt be extinguished forthwith!"

Patriotic overtures were at once made to fulfil the King's wishes, and both the South Sea Company and the Bank of England laid their plans before Parliament in May that year. After debating these proposals for a considerable time, three acts of Parliament were passed. (13)

The First Act was passed in acceptance of the plan furnished by the South Sea Company. However, when viewed in a dispassionate light, their plan amounted to no more than an audacious promise of a down-payment against future favours from the king and country. At the behest of the state, the South Sea company would advance the sum of 2,000,000 pounds which could then be used to discharge a portion of the still unpaid debts incurred during the reign of Queen Anne.

In the Second Act, it was agreed that the Bank of England would receive a lower rate of interest on the 1,775,027 pounds it had already advanced to the state. As a further part of this transaction, the Bank agreed to have 2,500,000 in

Exchequer Bills cancelled in return for an annuity of 100,000 pounds. In recognition of this annual sum, the Bank was asked to be ready to advance, at the crown's behest, a contingency sum not exceeding 2,500,000 pounds at a rate of 5% interest, redeemable by parliament.

The third, the General Fund Act, identified certain deficiencies that were to be 'made good' from the funds provided by the foregoing sources. From the point of view of the South Sea Company, a great deal of this newly formed political framework was of secondary consideration. The Company's prime objective was to continue to thrust itself into the limelight, and these political manoeuvres were deemed to be an excellent opportunity. Accordingly, there was a marked appreciation in the value of its shares; however, the increase in revenue that was so vital to underpin such a rapid spurt was commensurately weak. (14) This was recognised by the directors of the South Sea Company. In addition, they had been influenced by the dealings of John Law, and were envious of the headlines that he was attracting with his Mississippi Scheme in France. This served as a spur, so they eagerly sought other ways to increase their holdings.

Extremely bold and ambitious ideas now started to emanate from the directors of this popular English Corporation. To curry favour with the state, what better way could there have been than to put forward yet another plan to pay off the national debt. They knew that this would certainly appease the King. The problem was that, by 1720, the debt had tripled to 30 million pounds. However, the directors of the South Sea Company, who were now disciples of their own conceit, still had the audacity to place their scheme before parliament.

In competition with the proposals of the South Sea Company, the Bank of England now placed a counteroffer before parliament to pay off the 30 million pounds of national debt. This started a bidding war and, not wanting to lose out, each side tabled improved offers, which became the subject of much debate in the house. Recognising that the South Sea Company was now a firm favourite with the public, as well as certain anonymous members of the house and other people in high places, its proposals were favoured. The news was received by members of the public almost as though a pathway to riches had thrown open its fettered gates. Straight away, the company's shares rose from 130 to 300 pounds in anticipation that a bill would now be passed in its favour. (15)

The Whigs spoke vigorously against this resolution. They argued that stock-jobbing would divert the public's focus from the more pressing matters in every-day life – presumably indicating that work, and daily toils, were more likely to feed hungry mouths than gambling in the stock market. Their eloquent pleas were unable to change the hearts and minds of most of those present, and the bill was passed by a very large majority.

In fact, the Whigs had gone out on a limb to explain the consequences if the South Sea Company's capricious surge went unchecked. They were adamant that it would carry the nation with it, and into grave danger. In determined opposition to the possibility of such restraint, there was Chairman, Sir John Blunt, his board of South Sea Company directors, and many furtive agents and emissaries. These were the people who knew they would profit handsomely if all caution was thrown to the wind. Sadly, they were granted their leave, and the bill was passed through the Lords and given Royal assent.

Unsurprisingly, shortly after the passing of this bill, the shares in the South Sea Company pulled back quite sharply from 310 to 290. This was caused by a bout of timely profit-taking by the intuitive few, including the directors. (16) With these cheaper prices, members of the public were unable to say no, and stepped in once again to indulge themselves, so the South Sea Company's share price reaped yet another welcome benefit.

Pumped-up by hot air rather than fruitful enterprise and earnings, the South Sea Company's stock price skipped along, and gullible speculators came out in droves to continue their search for blue sky. But with aristocrats and other powerful individuals also having a vested interest in the performance of the company's shares, the need to please these higher echelons exerted another kind of pressure. There was not only a requirement to sustain the share's current position, but also a need to blow more smoke up the rear of this Company to keep its share price growing. Consumed by their own importance in the early days, but now confronted by this stark reality, the board had to face the fact that the company's shares were carrying a very hefty premium. They knew, at some point in the not-too-distant future, that this could be an embarrassing burden. But the vast majority of shareholders were unable to relieve themselves of their mental stupor, and get a handle on the company's figures, as they were critical.

Fortunately, this was a time for exuberance and optimism, so there was little sign that stockjobbers and speculators, now from all walks of life, might wakeup soon and understand this critical tenet. Those who did understand it wanted to make sure that others didn't, as this created opportunity. Consequently, the game continued, and the rules completely ignored foul-play. Therefore, in order to satisfy the voracious appetite of the crowd for further prodigies, plenty of rogues duly obliged by the creation of more 'hot-air bubbles' – officially known at this time as joint-stock companies. Now, the whole nation was besieged by a speculative frenzy, and this was the type in which the knaves would be enriched, whilst fools would be fleeced – if they continued to live with their heads buried in the sand.

Keen to maintain a state of ignorance, South Sea Company board members were never going to allow the corporation's stock price to retreat to its intrinsic value (*); amongst other things, this would expose their sinister, fraudulent game. The attention of the crowd was therefore refocussed on a regular basis by hyperbole and rumour, and the company's stock thereby preserved its synthetic value. With plenty of tricks up their sleeve, the board decided to pay a 10% dividend following the enthusiastic uptake of a new issue, and this drew more and more credulous speculators into Exchange Alley.

With the South Sea Company leading the pack, this period of chicanery took another sinister turn – companies were now being set up to fail. (17) As soon as their shares increased in value, those behind these sordid schemes took hold of the money and disappeared. It had simply become open season for dishonesty and unethical dealings. This was the source of much sorrow and alarm, not only for those who had been fleeced but also for the honest souls involved in the much-needed development of new enterprise, as short-term scams were derailing genuine efforts.

Back in the day, the wheel of perpetual motion was a best seller!

During this free for all, the prince of Wales became the Governor of one of the new joint stock companies, and he is said to have cleared around 40,000 pounds from his timely bout of speculation. Amongst their many connections, the South Sea Company's principals were now rubbing shoulders with members of the ruling class and the highest aristocracy.

The official title and description of some of these bubble companies, more often than not, gave away the real motives behind their floatation. In fact, crazy ideas could often become valuable assets to those responsible for their invention. The proposal for *'a company to create a wheel of perpetual motion'* ranked very high on the dishonest list, along with *'a company for taking up ballast'*. These ideas might be viewed as hilarious right now but, with the public's receptive state of mind at the time, these were downright dangerous proposals.

Recognising that these deceptions had now become a threat to the state, the King published a proclamation on the 11th June, 1720, which declared that all unlawful projects should be classed as public nuisances and prosecuted accordingly. (18) This forbade any broker, under the threat of a penalty of 500 pounds, from buying and selling shares in any bubble. On the 12th July, 1720, an order was published which had been handed down by the Lord Justices assembled in the privy council. It dismissed all the petitions that had been presented for patents and charters, and the dissolution of all bubble companies.

The great pity was that some of the propositions and bubble companies that had fallen, were probably associated with plausible and rational thought. However, some of the companies that were 'screaming out' to be struck-off are listed below:

A company for carrying on a trade in the River Oronooko (sic); A company for extracting silver from lead; A company for making iron with pit coal; A company for taking up Ballast; A company for the transmutation of quicksilver into malleable fine metal; A company for trading in hair; A company for carrying out an undertaking of great advantage, and this would be disclosed one month after people had paid their first subscription; A company for improving the art of making soap; A company to produce a wheel of perpetual motion; one million needed; A proposal to make deal boards from sawdust was soon dismissed ...

Now alarmed by the emerging political and financial scene, some shareholders were unable to hold their nerve, as they had large open positions with the South Sea Company. Between the late spring of 1720 and the King's intervention on 11th June that same year, the company's share price went through an unprecedented period of turbulence. It eventually reached a critical point where it went on a very steep climb, spiking at almost 1000 pounds after it had been manipulated from within, then it was finally exhausted. The huge sell-off began and the fatal imbalance soon appeared – there were sellers, but no more buyers. One of the most notorious periods of speculation in the nation's history was over. At first, there was widespread panic, and then there was a state of shock.

Deservedly, the directors of this once lauded company now had to face the wrath of all the people who had been duped, as well as the angry politicians who were on their case. After all, Walpole had been right in his early mental projections, as he had envisaged a far greater financial picture in which the South Sea Company was only part. He had realised that this flagship enterprise would be the catalyst for the joint stock company boom, which would then lead to devastation. At this opportune moment, a great many goldsmiths decided to take-off and, over the next few days, others followed in their footsteps.

Emotions were now running very high indeed, and both the Duke of Portland and Mr Hungerford stepped into the proceedings with carefully chosen words of appeasement. (19) In vain they attempted to remind everyone how much the South Sea Company had done for the state and how well it had served the interests of the people. Such words could not detract from the fact that this was a Company that had swallowed the fortunes of many thousands of souls, who would never recover. Their insincere words were immediately received by the house as most unwelcome and patronising – and hissing ensued.

At the same time, it was well known that the both the Duke of Portland, and Hungerford, had cashed out when the company's stock price was at its highest. So had John Blunt and most of the South Sea Company directors. Of course, they were in full knowledge that this once lauded share was completely exhausted, and at the edge of a steep precipice. A number of government officials, who were on annual payments from the company, were also privy to this same inside information, as were other influential shareholders.

Vehement speakers from the house soon started to appear, and they set about those who were responsible for this huge deception. One speaker was Mr Broderick, who said, "They have secured themselves with the losses of the gullible, and thousands of families will now be reduced to beggary." (20)

Significantly, he went on to say: "I founded my judgement of the whole affair upon the unquestionable maxim that 10 million, which is more than our running cash, could not extend 200 million beyond which our paper credit extended." (21)

Now there were riots and rampant public disorder, and it was not safe for the South Sea Company directors to be out in public. However, in a last-ditch effort to salvage, a least, a modicum of hope from the wreckage, Walpole made attempts to bring the directors of the Bank of England and the South Sea Company together. This was not easy as deep-rooted animosity had always existed between these two cliques, but now the nation's interests were at stake. As a relief measure, it was decided to circulate the bonds of the company, with the amounts and duration to be decided. However, the South Sea Company, and its bonds, were now held in such disrepute that the panic continued and there was a run on the remaining goldsmiths, and even the Bank of England. The South Sea Company's stock had now hit 35.

With the country's finances now in tatters, King George 1st returned from Hanover to address parliament on 8th December, 1720. Following his speech, a particularly vehement member stepped forward, Lord Molesworthy, who made it plain that he was seeking the death penalty for the directors of the South Sea Company. He suggested that they should be thrown into the Thames in sacks.

(22) Walpole stepped forward to diffuse the pent-up emotions now choking the judgement of a number of normally sane men. He pointed out that, before punishment, several important fires need to be extinguished. But his pleas failed miserably, and the vengeful got their way. Hence, it was resolved that both remedy and punishment should begin.

First the directors were forced to hand over the records of their dealings. Next, a bill was introduced which prevented all of the South Sea Company board, and its Chairman, John Blunt, from leaving the Kingdom. But it was well known that certain members of the house should have been hanging their heads in shame alongside them. Lord Stanhope said, "Every farthing possessed by the criminals, whether directors or not directors, ought to be confiscated to make good public losses." What a hypocrite he turned out to be. By now, the South Sea Company's treasurer, Mr Knight, had left the country with documents containing all the dark secrets of this organisation's fraudulent acts against both the state and its people. (23)

The King immediately dispatched envoys to secure the ports and likely escape routes in an effort to apprehend Knight, He was also keen to retrieve the vitally important papers he was carrying. Fortunately, Knight was later caught near Liege and locked in a citadel. Inevitably, Sir John Blunt and a number of his directors were now taken into custody, and a campaign was started to seize their possessions and ill-gotten gains. But when Blunt was first questioned by the house, he was evasive and aloof. Soon tired of his taciturn display, he was vehemently asked if he had ever sold any portion of the company's stock to any member of the House of Parliament for the passing of the South Sea bill. His refusal to answer spoke volumes.

Examination of the various papers and records set before the house revealed blatant falsehoods, alterations, erasures, blank spaces, fictitious entries and, when scrutinised more closely, damning proof that bribes had been handed out. By false accounting, shares had been set aside on the orders of Blunt so that they could be cashed-in at a profit, once the bill had been passed in the company's favour. The beneficiaries of this cash were often those who had remained unnoticed, behind the scenes, calculating in unison to deliver this outcome. Involved were many key members of the government and high-profile figures—including the Earl of Sunderland, the Duchess of Kendall, the Countess of Platen, Charles Stanhope—Secretary of the Treasury and sadly, the Chancellor of the Exchequer, Mr Aislabie. The scandal even extended to two of the King's mistresses who, no doubt, were profiteers with royal assent.

Culpable politicians were impeached, and the treacherous Mr Aislabie was taken to the Tower. Throngs of people now started to assemble on Tower Hill, where they lit fires and danced into the night in animated joy, but this was cold consolation for their financial suffering. Probably through the influence of those with privileged status, some of whom were also fraudsters and co-conspirators, the eventual punishment for persons already in custody didn't always fit the crime. After all, around 1.5 million in sterling had been won and lost and it was estimated that attempts had been made, through the creation of bubbles, patents and fraud, to rake in a figure upwards of 300 million pounds. (24) Indeed, the people had been lured by an orchestrated campaign of misinformation and lies, and their fortunes had been swallowed by those with a perfect vantage point – they were working on the inside. It was these treacherous and reckless beings who were responsible for shaping the affairs of this infamous period of history.

Finally, it would be difficult to leave this chapter without, at least, attempting to provide a snapshot of certain values as a yardstick. During this period of 18th century speculation, someone reasonably well-off would have earned a few hundred pounds a year. Further down the social ladder, a domestic servant would have earned around ten pounds a year, and most artisans would have made only a few shillings a day. On the other hand, anyone living at this time with £100,000 would have enjoyed similar status to that of a multimillionaire today. (25)

Another hare-brained proposal – 'A Company Trading in Hair'

If we consider these financial snippets alongside the sums said to have been won and lost during the South Sea Bubble, the nation's running cash of 10 million at this time, and the fraudulent companies purportedly in the pipeline requesting cash of 300 million, a truly terrifying picture of colossal scale emerges.

As for the people, the meagre existence of so many tells its own story. In their delusion, they believed that there was an opportunity to shed the tired apparel of a humble life, and don the splendour of silk. In order to fulfil this dream, they took an impulsive leap of faith – and were fleeced.

Chapter 3
John Law and the Mississippi Scheme

Blessed by the good fortune of a very privileged upbringing yet, deserted by the self-control one would expect from a man of his station, John Law accepted Edward Wilson's challenge to a duel, and shot his adversary dead on the spot.

Captain, John Law unmasked!

It was Bloomsbury in London during 1694 and, probably through infatuation, or maybe love and honour, both men had quarrelled over a certain Elizabeth Villiers. (1) Although she was well known in racy social circles, it seems that Law was unaware of rumours that she was also a mistress of the King. The temperamental young Law was arrested immediately and brought to trial for his ill-fated display of masculinity. But, as his life unfolded, this would not be the only occasion when he would make the headlines.

Some historians believe that Law was a knave and a madman, whilst others suggest that he was an innovative but wayward genius. (2) However, in view of his intemperate disposition, any or all of these descriptions might have been fitting from time to time.

Born in Edinburgh in 1671, Law was the eldest son of a wealthy goldsmith and banker who had acquired the estates of Lauriston and Randleston, thereby elevating his family name to the 'Laws of Lauriston'. This was where Law spent most of his formative years and, at the tender age of fourteen, he started his working life in the counting house of his father's bank. From the outset, it was obvious that the young Law had an extraordinary affinity with numbers and, with the pathways that he would later take in his life, this gift certainly served him well.

Over the following years, Law developed into a tall, good-looking young man, even though an attack of smallpox had scarred his face quite badly. However, with an intelligent countenance and great confidence, he soon became aware that he was able to capture the attention of certain ladies within his social circles. Unfortunately, this nurtured his vanity, as well as a liking for garish attire, and he became known as 'Bea Law' with the ladies, and 'Jessamy John' within his circle of male friends. Wishing to play a wider field, he became restless in his father's business and started to neglect what he felt were irritating duties. By this time, however, his numeracy had helped him to develop a basic understanding of the principles of Scottish banking and, in particular, the provision of credit.

Sadly, Law's father died in 1688 and he decided to take-off soon after, but he was able to depart as the beneficiary of the revenues from the family estate of Lauriston. Indeed, this was certainly needed to support the extravagant lifestyle that was to follow. London became Law's favourite playground where his preferred game of chance was cards. With an early run of sweet luck, assisted by his ability to use a high probability counting system in order to calculate the odds, Law consistently amassed large sums of money. An air of confidence accompanied Law into London's gaming houses, as well as admiring ladies, and an entourage of gamblers who wanted to see him play his hand.

Over a period of nine years his disciplined game and winning streak were gradually reversed when frivolity and excessive behaviour took control. He was now riding a storm instead of a streak of good luck, and addiction followed. Law attempted to recover his losses by placing even bigger bets, which was a fatal mistake, and he had no choice but to cover one large loss by mortgaging the family estate. Completely intoxicated by London's high life, he had foolishly accepted Wilson's challenge to a duel, and was currently facing a murder charge.

Sobered by the possibility of being put to death, Law eloquently pleaded his case, and his sentence was commuted to a fine and manslaughter. To his absolute horror he was still sent to prison but, somehow, managed to escape very shortly after. This seedy episode of his life was to blight his reputation for several years to come and would, in fact, delay the introduction of ground-breaking ideas to the nascent world of banking, finance and commerce. In the eyes of the many Londoners and Scots who had admired him, he was no longer worthy of the flattering title of 'Beau Law'.

'Fugitive Law' continued to evade capture and managed to make his way to Europe, in spite of the many wanted posters on display in his homeland. It is said that the posters were of little use as the description of Law was no more than a caricature. Clearly, he had been favoured by somebody in London with enormous influence, although it was unclear who this furtive agent was. Law therefore travelled to various European capitals for the next three years and, with lots of time on his hands, he devoted part of his daily routine to studying the local banking systems and trading policies, and the latter part of his day in gaming houses. In spite of the fact that he had returned to the tables, he was able to play his hand with a sober mind and thereby started another winning streak.

With his self-esteem and confidence now restored, it is believed that Law almost certainly visited Scotland and audaciously published a document in or around 1700, outlining his revolutionary proposals for the world of commerce. It was called 'Reasons for Constituting a Council of Trade'; a title which clearly reveals Law's very advanced mode of thought at this point in his life. Unfortunately, Law's thesis was largely ignored by those he had set-out to influence. However, the irrepressible Law then decided to place another publication before the Scottish Parliament, this time under the guise of an author by the name of 'Squadrone'.

'Squadrone' – or Beau Law?

Yet again, this evoked very strong suspicion about the pamphlet's origins and, following quite lengthy discussions, Parliament concluded that the contents of the document entitled 'Land Bank' would not be suitable for Scotland. With misplaced humour, it was even suggested that an alternative title might have been 'Sand Bank'. (3) To pour such scorn over the idea of a Land Bank was extremely short-sighted as the commercial Bank of Amsterdam had just started to examine similar concepts.

Indeed, the early eighteenth century was a time when the winds of change were already blowing over the monetary policies of a number of important domains, including Sweden, Genoa and Venice. In these centres, they had adopted the use of promissory notes as an early form of paper money and were using this process as an adjunct to metal currency. The problem with coins was that they were often 'clipped', thereby losing some of their weight and value. In addition, they were extremely cumbersome in large quantities, so the transportation of chests of money posed obvious risks. It seems, however, that this had been a long-standing problem. As early as 13th century, Venetian traveller, Marco polo, is said to have reported the use of rudimentary promissory notes written on parchment, following his visit to China between 1271 to 1275. (4)

Through an intermediary, Law had also made attempts at this time to gain a reprieve for the manslaughter of Edward Wilson, however, his pleas were summarily rejected. In a sombre mood, Law departed for Europe once more to resume the life that he knew best. After all, he would always feel at home in the busy capitals, where there were gambling dens galore, and ladies aplenty. With valuable lessons learned from his earlier escapades in London, he went on to amass another fortune. Widely regarded as the best gambler of his generation and, so often in the limelight, he started to attract the attention of the nobility and certain influential figures. At the same time, he attracted the wrath of the magistrates in Venice and Genoa, where he was expelled on the grounds that he was a bad influence on the local youth. (5) This did not bother Law at all, and he simply moved on, but now in the knowledge he had established contact with certain prominent figures who might, one day, promote his wider ambitions.

With this in mind, he roamed through Flanders, Holland, Germany, Hungary, Italy and France for well over a decade, studying the local customs, absorbing new developments, and exchanging ideas within influential circles. (6) Meanwhile, in 1707, England and Scotland had become Great Britain and, four years later, Robert Harley had launched the South Sea Company in a blaze of glory. This news had stirred Law, and it served to hasten his quest.

Law reached the conclusion that the paper money issued, and the accrued interest from loans, should never exceed the value of the entire lands of the state. He had therefore grasped that the face-value of 'promissory notes' (*) needed to be underwritten by some other asset – and that this asset should be one of recognised value. His earlier deliberations on 'Land Bank', in fact, had outlined such a belief. Law was now convinced that no economy would survive in an increasingly competitive world without the use of paper currency. However, would any nation in Europe ever adopt his ambitious plans?

During one of his many frolics with high society, Law made the acquaintance of the duke of Orleans and there was an instant rapport. In fact, this was an opportune moment in the life of both men and, of course, they soon seized upon this fellowship to assist with personal and pressing challenges. With a degree of desperation in both camps, each believed that the other could provide a solution.

The duke of Orleans became the Regent and controller of France upon the death of Louis 14th in 1715, who had an heir of just seven years old. Clearly, it would have been foolish to burden the young Louis 15th with the affairs of state, particularly amid the turmoil that was blighting the nation at this time. Law's new friend, in fact, had taken the reigns when France's financial position was so desperate that the duke had been advised to declare a national bankruptcy. The extravagance of the deceased King had taken the nation to the very brink of ruin and, although he was flattered in life, he was most certainly despised in death. At this time, France's national debt stood at no less than 3000 million livres, against which there was a revenue of only 145 million, and 142 million of this was earmarked for the government's coffers. (7) The remaining three million livres were set aside to, somehow, service the interest on this humungous debt. The position was almost irrecoverable, but there were those who were willing to try and, of course, John Law would be one of them.

But first, the hapless government decided to heap more pressure on the nation by instigating certain drastic measures – ones that would only deepen the rift between the state and its people. The administration decided that the currency should be depreciated by one fifth. As it turned out, this was really a self-serving exercise, in which coins were 'clipped' by one fifth of their weight, and the 'clippings' went into the coffers of the treasury. Although the nominal value of the re-circulated coins remained the same, they were twenty percent less in weight. In reality, it was the livelihood and wealth of the nation that had been 'clipped' by a dishonest state-run initiative. This is said to have raised 72 million livres but, at the same time, it severely disrupted existing commercial operations and, through public outrage, taxes therefore had to be reduced.

Coin clipping boosted the Treasury's coffers – but the public paid the price!

A Chamber of Justice was now set-up, and its task was to look into the affairs of certain well known 'loan-sharks', as well as the dealings of corrupt agents who were responsible for collecting taxes. The government was offering a percentage of any money that was recovered from these 'double-dealers', as a reward for anyone who would give them up. With the fate of the revenue collectors now in the people's hands, they unleashed their wrath. Hundreds of ministry men were sent to the Bastille and one very rich banker, Samuel Bernard, received the death sentence. (8)

The money that was seized from these crimes amounted to around 180 million livres, but there was another cruel twist. Only 80 million went towards the payment of real debts, and around 100 million found its way into the pockets of the courtiers. (9) The long arm of the law then reached tradesmen and practitioners of good character, who were the victims of greedy individuals looking to collect reward money. Evoking a ferocious hue and cry, this had to be abandoned as France was simply alienating the people it desperately needed to rebuild its future.

John Law surveyed this calamitous scene and, as usual, weighed-up the odds. He was convinced that France's strife could provide a unique opportunity for him to become their new messiah, even though he would need to revive a bankrupt state. Law could most certainly bring a credible game-plan to the table, albeit one that was unproven. He therefore published the two theses that had been rejected in Scotland, and they were very well received by the French.

Law sensed, at last, that his dedicated theories could now become operational. At the same time, the duke sensed that he had found his golden goose. In fact, the duke is said to have been so anxious, that he signed certain documents presented by Law without proper examination and, in haste, delegated matters that he should have attended to personally. (10) Law then gave a presentation to the court and proffered reasons for the country's economic plight. Of course, he dovetailed this with the remedies that his ground-breaking ideas would bring, thereby extolling the virtues of paper money and credit. As a lure, courtiers were also made aware that Great Britain and Holland had started to use paper money, but not in the highly structured way that Law was now postulating.

Law therefore recommended that a new bank should be set up forthwith to manage the crown's revenues and taxes. In turn, this would support the paper notes issued, which could also be secured on landed assets. To sweeten the pot even further, he said that the bank should be administered in the king's name, and subject to the control of commissioners. After hearing Law's proposals, a royal edict was published on 5th May 1716, in which Law was thereby authorised to establish a bank called Law and Company (11) which would later become the Banque General Privee and, eventually, the Royal Banque. Most certainly, Law's thirty odd years of deliberations, mental projections, and research now seemed to have set him on the road to great fortune.

The capital of the Bank was fixed at six million livres, and made-up of twelve thousand shares of 500 livres each, with billets d'état for the remainder – the latter being 'state issued public securities'. (12) Upon the presentation of paper notes, coins (also known as specie at this time) were handed over to the bearer, but a small problem lingered. More often than not, the notes were worth more than the coins for the simple reason that precious metal currency could still be clipped and tampered with.

Rival bankers with insufficient reserves to support their demands were now denounced by Law who proposed that they should face severe punishment – a suggestion that would certainly come back to haunt him.

Dreams become reality for Law!

Law's early bank notes started at 1% in premium value against specie (coinage), and eventually rose to 15%, thereby indicating that the public had great faith in them. Billets d'état were down by almost 80% as there was very little confidence in anything connected to the state. However, an optimistic new mood swept the nation as commerce moved out of the doldrums and people's work ethic pickup with it. Against the backdrop of this much improved economic scene, other branches of Law's bank were therefore established in Lyon, Rochelle, Tours, Amiens and Orleans. (13). Enormously impressed by events, the duke would now grant the Scotsman almost anything, and his bank was given a monopoly on the sale of tobacco, and the exclusive rights to refine gold and silver.

Law therefore sensed that it would be opportune to float another of his grand ideas and, this time, it would be a daring venture into the world of trade and commerce. However, a similar flagship enterprise in Great Britain, the South Sea Company, had hardly found its way out of the dock during the past five years. This appeared to be a bad omen as international enterprise over the high seas was proving to be a risky business for this corporation. To make matters worse, the rapid increase in the formation of joint stock companies had caused a speculative frenzy, not only in stocks and shares, but hapless souls were now gambling on anything and everything. News of this surge had crossed the channel into France, where there were also signs of a similar ethos. In spite of the current lethargy of the South Sea Company, a French corporation was formed at Law's behest in August 1717, which would have the privilege of exclusive trading rights in Louisiana, up to the western bank of the great Mississippi. (14)

Law's bank now changed from a private enterprise to one with royal assent, thereby taking the prestigious title of 'Royal Bank of France'. However, this move soon brought attendant problems as the bank's affairs were well within reach of the meddling Regent, who chose to ignore one of Law's critical tenets. Law had insisted that the total face value of all the banknotes produced should be identical to the total value of the coins lodged with the bank. With royal hubris, the Regent started to print money and failed to align his production of notes with the underlying security that Law, at the outset, had demanded from all other bankers. Law's earlier message to his rivals had now come back to haunt him.

The realm was now flooded with 1,000 million livres of 'paper'. This surfeit escalated the already buoyant mood of the people and led to a speculative frenzy, as well as depreciating the value of existing money. Law knew, sooner or later, that this would create enormous difficulties unless, somehow, a realistic ratio between 'paper and metal' could be restored. Up to this point, he had operated conservatively with an issue of just sixty million paper notes.

The Great Paris Flood

The French chancellor, D'Arguessau, was also aware of the imbalance, and immediately started a quest for Law's head. (15) Fortunately, the chancellor was soon dismissed and replaced by D'Argenson who was more sympathetic towards Law, no doubt as a result of his close ties with the Regent.

However, Law realised that he was in a position of weakness and was conducting his affairs under a repressive regime where jealousy had turned the heads of certain courtiers and rivals. The new chancellor now instigated a 'royal manoeuvre' in order to alleviate the current difficulties – one in which the people of France would pay the price for the Regent's meddling. D'Argenson issued an order that coins should be recalled to the mint and anyone who brought 4,000 livres of metal currency and 1,000 billets d'état would receive 5,000 new coins. The billets d'état were useless government securities, which the people couldn't wait to offload, so this appeared to be a fair exchange. However, the 5,000 re-minted coins were of lesser weight so the people had inadvertently become victims of a further devaluation of their currency.

Of Course, the 'clippings' appropriated by the mint were used for the benefit of the treasury. People of the realm were oblivious to this as there was an abundance of paper money floating around, as well as the re-minted coins issued to replace government securities. Amid these tenuous circumstances, Law's Mississippi scheme was firmly in the spotlight, particularly for avid gamblers who had driven the Mississippi Company's share price to new highs. It was really a question of whether the company's earnings would ever be sufficient to support such a high price, but the majority of speculators were completely unaware of such an important matter.

At the beginning of 1719, an edict was published which granted the Mississippi Company the exclusive right to trade in the East Indies, China and the South Seas. (16) Of course, this immediately sent a shot over the bows of Great Britain's South Sea Company. At the same time, Law's enterprise now absorbed the French East India Company set up by Colbert, thus creating a potentially titanic enterprise. Once speculators caught scent of this, they literally beat a pathway to Law's front door to acquire shares, where he was besieged from morning until night. He was living on the Rue de Quincampoix, and the scene soon resembled that of the frantic Exchange Alley in London. Aware that Law was now revered by the French people and favoured by the Regent, he received a pardon from the British in 1719 for the murder of Edward Wilson.

At least three hundred thousand applications were made for a new issue of fifty thousand shares, as Law had projected an enormous dividend. As still more shares were issued, there was loose talk from ministers that the realm's new surge of confidence might even generate enough money to pay off the national debt of 1,500 million livres. Law had whipped-up a frenzy and both he and other locals were unable to cope with the frantic scene in Rue de Quincampoix. Desperate for respite, he moved to the Place Vendome but was still pestered, and local residents became very angry at Law for this upheaval. (17) The insatiable desire of the French people for shares and money, had a profound influence on Law's ability to maintain control over his thoughts and, more importantly, his project. He knew that there was a point at which his operation could become overloaded by the sheer weight of public expectation and dragged beneath the surface.

In an effort to calm the waters somewhat, Law now moved to Hotel de Soissons, which had a convenient expanse of garden at the back. Pressured by

Law's persistence, the owner accepted his offer to buy this prestigious property. An edict was now passed which proclaimed that stock jobbing could only take place in the hotel's gardens, thereby constraining any potential nuisance from share dealing and crowds. Now, speculators were camped outside Law's back door instead of his front. Swirling amongst the throngs of people were dukes, marquises, counts with their duchesses, marchionesses, countesses, noblemen, men of politics, jesters, and many humble people of the realm.

This was indeed a colourful scene but, hardly surprising for these times, the crowd was infiltrated by those who were up to no good. However, people were completely taken aback when the Count d' Horn, who was the younger brother of Prince d' Horn, resorted to murder. (18) Their lineage stretched as far back as the families of D'Aremberg, D'Ligne and De Montmorency. As it transpired, the Count would need to call upon these very influential connections in an attempt to save his skin. With two accomplices, the Count had arranged a meeting with a very rich broker and, in a bout of crass stupidity, set about him with a knife and killed him in a very public place.

The Count stole 100,000 crowns from his victim but was caught trying to escape. In spite of his pleas to the Regent for mercy, Law was consulted – and the Count was 'broken' by the dreaded wheel.

Indeed, temptation was difficult to resist during these times – even for humble souls in lowly positions.

Count d' Horn is measured-up

A servant's master sent him to the Hotel de Soissons with express instructions to check the share price of the Mississippi Company. The dutiful employee found that the share was trading in a band between 800 livres a share and 1,000 livres, with rapid movements between these two prices. The astute servant managed to buy 250 shares at the lower figure and sell at the higher figure. However, the servant reported to his master that the shares were bought at 800 and sold at 900 livres. (19) Eureka! The servant had just become a wealthy man and, in the bargain, he had also managed to keep his master happy with a handsome profit.

Paris had such an air of affluence that well over 300,000 foreigners were drawn to the city and, although this overstretched its facilities, it created a vibrant scene for its visitors. With an abundance of paper money floating around, these halcyon days were hardly surprising, but there were deep concerns elsewhere. Some parliamentarians argued that too much paper money had been issued, and this merely created an illusion of wealth, which could only bring the country to bankruptcy. Indeed, as the Indian and Mississippi stocks rose, more 'billets de banque' were printed to keep pace. (20)

Although the virtues of paper money could not be denied, there simply had to be an equal value between 'paper' and 'coins' – but this was not the only problem. The earnings of these two flagship companies were way too low for their share price, and it was now a mirror image of the dire scene in London. Unfortunately, the Regent had a puerile way of thinking. He believed that if 500 million livres in banknotes could lift the economy, then printing a further 500 million livres would double the effect.

But, as that printing-press kept on rolling, this amounted to double trouble.

Law was now at his pinnacle and regarded as the most important man in France, where some even called him the new Plutus. The Regent asked Law, who was not a religious man in any way, to adopt the catholic faith, but this request was accompanied by an offer. The Regent asked Law to become the Comptroller General of French finances and, upon hearing this, Law became religious on the spot. These heady times lasted until early 1720 in both France and England. During the previous five years, there can be no doubt that speculators had been gullible, but this state of affairs had largely been created by the deceitful and incompetent government of these nations.

Of course, there had to be a tipping point. For France, the early cracks began to appear in their monetary policies soon after a dispute erupted between Law and Prince de Conti, when the latter had requested a discount on his proposed acquisition of India Company stock. Upon Law's refusal, the prince withdrew three huge waggon loads of coins (specie) after inundating the bank's cashiers with paper notes. (21) Effectively, this was an impetuous 'run on the bank', prior to which there had never been any problem making withdrawals in specie. The furious Regent ordered the prince to pay two thirds of the coins back into the coffers, and the news of this iron fisted demand spread like wild fire.

Yes, in fiscal matters at this time, small cracks often had the uncanny ability to develop into gaping ravines.

In the discerning eyes of the people, the prince had been unjustly prevented from withdrawing money that belonged to him. So they soon began to wonder, if push came to shove, how much control the state would really have over their own monetary affairs. Stock jobbers now sensed that a storm was brewing, and started to secretly convert paper currency into gold, silver and jewellery, which they smuggled to England, Holland and elsewhere. Other French citizens soon followed their lead and, in the midst of this sudden storm, paper money became taboo and was shunned. Immediately, share prices fell and things began to look extremely bleak.

In order to restore the nation's confidence in paper money, the government decided to resort to drastic measures. However, the steps that were taken simply had the reverse effect as they ran into the intractable will of the people. To begin with, the government devalued coins against paper money, first by 5% and then 10%, but this failed miserably. Next, they restricted withdrawals from banks to 100 livres of gold and 10 of silver, and this did not work either because whatever people withdrew, they hid or sent abroad. Now there was such a wealth of coins in foreign coffers or hidden, that French trade and commerce could not carry on.

In desperation, Law even suggested that the use of coins should be banned altogether. However, an edict was published in February 1720 preventing anyone from being in possession of more than 500 livres of coin, and it was forbidden to buy plate, jewellery or precious stones. Instead of restoring the people's belief in banknotes, it destroyed it, and brought France to the cusp of revolution. Servants betrayed their masters and accused them of hiding coins, and the poor seized upon this rare opportunity denounce those who had once been garishly rich, but who were now stockpiling their wealth.

In the midst of what became a national outcry of tyranny, Law and the Regent were now despised, and the streets were littered with graffiti and seditious posters bearing their names and images. As the value of the Mississippi stock plunged, 6000 poor wretches were snatched off the streets of Paris and, after being paraded through various thoroughfares with picks and shovels, were pressed into servitude. Supposedly they were sent off to work in the 'goldmines' in New Orleans. This grotesque abuse of these impoverished souls momentarily raised share values, but then they plunged to new lows – in keeping, perhaps, with the integrity of the French government.

A Council of State meeting was held at the beginning of May 1720 in which Law, D'Argenson and all ministers were present. (22) It had been calculated that 2,600 million livres of paper notes were in circulation, whilst there was half of this amount in coins. Council members therefore decided to try to equalise the value between paper notes and metal currency. They discussed the possibility of raising notes to the value of coins, or raising the nominal value of the coinage until it was equal to the value of paper notes.

In reality, they were trying to create value through manipulation and very wishful thinking. In relation to fiscal efficacy, these manoeuvres were no more than wild cards, as the Council of State members didn't really know which way to turn.

Perhaps with similar odds for success as a 'toss of a coin', an edict was issued on 21st May 1720 to devalue notes by 50%, but parliament refused to register it. On the 27th May 1720, an edict restored notes to their original value, and stopped the payment of all coins.

However, on this very same fateful day, Law and D'Argenson were dismissed amid chaotic scenes, and Law's carriage was now stoned whenever it appeared in a public place. During one particularly violent outburst, the mob overturned his cart and broke it to pieces.

Fortunately, Law was not inside, but this caused both he and his family to go into hiding. On a night of protest, the Hotel de Ville was illuminated by a number of large bonfires at its façade, and cheering crowds used piles of banknotes to fuel the blaze. (23)

The people had spoken. With no choice, the government reverted to the use of coins and, on 10th June 1720, the bank reopened to reissue them in silver and copper to anyone who submitted banknotes The paper currency consumed by flames most certainly helped the bank as, effectively, these were receipts for coinage. Almost the whole of Paris had turned out and, in the melee, at least fifteen people died when they were crushed or trampled, as well as another poor soul who was shot by soldiers.

Law's buggy wrecked!

By October 1720, the government had no choice but to withdraw all the privileges of the India and Mississippi Companies and they were thereby turned into private enterprises. Soon after they were cut adrift, these national flagships were unable to fulfil their obligations. In a witch hunt, government officials now started to seize anyone who was suspected of peculation and fraud, which enabled the state to cast a very wide and treacherous net, and trawl for people's assets.

Law now asked for the Regent's permission to retire to his country home, and his request was granted as Paris was now a dangerous place. The Regent harboured a great deal of sadness about this turn of events, as he knew that his own errors had placed a hefty burden on the machinery of Law's fiscal policies.

In their very last meeting, the Regent admitted this, but Law graciously informed him that even one so eminent could never be immune to innocent error. Shortly after, the Regent sent Law a very kind letter, with an offer of money to expedite his departure from France, as Law and his family were now penniless. His estates and vestiges of wealth in France, had been seized by the insolvent French state. Consumed by the pressure, the Regent passed away in 1723. As for Law, he had to make ends meet, so he returned to the European gaming dens where he embarked on another roller-coaster ride, but managed to stay in front.

However, upon the invitation of the British government, who had witnessed their own problems during the 'South Sea Bubble', Law and his family returned to England. Law felt honoured when he was asked to appear in the House of Lords, where he spoke to a regaled audience about the strife that had befallen both France and Great Britain. However, after just a few years in his homeland, the allure of the continent's gambling dens pulled him back, where he continued with his beloved 'games of chance' – until he died in Venice in 1729.

Ambition is indeed a powerful driver but, if you shoot too high and miss, it can be extremely dangerous. Law desperately wanted to launch very credible ideas, and France wanted a messiah, but they started life together in a bottomless economic pit. To make matters worse, the French people and their government frayed the lifeline extended by Law – until it gave way.

In spite of this huge economic failure, it is generally held that Law understood monetary matters and credit better than any other man of his day and, in many ways, provided the rubrics for modern-day banking. However, during the decades that followed, it proved to be very difficult to build on Law's early initiative, even though his key principles were reflected in the 'gold standard', which was widely adopted by the 1800s.

The Enigma from Lugo, Italy

In the earlier chapters, we have seen how legions of gullible individuals in eighteenth century England and France lost money on an enormous scale when ethical and legal boundaries were flagrantly breached by two flagship companies, the establishment and the monarchy.

In this chapter, we are about to see how just one man, Charles Ponzi, also managed to wreak financial havoc on a grand scale during the twentieth century, when he finessed money from members of the public by marketing a phony get-rich-quick scheme. Expressed in hard cash, this might give the impression that Ponzi was more interested in pocketing an easy $10 from a scam, rather than making a hard $20 by legitimate business endeavours and respectable means. However, let us reserve judgement on this Italian enigma because on the other side of his intriguing personality he was extremely charming, generous to a fault, and often kind to the ill-fated. Setting aside these opposing facets, it would be difficult to dispute Ponzi's creative ability, whilst his record would lead most people to the conclusion that he had an irrepressible desire to misuse it.

'Carlo' Ponzi's full name, in itself, was almost like a hazard warning.

Charles Pietro, Giovanni, Guglielmo, Tebaldo Ponzi was born in Lugo in Italy in 1882 and, after an arduous fourteen-day journey across the Atlantic on the S. S. Vancouver, he settled in Boston, USA, in 1903.

At this time, America was already well established as a world power. The Indian Wars were over after the defeat of the Sioux in 1891 at Wounded Knee. The buffalo were now gone, and vast areas of open range had been placed within the confines of barbed wire, where homesteads and settlements were springing up everywhere. Over a period of just a few years, America experienced rapid economic growth and the country's Republican President, William McKinley, had returned for a second term in office in 1900. It was during this term that he reinforced his belief in certain fiscal measures, the most prominent being 'The Gold Standard'. The value of currency was thereby defined in terms of gold, for which bills could be exchanged. This meant that gold served as a point of reference against which other things of value could be measured.

Indeed, trailblazing feats were sweeping the nation and 193,000 miles of rail track had been laid, with five rail-road systems spanning the continent. Major oilfields were being tapped in Kansas, Illinois, Louisiana, Oklahoma and Texas, and John D. Rockefeller's Standard Oil Trust dominated the world's petroleum markets. (1) Back in the 1880s, Andrew Carnegie had constructed the world's largest steel mill in Pittsburgh and, as the nineteenth century rolled into the twentieth, the United States had become the largest steel producer in the world. The country's major cities were in the process of being electrified, which soon enabled the use of 1900 telephones and, only a couple of years later, the Ford Motor Company was founded in 1903. (2)

But there had been a very tragic set-back during this notable era with the assassination of the visionary President McKinley in 1901. After just a short term in office, he was therefore succeeded by his Vice President, Theodore Roosevelt, and America's economic advancement thereby continued. Architect, Louis Henry Sullivan would become known as 'the father of skyscrapers' and his protégé, Frank Lloyd White, followed him and carried his creative spirit upwards and onwards.

This was the political and economic vista that welcomed Ponzi when he first stepped onto the continent – and into a promising new world.

However, his impulsive tendency to deviate from the truth was soon betrayed when, having paid for an affordable second-class passage, he claimed to have made the journey in the style and comfort of first. This is said to have occurred as soon as he stepped onto American soil, so it was perhaps a very early warning of how his mind worked – and also of things to come.

Following a visit to Canada, which included a prison term, Ponzi roamed through various parts of the US in a quest for fame and fortune but found himself scratching around to make ends meet. During this time, he was extremely keen to learn from the exploits of others and felt sure that one day he would have his very own 'eureka moment.'

At the beginning of the 'Roaring Twenties', this tiny Italian immigrant would therefore become one of the most notorious confidence tricksters in America's history. It seems that all of Ponzi's names, and aliases, were useful when he needed to go incognito, as his reputation eventually spread throughout the whole of the U.S. and Canada. In spite of his notoriety, he still managed to find gullible investors, and he did this by keeping the truth about his illicit campaigns hidden within a thick fog of deceit.

But what was really at the heart of Ponzi's curious behaviour? He reportedly told a relative in the early days that he wanted to make so much money that he would be as rich and famous as America's wealthiest families – the Carnegies and the Rockefellers. (3) However, his chimerical ambitions eventually drove him towards dire consequences, and this resulted in numerous brushes with the law, court appearances and jail terms.

So, let's move on with the life and times of the progenitor of 'Ponzi Schemes', and see how this confident, dapper, Italian immigrant provided the cradle for some of the feckless money-making rackets that would surface during the following years.

Chapter 4
Charles Ponzi

The difference between success and failure in the business world sometimes amounts to no more than a stroke of luck.

Charles Ponzi at the pinnacle!

On occasions, however, a real maverick appears on the scene, who prefers to manufacture his own brand of luck.

It was 1920 in Boston, Massachusetts, and Ponzi's heyday. But it was also a time when plenty of bitter memories were stored in the emotional junkyards left behind by corruption and scams. Most of these schemes had at least one thing in common – they promised riches beyond people's wildest dreams. Instead, the usual returns amounted to zero as the investment money handed to the confidence-tricksters was, more often than not, lost forever. Certain scams were remembered for their audacity and the sheer volume of money they raked in, whilst others were recalled for their cold-hearted guile and the notoriety of the characters involved. For the gullible people who were duped by these hopeless get-rich-quick schemes, there was certainly an everlasting mark.

There was an age-old scam known as 'robbing Peter to pay Paul', in which one man would be paid with another man's money. The undisputed master of this scam had been William Franklin Miller who, around 1899, set-up for business as the Franklyn Syndicate in Brooklyn, and then opened an office in Boston. (4) He audaciously told investors that he could replicate the techniques of Wall Street gurus and was privy to inside tips. Based on his fantasy-world assessment of the annual returns his investors would receive, he became known as '520% Miller'. These were truly extraordinary projections and would only appeal to the most gullible, yet he enjoyed enormous success for a short while. After raking in a million dollars, he was exposed by the New York Herald and sentenced to ten years in Sing-Sing. (5)

However, C. D. Sheldon, alias Wilson, alias Hoyt, alias O. D. Washburn soon followed him with another 'Peter to Paul' scam in Canada. Fortunately, this imitation of Miller's scheme was soon brought to a halt. (6)

The charming Martin Kolega had audaciously gone door to door selling no less than a 'double your money machine'. This was not a 'pennies from heaven device' as it purportedly discharged new bank notes. Amazingly, some people were actually taken in by this early version of a domestic counterfeiting kit. Fortunes had been promised from silver-fox fur farming, as well as engines that used water instead of fuel. In such uplifting times, it is hardly surprising that people had a tendency to fall for the proverbial – 'hook, line and sinker'.

During a 'heavenly vision' the Baptist Minister, Prescot Ford Jernegan, claimed that he had discovered how to turn sea water into gold, and the captivated public suddenly had faith. Yes, it was a time when the impossible was certainly possible, simply because so many people were ready to believe that the rainbow's end, one day, would land in their lap. In his late 1890s scam, Jernegan is said to have collected around $200,000 and his accomplice, Charles E. Fisher, about half that amount. It is believed that Fisher lived out his life in the Philippines whilst, during a pang of guilt, no doubt caused by divine intervention, Jernegan decided to return as much as $175,000 to his victims.

For ruthless confidence tricksters, there were no limits at this time!

Through a network of salespeople, Ferdinand Borges and the Consolidated Ubero Plantation Company sold bonds which promised to give investors a share of the operating profits. The salespeople were on 5–15% commission but Borges and his cohorts managed to net as much as $2 million from gullible victims. In 1906, Borges was convicted of conspiracy and seventy-three counts of larceny and sent to prison. Two million dollars was a truly humungous amount of money at this time but, as well as the commission paid to sales agents, it was long gone.

Then there was the law – the trusty vanguard of financial probity. It was well known in some parts of 1920s America, that certain criminals had bought their pardon, simply because they had connections, and were able to pay enough money. In a prominent case, Dan Coakley, Ponzi's eventual high-profile lawyer, and the District Attorney for Massachusetts, Joseph Pelletier, were found to have joined forces to operate a lewd extortion racket known as 'the badger game'. (7) Useful or important people were set-up so that they would engage in sexual activities – then they were blackmailed and used as marks. As for the local police, many were enthusiastic investors in Ponzi's scheme, and some could even be called on as trusty gatekeepers. This was indeed a bonus as there were some in the political arena, the newspaper world, and high office who were out for Ponzi's blood.

With not drop of alcohol to be found anywhere in the nation, Bostonians were sober minded citizens or, at least, alcohol free, as 1920 began the second decade of the American Prohibition era. However, it was also the beginning of the Roaring Twenties, an era which would eventually become noted for overindulgence, exuberance, glitz and glamour.

During the early part of the 1900s, Brahmins were at the forefront of the social scene and, in the manner of true aristocrats, they ran the towns of New England, including Ponzi's stamping ground, Boston. This elite group consisted of people from old, respected families with wealth and high public status, which made them intellectually aloof and cliquey. They could therefore wield considerable political power and were prepared to use it if needed. Bostonians certainly respected this, including Ponzi.

On 24th July 1920, a huge chauffeur driven limousine known, back in the day, as Locomobile purred slowly through the Boston Streets and gently negotiated its way through the surging throngs of adoring Ponzi fans. (8) This vehicle was a custom-built model, finished in azure glass, and its driver was the young Irish immigrant, John Collins. He looked extremely smart and wore a hat and brass buttoned uniform. At $12,600, the revered Locomobile was a class apart from Henry Ford's behind the times Model T, which would never be the choice of elite citizens – like Ponzi.

The air close to the harbour was pungently seasoned with odours of fish, livestock, fruit, and leather goods, but these were all customary smells in this part of town. (9) This minor irritation soon became an irrelevance as members of the adoring crowd caught a glimpse of the great man in the rear seat of his fabulous vehicle. This was more than enough; sufficient to transfuse the atmosphere with another kind of smell – the sweet smell of easy money. The adoring crowds in this part of town had achieved what they wanted. They had seen Charles Ponzi, cheered him loudly in a manner befitting a true financial wizard and, reassuringly, he had waved back. But there was something the crowd didn't know. Deeply etched in the back of Ponzi's mind was the graphic image of their desperately disappointed faces. He knew that the hopes of his adoring fans had been vested in him, as millions of dollars had been placed in his hands.

No._____   Boston, Mass. _____ *(date)* _____

The Securities Exchange Company, for and in consideration of the sum of *(amount invested)* dollars, receipt of which is hereby acknowledged, agrees to pay to the order of *(investor's name)*, upon presentation of this voucher at ninety days from date, the sum of *(invested amount plus 50 percent)* at the Company's office, 27 School Street, Room 227, or at any bank.

$ ___ *(amount due)* ___   The Securities Exchange Company
                                                            Per Charles Ponzi

---

The receipts issued became the first Ponzi Notes

In just forty-five days, Ponzi had promised to turn $10 into $15, $100 into $150, and $1000 into $1,500 – then the sky itself would become the limit. In fact, with a ninety-day investment, people could even double their money, and this had most certainly caught people's attention. To back this up, Ponzi's Securities Exchange Company issued written receipts for the cash it received and these clearly stated that investors' capital and interest would be repaid in either forty-five days, or ninety days, thereby reflecting the arrangements that had been made. (10)

As reassurance, the Notes were backed by a verbal promise from Ponzi himself, which seemed to carry even more clout than the paper he had issued. With such an ambitious arrangement, there were bound to be those who preferred to harbour doubt, or those who would resort to derision, as these sceptics felt that Ponzi simply had to be involved in something sinister. In fact, many believed that this was simply an exchange of cash for trash.

However, news of the astonishing 50–100% return had spread throughout the different walks of Bostonian society like wild-fire and, ironically, the flames had been fanned by sceptical news coverage from the Boston Post. (11) Perhaps the Post had worked out that Ponzi's financial alchemy represented an annual return of several hundred percent for those who would be willing to place all their money back on the casino table every forty-five, or ninety days. As a result, the Post even recruited the renowned financial expert, Clarence Walker Barron, to investigate Ponzi's scheme but, in spite of his very cynical reports, money still flowed into Ponzi's coffers at a remarkable rate.

This was noteworthy for two reasons. First and foremost, it flew in the face of the Boston Post's negative crusade. Secondly, it was a sure-fire indication that masses of people would still take a headlong leap of faith to join another get-rich-quick bonanza – provided the potential rewards were large enough. At this time, all the scheduled repayments to investors had been met by the Securities Exchange Company, yet, Ponzi's scheme had also caught the eye of Banking Commissioner, Joseph C. Allen, as well as the belligerent Post. (12)

A few minutes later that same morning—24th July 1920—the twelve-mile journey was completed and the huge Locomobile arrived at the Securities Exchange's offices in the Niles Building at number 27, School Street. As the door of Ponzi's vehicle opened, the tip of his trade-mark Malacca walking-stick touched down, and out he stepped. (13) Here was a beacon of sartorial elegance, grace and charisma – yes, a giant of a man in his investors' eyes, even at five feet two inches tall.

Elevated by fame and fortune

On School Street, fascinated onlookers were once again standing shoulder to shoulder with just one focus. Within the throngs, were immigrants from all over the world, together with people from all walks of Bostonian life. Several Brahmins had momentarily stopped to take in the amazing scene. With his customary beaming smile, Ponzi graciously gestured to everyone present and then entered the building to attend to business.

The office itself was anything but plush, and neither was it an operational masterpiece. Instead, it was reminiscent of a giant moneybox in which there was almost a frenetic eagerness amongst those in the queue to deposit their cash. But the abundance of ready money brought its own problems and there was a particularly uneasy alliance in the office between Ponzi and Louis Cassulo. Ponzi knew that Cassulo was pocketing money on a regular basis but, rather than fire him and cause a scandal, Ponzi preferred to maintain the status quo. Ponzi knew that it would only need one scandal to derail his scheme. To add to Ponzi's woes, the Old Colony Foreign Exchange Company had set up a copy-cat scheme just down the hallway from his office. He knew they would have to be dealt with.

This particular day, the atmosphere had been alive with banter and exuberance from the moment the doors of the Securities Exchange opened. Some months earlier, Ponzi had hired a twenty-year-old graduate, Lucy Meli, to run the bookkeeping and the office. She had an impeccable manner as well as an assured steadiness about her for one so young. This was a day when she needed it. Lucy was supported by other office staff, as well as Ponzi, who was usually around when important things were afoot. Right now, the tellers were inundated with money. The people who were patiently waiting in line, slowly but surely, made their way to the front of the queue and eventually found themselves face to face with a one of the Security Exchange's tellers. After they had deposited their cash, the investors received promissory notes, or receipts, which guaranteed their investment, plus 50% interest in 45 days, or 100% in ninety days.

The fancier type of Ponzi Note that was used later

Ponzi did not believe that his clients should be bogged down with soggy text, so he just gave it to them straight and trusted that his promise of 50–100% return would appeal to their better judgement. But what was really underpinning Ponzi's intriguing offer, and how had he arrived at this juncture in his life after stepping onto the American continent as a penniless immigrant?

After showing enormous promise as a kind-hearted and ambitious lad, Ponzi's attitude seemed to change in his late teens. At the University of Rome, he turned out to be a miserable failure. From the off, he started to look for shortcuts in order to circumvent the academic workload that comes with student life. He preferred to stay out all night and then sleep all day, a routine which he could never break. Good excuses were always close at hand for this wayward young fellow and, in spite of assurances that he would get his head down, he was unable to dedicate his mind to scholarship – simply because his mind worked in another way.

For a time, young Ponzi's life began to drift along aimlessly so, to set him on the right track, his family suggested that they should club together to pay for his passage to America. Ponzi was swayed when one relative told him that this was a land that offered enormous opportunity – a place where 'the streets were paved with gold'. This proved to be a confusing metaphor for young Ponzi, and he boarded the S. S. Vancouver in Genoa – post-haste. Several days later, he touched down in Boston when he was just twenty-one years old.

He soon found that the 'gold paved' streets were clad in the cold, harsh reality of stone, where he encountered many setbacks, misadventures, and a string of failures. Although Ponzi had always been keen to promote the image of a successful and wealthy immigrant, during his first four years in Boston, he worked as grocery clerk, a road drummer, a factory hand, and a dishwasher. (14) He repaired sewing machines, pressed shirts, painted signs, sold insurance and waited tables. Of course, this was hardly the persona that would endear him to the rich, privileged and influential; a scene that he so desperately wanted to be part of.

In July 1907, Ponzi packed his possessions, what few he had, and scraped enough money together to pay for a train ticket to Montreal. When he arrived at the Gare Bonaventure, he did not have another penny in his pocket, so he decided to seek a charitable overnight arrangement. Within a couple of blocks of the station, Ponzi found himself looking up at the sign for Banco Zarossi, and realised straight away that this was probably a bank with Italian connections. The very next day, a spruce looking Charles Bianchi—yes, Charles Ponzi—was hired by Banco Zarossi as a clerk. Whilst it was unclear as to why Ponzi decided to adopt a false name, it had been clear from his youth that his mind would work in mysterious ways. There was very little indication of anything untoward in his life at this stage, except hardship, and probably no real need for an alias. What a serious error of judgement this would turn out to be in more ways than one.

Shortly after Ponzi had taken up his employment with the Bank, the corrupt owner, Louis Zarossi, promised to pay the unheard-of interest rate to depositors of 6% per annum, as it was twice as much as the other banks were paying. A year later Zarossi went missing after dipping into the money generated by his ploy. Just before Zarossi absconded, the extremely charming and ambitious Ponzi, or rather Bianchi, had become manager of the Bank and was now worried that he might be implicated. Unsurprisingly, Banco Zarossi collapsed under the weight of a huge scandal when it was discovered that Zarossi, like William Miller and C. D. Sheldon before him, had embarked on the very same old 'robbing Peter to pay Paul' scam. (15) No doubt, this had created a flicker in Ponzi's mind, which would ignite a raging fire further down the road. In the meantime, Ponzi made another bad error of judgement.

Now realising that he was out of work, the twenty-six-year-old Ponzi decided to play on his position as ex-manager of Banco Zarossi. On 29th August 1908, he paid a visit to the offices of one of the Bank's clients, Canadian Warehousing Company. (16) Ponzi had been there before on behalf of his employer, and was quite well known to their staff. This time, during a fateful moment, Ponzi decided to steal a cheque from the back of the company's chequebook, which he promptly cashed for $423.58 at a nearby bank. The French owned Bank of Hochelaga became suspicious about the signature as it was purportedly that of the manager of Canadian Warehousing Company – D. Fournier. Montreal Detective, John McCall, who had been alerted by suspicious staff at the Bank, confronted Ponzi at his boarding house. (17) When he asked Ponzi if his name was Bianchi, he said that it was Clement. This bout of stupidity sent Charles Ponzi, alias Bianchi, alias Clement, to prison for the first time. He was sentenced to three years at the Saint Vincent de Paul Penitentiary in Montreal for forgery.

Ponzi's cellmate was swindler, Louis Cassulo, who, a decade later, was in the thick of things at the Securities Exchange on that warm day in July 1920. (18) Afraid of what he knew, Ponzi simply had to give this extremely dangerous skeleton from his past, a job handling cash. Perhaps this dubious arrangement could have been classed as 'robbing Peter to pay Cassulo'. In order to keep his nemesis silent, Ponzi bought him a house.

On July 13th 1910, Ponzi was released after serving twenty months in prison, but there were daunting issues that he would now have to live with. He was a convicted forger, ex-convict and strongly suspected of having fleeced depositors at Banco Zarossi. Against this milieu, the normally ebullient Ponzi was feeling down on his luck so, just seventeen days after regaining his freedom, he decided to take a southbound train towards the Canadian American border. (19).

Assisting fellow countrymen – really?

Ponzi was accompanied by five ex-countrymen, none of whom spoke English or had proper papers. Customs inspector, W. H. Stevenson, boarded the train just before New York and, sure enough, Ponzi was in trouble once again. Ponzi claimed that he had been asked by an old friend to lend his compatriots a hand, but didn't let on that this was Antonio Salviati – a fugitive from the Zarossi bank scandal. After spending two months in Plattsburgh Jail in New York, Ponzi sought leniency and tendered a guilty plea. However, he was sent to federal prison in Atlanta, Georgia, for another two years – in spite of frantic protests about the length of sentence. Now, Ponzi was a convicted smuggler, as well as forger.

During his second spell behind bars, Ponzi constantly rolled out new ideas for financial schemes, and looked upon fellow prisoner Charles W. Morse as a kindred spirit. Following reckless speculation, this crooked paradigm of American prosperity was said to have been responsible for a national financial panic in 1907. (20) But in 1910, Morse got his come-uppance when he received a fifteen-year sentence for misuse of bank funds. Nevertheless, this very rich man was able to let his money do the talking, thereby securing an early release in January, 1912. Indeed, the 'Atlanta Academy of Crime' was a place where inmates could certainly hone their tradecraft if they so desired. Ignazio 'the Wolf' Lupo was boss of the Mafia gang, Black Hand, and controlled the prison's underworld with an iron fist. Up to the very day of Ponzi's own release in the summer of that same year—involuntarily—he was made to breathe the same rancid air as Lupo, as they became cellmates at Lupo's request.

Ponzi was now thirty and decided to head to Birmingham, Alabama, where he met an acquaintance who was operating a medical insurance scam. Fearful of even the slightest implication—and then a spell on the chain-gang—Ponzi soon made his way to the Appalachian mining town of Blocton. (21) Here, he managed to scratch a living as a translator, a part-time bookkeeper and even a nurse to injured miners. However, it was in this unremarkable place that the kind and generous side of Ponzi's complex character emerged.

Pearl Gossett worked in the mining company's hospital and, whilst she was cooking a patient's meal, the gas stove burst onto flames. Her left arm, shoulder and breast were so severely burnt that Dr Thomas informed Ponzi that her position was desperate, as gangrene could set in at any time. (22)

Ponzi knew that this young woman was very kind and caring, so he asked out of heartfelt concern if anything could be done to help her.

Always willing to oblige!

Dr Thomas informed Ponzi that skin grafting was the only option, and she needed around forty or fifty square inches. That same day, Ponzi had seventy-two square inches of skin removed from his thighs and, on 5th November 1912, he donated another fifty square inches from his back. Soon after, Ponzi fell

83

seriously ill with pleurisy, and was completely prostrate for several weeks. Mercifully, both he and Pearl were able to complete the journey from the lap of the gods to a reasonably normal life, but they would bear the scars of this tragic accident thereafter.

Looking for a scoop, the newspapers latched onto Pearl. Not wishing to bask in the reflected glory from his humane act, Ponzi decided to seek new horizons and left Blocton a few weeks after his recovery. First, he went to Florida, followed by Mobile, Alabama, and then set off for New Orleans in 1915 with hardly a penny in his pocket. From here, Ponzi moved to the cattle and cotton town of Wichita Falls, Texas, which was 'owned' by Joe Kemp and Frank Kell. (23) They controlled its banks and the dry goods business, but also had a company which sold flat-back trucks, and this provided an opening for Ponzi. Fluent in several languages, he took a job as a clerk and, during the company's dealings in North and South America, Europe, India, China and the South Sea Islands, Ponzi had to grasp the rubrics of foreign exchange – a skill that would become essential later.

In December 1916, however, Ponzi felt that he should return home to reinforce his country's effort in the Great War but, shortly after boarding an ocean liner to join the noble cause, he was shocked to discover that his passage would not be given to him for free. Without further ado, a disgruntled Ponzi jumped overboard and swam back to the pier. He remained in New York for a further year and, well and truly tired of having to scratch around for a living, he constantly scoured the newspapers for opportunities. After spotting a promising advertisement by J. R. Poole and Company, Ponzi decided to return to the place where he had first set foot on the American continent – Boston.

It was now 1917 and Ponzi had become an import and export clerk with his new employer, and things were certainly looking up. During this very same year, Ponzi met his beloved Rose Maria Gnecco, and they were married on 4th February 1918. (24) However, during another mental aberration shortly after wedlock, Ponzi misled an American newspaper reporter in what was no more than a brazen effort to elevate his own pedigree. Ponzi told the reporter that he was the son of wealthy parents with aristocratic titles. In fact, it was his wife's parents and grandparents who were referred to as 'Don' and 'Donna', thereby denoting their place within the nobility of the Dutchy of Parma. In spite of Ponzi's protests and denials, he had hailed from Humble beginnings in Lugo, Italy. Ponzi's father was the well-respected local post-man in Lugo, and his doting mother had brought young Carlo through his formative years under his grandmother's roof. But, in spite of this senseless encounter with the reporter, Rose adored Ponzi, and would forgive him almost anything.

During September 1918, Ponzi left J. R. Poole in order to help with the bail-out of a distressed family business, however, after being given full charge of its affairs, his efforts failed miserably. In January 1919, Gnecco Brothers wholesale fruit business went into bankruptcy and, under financial pressure once again, it seems that Ponzi made another bad error of judgement. Shortly after the collapse, he was served with a warrant which charged him with stealing 5,387 pounds of cheese valued at 45 cents a pound. (25) He pleaded his innocence in the Boston Municipal Court and, only through a clerical error in which his name was spelt 'Pouzi', was he able to avoid another sentence. This lucky escape shook Ponzi to the core. The thought of being away from Rose—in jail—was too much to bear.

Within a few months of his brush with the law, and following seventeen long years of misadventure and chancing it in the margins, promising developments finally started to shape Ponzi's life. Inspired by his truly eventful journey on American soil, he set up – 'Charles Ponzi Export & Import'. (26) In order to deal with marketing for his new venture, he decided to follow up with the 'Trader's Guide'. This second business, in fact, was more a necessity than an afterthought. After discovering that postal marketing would cost a nickel per circular for domestic companies, and eight cents for international firms, Ponzi worked out that his production and distribution costs for the magazine would be $35,000, and his income would be $80,000. This would yield a nifty profit for each edition, as well as promote his export and import business – but Ponzi soon ran out of money. (27) He therefore discovered that creating reality out of a brainwave is not an easy task. Permission for him to continue trading was now in the hands of an elusive demon – and its name was 'funding'.

The sweet-talking Ponzi sought outside investment and then a bank loan, but failed miserably. It was now the summer of 1919 and, despondent once again, he went into his office in the Niles Building at 27, School Street to look through his post. A letter writer from Spain had requested a copy of the 'Trader's Guide' and enclosed with his correspondence was a 'Postal Reply Coupon'. (28)

As Ponzi poured over this intriguing item, it certainly stirred his curiosity. The Postal Reply Coupon, in fact, bore all the hallmarks of a typical financial instrument. Its design was sufficiently impressive for Ponzi to recognise its unmistakeable air of authority, and this attracted him. In his eyes, the coupon looked as though it was begging to be exchanged for something with far greater importance than just postage stamps. Indeed, the more Ponzi looked at the coupon, the more he could see the word 'opportunity' staring him in the face. During the deliberations that followed, Ponzi scribbled his thoughts down on a piece of paper. He was desperately looking for ways in which he might convert his revelation into a money-making opportunity. His creative sparks and flashes were interrupted by any number of voids, but following a couple more days of rummaging, the lights finally came on. Ponzi's eureka moment had arrived.

International Reply Coupon – and a wonderful vision

Ponzi saw Postal Reply Coupons as a kind of global currency, and therefore a mechanism by which he would be able exploit international exchange rates against the fixed price of the Coupons.

The Universal Postal Union had been founded in 1874 and, following a meeting of sixty-two nations in Rome in 1906, it was decided that Postal Reply Coupons would make it easier to send mail across national borders. (29) Coupons were urgently needed because it was not possible, for example, to use Italian stamps on America soil, to reply to the original correspondent back in Italy. The receiver of the International Reply Coupon in America could therefore redeem this piece of paper at his local post office for international stamps. The treaty writers wanted to ensure that no one would try to make money from the redemption of the coupons. Therefore, they created a regulation which set the rate of exchange between the currencies of the member states and International Reply Coupons. This meant that one dollar's worth of coupons would yield one dollar's worth of stamps in any of the sixty-two member nations. But when Ponzi first set eyes on an International Reply Coupon, thirteen years had passed since the 1906 treaty, and certain things had changed.

The Great War, in fact, had created enormous fluctuations in currency values, and Ponzi knew that the value of the Italian lira had fallen to 20 to $1. The same dollar that could buy 20 coupons for 5 cents each in America, in fact, could buy 66 International Reply Coupons in Italy. This meant that 66 coupons purchased in an Italian jurisdiction for $1 would be worth $3.30 in an American state. By Ponzi's calculations, this would provide him with a gross profit of around 230% – and Spain could provide him with similar margins. After consulting with Robert de Masellis, a foreign exchange expert at Fidelity Trust Company, Ponzi discovered that, in certain other European countries, the exchange rates against the American dollar offered even bigger opportunities. At this time, the Austrian krone had fallen from the equivalent of 20 cents to just a penny. (30) This meant that $500 would buy the staggering sum of 70,000 kronen. Theoretically, this could purchase more than 250,000 International Reply Coupons which, if redeemed in America, would turn a $500 investment into stamps worth $12,500.

But of course, there was absolutely no provision in the 1906 treaty which would allow $12,500 worth of stamps, or International Reply Coupons, to be converted into local money. Ponzi learned about this irritating detail shortly after seeing his first coupon, but this indefatigable Italian immigrant often chose to live in a state of denial. With his 'devil may care attitude', Ponzi was therefore confident that he could tie-up all the loose ends as the details of his new idea unfolded over the next few days. Besides, he suspected that if he started asking questions about cashing in postage stamps, or the redemption of International Reply Coupons, someone in authority might become suspicious. Even worse, he contemplated the possibility that a copy-cat scheme might emerge from his very own stroke of genius. Ponzi had always been an optimistic soul but, at times, his enthusiasm could cloud his better judgement. Ponzi's ability to redeem stamps or coupons for cash was the key to his success. In addition, the availability of very large quantities of coupons was just as important. But, instead of seeing where he actually stood on these critical matters from the start, Ponzi 'put the cart before the horse' and decided to ride it. So what was it, exactly, that he had he attempted to set in motion?

During his paper exercise, Ponzi's had reached the conclusion that his scheme would work, simply because the favourable currency exchange rates supported the projection of enormous future profits. With this in mind, the promise of fifty percent interest on any monies invested would work in theory, thereby assisting Ponzi quest to raise money. But these apparent 'positives' were only part of a much bigger picture – one in which there were large gaps. Of course, it's quite easy to project enormous returns from almost any imaginary scheme, but making impetuous ideas work in reality is an entirely different matter. This is, perhaps, reminiscent of a situation that I encountered in the late nineteen eighties, so please stay with me on a slight detour for a moment or two.

A friend of mine asked me to assist him with the creation of a business plan, as he had come up with an idea that would assist almost every housewife in the land. He told me that he intended to take his idea to a congenial bank manager, who had been recommended by a friend. Indeed, the names of congenial bank managers were certainly passed around back in the day. Anyway, Freddy and I met in a local coffee shop and he proceeded to explain how he intended to manufacture metal clothes props to hold up the washing lines in people's back gardens. In very convincing tones, he assured me that the traditional wooden props were not nearly strong enough when the clothes were wet, particularly when there was a strong wind. He was therefore certain that there would be a good market for his wonderful idea. Yes, it did cross my mind that the actual fabric of the washing lines might need strengthening too, but I refrained from asking him if he had any bright ideas on that front.

So, Freddy proceeded to give me the manufacturing costs and sales values for his ground-breaking new venture, and then continued to eat his cake and sip his coffee. Itching for more, and quite fazed by his ingenuity up to now, I just kept nodding. As it turned out, the notes I had scribbled down at that point proved to be the full extent of Freddy's brainwave. With no choice, I had to interrupt his obvious air of expectation. I suggested that he would need far more than a congenial bank manager to get this one over the line. I explained to Freddy that it was possible to do almost anything with projected figures. I could create the impression that his scheme would earn him a decent living, or provide numbers that would reflect a really profitable enterprise. With an even more optimistic outlook, I suggested that I could probably make him a multi-millionaire. I asked him for his thoughts.

He said, "Ralphie, I think we'd better go somewhere in the middle – this bank manager might not be all that he's cracked-up to be."

My friend and I have laughed about his 'prop-job' ever since. Freddy decided to start with small scale production, but sold just a handful of props. Now realising that his brainwave needed a very serious reality check, he considered my suggestion that the property market might provide far better opportunities, and he has not looked back since.

At this juncture, Ponzi took a huge leap of faith with little more than the bare bones of a business idea. But, as always, he was confident.

Section Two

Was there a chance now that Ponzi could find a better life? He had always been keen to promote the image of a conscientious, clean-living immigrant so that he could mix with the right people. Would his potential new business give him this opportunity?

Chapter 5
'Ponzi's Scheme'

At the beginning of this book, we talked about the enormous importance of a realistic, well thought out, game-plan for involvement in speculation and business. Without doubt, Ponzi only had a very rough and ready sketch of an idea at this juncture, so let's take a quick look at its pros and cons.

Ponzi was not in a position to revise or abandon his scheme as he had set off during the conceptual phase, and had suddenly unleashed an unstoppable roller-coaster of inflows and outflows of cash. By July of 1920, Ponzi was raking in so much money, it was difficult for him to contain himself and keep his feet firmly on the ground. In spite of his euphoria, he knew that he had probably taken a premature leap of faith when he had dangled the promise of such enormous returns on any money invested. This had undoubtedly enticed his clients to join him in that very same leap of faith. Right now, there were waves of cash spilling over the counters at the Securities Exchange Company, and the tellers could barely cope, yet there were certain pressing matters that needed to be dealt with. Ponzi was still unsure how he should deal with the redemption of both Postal Reply Coupons and stamps in return for cash, and was in the dark about the availability of coupons in very large quantities.

He had made the fateful decision to contact postal officials back in March of that same year. (1) He proceeded to ask questions that would have been far better placed during the previous December, which was the point at which he had opened for business. Unfortunately, the response from Postal Union officials virtually put paid to Ponzi's scheme, as they stated categorically that the redemption of stamps or coupons for cash was not possible, emphasising that they were not intended for speculation. In fact, the postal officials went one step further and paid him a visit. Now between a rock and a hard place, Ponzi managed to blag his way through this unplanned encounter but, with a notable

93

degree of irony, money still continued to roll into his Securities Exchange Company at a staggering rate. In Fact, Ponzi's 'scheme' had become the talk of the town, so he decided that he would find a way round any obstacles later.

In spite of this, it was evident that Ponzi had simply conjured up little more than an unruly box of tricks, which needed to swallow money in order to maintain its very existence. But this very same box of tricks had little sympathy for those who—one day—would need to be repaid.

In spite of his setbacks, Ponzi believed that no man was ever licked unless he wanted to be. In the case of this feisty Italian immigrant, only time would tell. However, with the consolation of an ever-growing mountain cash to prop-up his naturally buoyant personality, the events of the previous day always seemed to be ancient history. He was well aware now that the Postal Union would not play ball so, almost living in a state of denial, he decided to attend to other pressing matters at his Securities Exchange Company.

Amongst the many skeletons in Ponzi's cupboard was one Joseph Daniels. Ponzi had borrowed $200 dollars from this opportunistic furniture dealer at the outset of his 'Ponzi Scheme', and had paid him back during the required period, in full, and with interest. But Daniels was not satisfied and decided to pursue Ponzi's newly found success with a lawsuit, making the truly absurd claim that his $200 loan entitled him to 50% of the Securities Exchange Company.

Daniels recruited the particularly aggressive lawyer, Isaac Harris, to run his case. Instead of simply 'running the case', Harris decided to go for Armageddon, so he filed a lawsuit on 2nd July 1920 against the Securities Exchange Company for a claim of $1 million. But that was not all. He made applications for attachment orders against a number of Ponzi's bank accounts, thereby freezing hundreds of thousands of dollars in cash. Potentially, this was capable of jeopardising Ponzi's ability meet the scheduled repayments to his investors – and in the event of widespread panic, there could be a run on the Securities Exchange.

Pressure of this nature often means that mere mortals lose their nerve, and they settle lawsuits as soon as they can, even though it may ride rough-shod over their notion of 'right and wrong'. But this was Ponzi, and he was blessed with guile and plenty of moxie. In spite of the fact that he was in the right for once, Ponzi recognised his vulnerable position, so he appointed a Securities Exchange client and lawyer, Frank Leveroni, to open settlement talks. (2)

The news of the $1 million lawsuit reached the Boston Post and this is where Ponzi's fun and games really started. On 4th July 1920, Ponzi appeared on the front page of the Post for the first time, and the headline read "Boston Man Sued For $1 Million." (3) To avoid an attachment order, Ponzi immediately removed $283,710.62 from his account at Cosmopolitan Trust Company, and performed various manoeuvres with accounts at other banks.

The news was not received well by investors, but their concerns soon passed. As the 'Ponzi Notes' fell due, Ponzi was able to honour all of his promises. Yes, reminiscent of his old employer, Louis Zarossi, as well as William Miller and C. D. Sheldon before him, Ponzi was now 'robbing Peter to pay Paul'. With Ponzi's revolving door of incoming and outgoing dollars, new investors coming through one side of the door, had to more than double those leaving via the other. In this age-old scam, each investor was being repaid with another man's money and, for every dollar Ponzi received, this carried a further 50–100% liability.

In these circumstances, Ponzi would have been insolvent from day one. After all, he was unable to look forward to the huge profit margins he had anticipated from foreign exchange, as the Postal Union had scotched this one. In order to maintain the charade, and the necessary flow of incoming dollars, Ponzi had promoted a system of managers, agents, sub-agents and hangers on, who were all investors, and commission agents in his scheme. This included a number of local policemen, and other demigods from within the corrupt 'system' itself. There can be no doubt that this part of the operation bore all the hallmarks of a pyramid scheme, with Ponzi at the pinnacle. So, under its current guise, how long could the Securities Exchange Company last before it was exposed?

Ponzi's 'robbing Peter to pay Paul' scam, would only last as long as the number of investors cashing in 'Ponzi Notes', did not significantly exceed those bringing in new investment.

However, Ponzi was well aware that another run on his scheme could easily be precipitated by some sort of adverse breaking news. His investors had been massively unnerved by the Post's headline on 4th July, and this was still foremost in Ponzi's mind. In spite of these negative vibes, there was still a constant stream of investors who were attracted by the staggering interest rates of 50–100% in just forty-five, to ninety-days. It is hardly surprising therefore that after a period of just nine months, Ponzi was said to be raking in $1 million a month by July 1920, and this would soon be $1 million a week. (4)

This ambitious Italian immigrant had started during the previous October, without a light, but was now reportedly worth $8.5 million and had over 20,000 investors. Indeed, Ponzi's financial alchemy was increasing day by day. With his bank accounts bulging, and with no possibility of cashing in Postal Reply Coupons or stamps, he decided he should diversify. He invested in businesses that he felt would be secure and profitable, and real estate was high on his agenda. However, the benevolent side of his nature was revealed when he made several unsecured loans to certain friends, associates and business people. But Ponzi was determined to gain control of one or more banks (5) as he believed that, not only would this give him access to more capital, it would deflect attention from his dealings at the Securities Exchange.

During this illustrious phase, new business auditioned for Ponzi and not the other way around. Ponzi bought shares in the Napoli Macaroni Manufacturing Company for $61,000, and then he issued a cheque for $30,000 to take over C. and R. Construction. Next on his list was J. R. Poole and Company, his former employer. Ponzi outlaid $240,000 for a controlling interest in this enterprise, which was perhaps acquired out of just 'pomp and swagger'. In another bout of gross extravagance, he extended Poole a further five loans for the expansion of his Company totalling $155,000. Then he bought a small tenement house in the west end for the modest sum of $6,000. However, when Ponzi eventually turned his attention to banks, (6) he proceeded far more subtly.

He bought 50 shares of Fidelity Trust for $60,000, 5 shares of Tremont Trust for $500, and 100 shares of Old South Trust for $12,500. He knew that these investments would give him no more than a toehold, and they would never earn enough money to dig him out of the hole he was in. However, Ponzi felt that if he could discreetly gain control of these institutions, or others, he might be able to weather the storm that was most certainly looming.

He eventually set his stall out to gain control of Hanover Trust, but these lofty aspirations soon came to the attention of the forty-two-year-old Banking Commissioner, Joseph C. Allen. He had just been appointed by Calvin Coolidge, the Governor of Massachusetts, who particularly respected Allen for his undoubted probity. Allen was not a man to be taken lightly, as he was both intuitive, and very tenacious. But Ponzi also got wind of Allen's recent enquiries, and decided to adjust his plans – for a short time at least.

But Ponzi was Ponzi, and there was a constant fight for his soul – between an angel on one shoulder and a demon on the other. During this endless tug of war, Ponzi's mind wandered off yet again.

Ponzi's turmoil!

With his usual swagger, this diminutive Italian immigrant was keen to let it be known that he now had big-bold plans for further extensive lines of business. With this sort of self-exerted pressure, Ponzi's mind was rarely still and the silhouettes of new business ideas appeared and disappeared as fast as night melted into day. But Ponzi knew that his deliberations were important because he was very wary of the intrusive Joseph C. Allen and the Boston Post. Although he had temporarily shelved his plans for control of a bank, Ponzi knew that he was still out on a limb with the Securities Exchange. As a matter of necessity, his mind was now completely focussed on contingencies for survival.

The US government had placed an advertisement asking for bidders for thousands of surplus freight and passenger ships from the Great War and they came with a $2 billion asking price. In a flash, Ponzi conjured up the notion of the 'Charles Ponzi Steamship Company' and the 'Shipping and Mercantile Company'. Once again, he envisaged that he would strike a deal with investors in which he would offer the Government only $200 million. It was at times like these that Ponzi's biggest liability was his fertile imagination, and this had just taken him on another fruitless journey.

Now in a corner, he decided to rekindle his earlier aspirations. Ponzi breezed into Hanover Trust as though he owned the place but, in the eyes of some of the staff, the reality of the matter wasn't too far from the truth. (7) When certain bank officials spotted Ponzi, they immediately greeted him with the kind of toadying reverence normally reserved for a vain celebrity, whereas more retiring employees graciously bid this self-proclaimed virtuoso good morning. Ponzi had no less than $2.7 million deposited in Hanover Trust which, as a medium sized but respectable Bank, had just five million in assets.

Clearly, Ponzi was the Bank's largest customer, hence his red-carpet treatment from some of the Bank's staff and stockholders. Without further ado, he made a beeline for Henry Chmielinski's office, who was a senior official at the Bank. Ponzi got straight to the point. He offered to buy all two thousand shares of the Bank's soon to be issued stock. One official immediately informed Ponzi that this was not possible as they would, effectively, be selling him control of the Bank. However, with a deposit $2.7 million, Ponzi knew he had the officials at Hanover Trust over a barrel. He eventually agreed to settle for fifteen hundred shares in the Bank and, as well as being given a directorship, he was elected to the powerful executive committee.

On 15th July 1920, Hanover Trust completed the sale of a large proportion of its stock to Ponzi for $187,500, effectively giving him control. (8) The extremely principled and morally upright Banking Commissioner, Joseph C. Allen, was now compelled to take a very close look at the Securities Exchange Company and its humungous profits, purportedly from 'currency speculation'. Allen had also asked for an opinion from the unrelated J. Weston Allen, the state's Attorney General. Between them, they decided to appoint a foreign exchange expert, Mr Abbott, from another Boston bank. (9) Amazingly, it was concluded that Ponzi's scheme was legitimate and, privately, Abbott is even said to have propositioned Ponzi for an investment with the Securities Exchange. However, the two Allens and the Editor of the Boston Post, Richard Crozier, still had massive doubts.

Ponzi liked to feel in charge by being pro-active, so he decided to purchase confirmation of his scheme's efficacy, even though he realised that he might need to ask some well-respected professional to sail close to the wind. Whether a scheme such as Ponzi's was perceived to be 'ingenious or reckless', would depend almost entirely on how the yarn was spun, and Ponzi realised this. So, on July 23rd, Ponzi hired the publicity professional, William McMasters, a former employee of the Boston Post, to step into his corner. (10) As it turned out, Ponzi would have been far better placed 'under the radar', thereby adopting a dignified code of silence, instead of drawing aggressive new battle lines. But Ponzi was Ponzi. He was larger than life and this was impossible. It is quite surprising therefore that Ponzi had been relatively ignored by the majority of newspapers, until the Post's disconcerting article of 4th July. But by 24th July 1920, the tide of scepticism had turned once again, and money continued to flow into Ponzi's office at such a rate, Luci Meli and her staff could hardly cope.

But even though Ponzi was increasing his liquid asset base day after day, this failed to mitigate his wider problems at his Securities Exchange Company. Somehow, he now needed to create sufficient breathing space to figure out what he might do with his 'robbing Peter to pay Paul' scam. On the one hand, he felt it would be unwise to stop the money coming in from investors but, on the other, he was tempted to do so – even though he still needed the income so that he could hand it over to those who needed to be repaid. For the time being at least, Ponzi decided to continue with his charade.

By now, the piqued Richard Crozier at the Post had just about staked his reputation on 'nailing' Ponzi and his Securities Exchange Company. However, the closest he had dared to go in a recent edition was to suggest that the Federal and State Authorities had looked at Ponzi's investment plan, and had not been able to discover anything illegal. However, articles on Sunday 25th and Monday 26th July certainly had a different tone, highlighting the comments of Clarence Walker Barron who had scoffed at Ponzi's scheme. (11) Ponzi now realised that he was being pulled from 'pillar to Post' in a media maelstrom, so he decided to act. He therefore sought the privacy of Chmielinski's office at Hanover Trust to make some important telephone calls. First, he called Dan Gallagher, the District Attorney for Massachusetts, to offer him and other officials the opportunity to investigate his business – and Gallagher agreed. Ponzi received the same response from Suffolk District Attorney, Joseph Pelletier, but Attorney General, J. Weston Allen declined Ponzi's offer to meet.

Ponzi attended the meeting with his publicity man, William McMasters, and dropped, what turned out to be, a bombshell. Ponzi volunteered to suspend all further investments into his scheme, until after it had been investigated, and said he would continue to meet any repayments that fell due. This was either a weight off Ponzi's mind, a mental aberration, or an enormous gamble. Now he would, somehow, have to stem the torrent of outflowing cash, or else he would drown in lawsuits. Yes, Ponzi was known to be extremely resourceful, but a run on his scheme started with vigour when the following notice was placed. Some even resorted to violence as the police had now abandoned Ponzi, but he still had his Pinkerton Agents as security who, somehow, managed to keep matters under control.

"PUBLIC NOTICE: *I have made a personal agreement with District Attorney Pelletier to cease receiving funds from the public for investment with the Securities Exchange Co. 27 School St. Boston and all branches, until after an official audit is made to determine my solvency and satisfy him that my methods of financial operation are thoroughly legitimate. Meantime, I shall pay all maturing obligations as fast as presented. Further, during the auditing of the books any person holding unmatured notes can receive back their original investment, without interest, if they desire.* **Charles Ponzi."** (12)

Instructions to this effect were immediately wired to all agents, sub-agents and introducers of business to the Securities Exchange. The Post's headline read – *'Ponzi Closes; Not Likely to Resume'*. Now, almost all the local newspapers, as well as some nationals, were on Ponzi's case. Ponzi had calculated that he had around $15 million in outstanding promissory notes and about $8 million in available capital, so he knew that he would have an extreme up-hill struggle in any attempt to fabricate his solvency. Thus, Ponzi decided that he would rob a bank to get the assets he needed and, as a member of the executive committee of Hanover Trust, he knew it had at least $5 million 'in liquid'. (13)

But it would only be a temporary bank robbery as the money would be returned after about an hour, once Ponzi had hoodwinked the auditor who was about to be appointed to investigate his financial status.

Ponzi felt that this manoeuvre would not be difficult as the authorities had made some of the most basic errors imaginable during their first investigation of the Securities Exchange Company under the stewardship of banker Abbott.

It's only me! Don't worry! I'll pay it back in tomorrow!

In fact, their blunders were almost puerile. They had failed to check the number of Postal Reply Coupons produced annually and worldwide, those currently in circulation worldwide, the number currently in circulation locally, or whether postage stamps or coupons could be redeemed for cash. After all, Ponzi's purported ability to engage in foreign exchange speculation, and generate enormous profits, relied almost entirely on these precepts. In order to support his cause, Ponzi now decided to appoint the corrupt but charming lawyer, Dan Coakley, who had 'connections' in high places. (14) The problem was that Coakley had gathered just as many enemies as connections over the years.

Ponzi's biggest worry was that he might run out of money before the official audit on his Securities Exchange but, in this double-edged sword conundrum, Banking Commissioner Allen was also worried that the current run on Ponzi's scheme might place any number of local banks in jeopardy. However, the 'Ponzi Alliance Group' stepped in and placed a petition, with a pledge for funding if needed, in front of Judge Leveroni. It was now unclear as to who was playing whom in this game of high stakes poker, and the fickle attitude of the crowd swung back and forth with every move. During the hostilities, the Post responded with the headline *'It Cannot Last'* and, on 28th July, the run on the Securities Exchange was far bigger than ever before. Right now, public sentiment was caught in the path of belligerent gusts so, sooner or later, something simply had to give.

But McMasters still took an aggressive stance and started to antagonise the Post, so the Post responded with the headline *"McMasters Expresses Contempt for Investigation."* Ponzi was even challenged by one reporter on how he cashed the International Reply Coupons, but said that it was a secret he simply would not tell – nor could he tell. (15) In the middle of this complex melee, Daniels' lawsuit was still pending and a hearing was due the following week. But on the brighter side, Pelletier said he was going to investigate the Colony Foreign Exchange Company but, when he did, they defiantly continued to take deposits.

By Friday 30th July, still more problems surfaced. Information provided by Thomas G. Patten, the New York Postmaster, was heralded by – *"Extra Coupon Plan Exploded: Postmaster Says Not Enough in the Whole World to Make Fortune Ponzi Claims."* (16) When confronted by the Post, Ponzi tried to blag his way out of the quandary, and said that he was purchasing the coupons directly from foreign governments. In reality, Ponzi had abandoned the idea of making money from Postal Reply Coupons a long time before. For possibly the first time, desperation now crept into Ponzi's psyche and he thought about running with whatever money he had at his disposal, as other large amounts of cash were still frozen in the Joseph Daniels' lawsuit.

Ponzi had even made enquiries about the possibility of selling the Securities Exchange for $10 million, but he knew in the back of his mind that any prudent businessman would take a close look at his set-up before he outlaid a single dime. It would then be discovered that the company was no more than a sham. In fact, Clarence Barron had just weighed-in with a direct accusation that Ponzi was running a 'Peter to Paul Scam' so Ponzi had immediately hit back with a $5 million lawsuit with applications for attachment orders against his properties. But this was not enough to make Barron back down. In the meantime, the shady Pelletier had somehow drawn the conclusion from his investigation that Ponzi had conducted his business 'normally'. Pelletier was promptly removed from the case by the frustrated Banking Commissioner Allen, who now took the drastic decision to have Ponzi's phones tapped.

But more devastating blows were yet to come. Having anticipated which way the wind was blowing, Ponzi's own publicity agent, William McMasters, switched his allegiance to the Boston Post, and sold Ponzi out for just $5,000. The Post now had what it wanted and, on Monday 2nd August 1920, it declared in its headline: *"PONZI IS HOPELESSLY INSOLVENT."* (17) This was followed by the sub-heading: *"Publicity Expert Employed By 'Wizard' Says He Has Not Sufficient Funds to Meet His Notes – States He has Sent No Money to Europe, Nor Received Money from Europe Recently."* Ponzi's last hope now was auditor, Edwin Pride, who had been appointed by Boston Federal Prosecutor, Dan Coakley, to audit Ponzi's scheme. (18) Pride was under enormous pressure and had been given just a four-day time span, including the weekend. As a result, Ponzi saw this as an opportunity to bamboozle the harried Mr Pride, and get him to sign-off on the Securities Exchange's solvency. Ponzi's bookkeeping system consisted of no more than index cards, with investors' names and other brief details, which Ponzi believed he could manipulate.

At this time, opportunists were working the huge crowd outside Ponzi's office. On the spot, they were buying matured Ponzi Notes from anxious or frightened individuals for the original amount they had invested. A quick 50% profit was waiting for these carpetbaggers once they reached Ponzi's tellers. They knew that the first man to be turned away would mean that Ponzi was 'bust'. But, in this calculated numbers game, most of them would be way in front by then.

Meanwhile, reporters were firing questions at Ponzi about the allegations made by his former employee, William McMasters. Ponzi's reply was that "My dog follows me and never goes ahead." With a sardonic smirk, Ponzi pointed out that very few banks in the city would have been able to survive the run that his Securities Exchange had withstood – and perhaps he was right. To Ponzi's delight, Pride reported on 3rd August that he hadn't found anything to suggest that any law had been broken, and he was already three days into his four-day audit. However, Barron published a story indicating that the Postal Union had only printed, worldwide, around $200,000 of coupons annually for the three years up to the end of June 1919. (19) This revelation dented Ponzi's claims that he was using vast numbers of coupons in his foreign exchange dealings but, when challenged, he simply would not comment on the matter.

Ponzi now realised that he would have to settle Daniels' lawsuit, which had frozen $700,000 in cash and $1 million in assets, so they met privately on 6th August. Ponzi managed to barter Daniels down from $100,000 to $50,000, and the matter was settled after they both attended the courthouse that day and Daniels withdrew the suit. (20) Ponzi immediately went to Cosmopolitan Trust with Daniels and, following confirmation from the very perturbed lawyer, Isaac

Harris, who had not been present when the settlement had been agreed, Ponzi walked out of the bank with $389,000. Assisted by Ponzi, Daniels had simply Duped Harris about the details of the settlement, and Harris only received a $9,500 contingency fee from Daniels. The very next day, Ponzi walked out of Tremont Trust with another $185,000 in cash.

Ponzi had gained the upper hand again, and he was now asked by the attendant reporters if he was acting as a financing agent for Soviet Russia. Beguiled newsmen even challenged him about his connections to Lenin and Trotsky. Indeed, wild stories abounded, whilst the authorities floundered, and 'The Boston American' declared soon after that Ponzi had become the most talked about man in the whole of America and Canada. (21) From Ponzi's point of view, he had lived to fight another day, but Allen had learned about a $250,000 loan from Hanover Trust and wondered why the affluent Ponzi would ever need to borrow money, so he decided make enquiries. To counter this by another charade, Ponzi now announced that he intended seek investment in order to follow through with a bid for the entire fleet of the United States Shipping Board. Oh yes, Ponzi was at it again. In his latest enterprise, investors would receive 1–2% a month but, annualised, this was 12–24%, and a staggering return.

Whilst relaxing on Sunday 8th August, Ponzi decided to entertain the cunning Post's reporter, P. A. Santosuosso, and in the tranquil surroundings of his own home, Ponzi lowered his customary smart guard. Ponzi let it slip that he had once been involved in 'confidential investigations' in Canada and the reporter knew that there were large gaps in Ponzi's background between 1906 and 1916.

Effectively, this was a self-inflicted bullet in the foot. A female contact of Santosuosso then came forward with a rumour that Ponzi had been in the Montreal jail. The reporter's interest immediately escalated to another level and, after conveying this to Richard Crozier, the Post's correspondent in Montreal confirmed that a man who went by the name of 'Charles Ponzi, alias Bianchi', had been convicted of forgery whilst working for Banco Zarossi in Montreal. When Ponzi was challenged about this, he scoffed – but admirably concealed the fact that he had choked at the same time. Ponzi didn't know that the Post's Montreal correspondent, Herbert Baldwin, had been given his current picture, and was touting it around and asking leading questions. (22)

Meanwhile, Banking Commissioner Allen had embarked on a crafty offensive by monitoring Ponzi's fictitious account at Hanover Trust in the name of Luci Martelli, and had received word that it was 'bust'. Without further ado,

Allen ordered Hanover Trust to stop paying cheques drawn on all of Ponzi's accounts and, following mild resistance from Hanover Trust, its principal, Chmielinski, agreed. In addition, Allen instigated a very underhanded 'straw man' set up in which certain people started bankruptcy proceedings against Ponzi. The newsboys now cried *"Ponzi Stopped."* (23) In the meantime, the Post had received confirmation from Eugene Laflamme of the Montreal Police that Charles Ponzi, the Boston financier, was most certainly same man who had been convicted of forgery and sent to prison in Montreal in 1908. Ponzi's ability to wriggle out of this one was now restricted by the equivalent of a straight-jacket so, instead of striving for salvation, he would certainly need to seek leniency – and some sort of legal deal.

Ponzi's Hanover Trust accounts were now overdrawn by as much as $441,788, and this was capable of sending Hanover Trust over the edge. (24) This soon led to Banking Commissioner, Allen, taking over the Bank, which would then provide him with a bird's eye view of Ponzi's shenanigans. But Hanover's problems went far deeper than Ponzi's affairs alone. Chmielinski had used the Bank's funds as though they were his own and had made internal loans that were illegal. In the meantime, auditor Pride was so confused that his audit, carried out under the duress of time, had estimated Ponzi's liabilities at $7 million with assets of just $4 million. With a deficit of $3 million, and Allen's custody of Hanover, Ponzi's outlandish plan to rob the Bank—temporarily—was gone forever. In any event, the idea had been yet another of Ponzi's daydreams.

Ponzi seeks leniency

The Boson Post now went for broke with the headline: *"Canadian Ponzi Served Jail Term. Montreal Police, Jail Warden and Others Declare That Charles Ponzi of Boston, and Charles Ponzi of Montreal, Who Was Sentenced to Two and a Half Years in Jail for Forgery on Italian Bank Are One and the Same Man. State Authorities Now Active and Promise One Arrest in Case Soon."* Ponzi's trademark smile had now gone, as he knew that his jail sentence in 1910 in Atlanta would also be revealed sooner or later. But a weight was lifted from his mind. His beloved Rose revealed on 12th August that she knew about his prison record when she married him, and she still loved him anyway.

But the Post's headline read, *"Arrest in Ponzi Case May Be Made Today –"* and this was accompanied by cartoons showing the two Allens sticking spears into the 'Ponzi Get Rich Quick Bubble'. Ponzi now contacted Gallagher and said that he wanted to turn himself in and was thereby charged, tenuously, with 'using mails in a scheme to defraud'. But, before the court, Ponzi pleaded his innocence, and made bail whilst he was also awaiting federal charges. However, shortly after, two police officers served him with a warrant from Attorney General Allen, charging Ponzi with three counts of larceny.

Indeed, the friction between the authorities and Ponzi had made the situation red raw, and the demigods of state, public office and banking would not let go. The Post's headline now read: *"Ponzi Arrested. Admits Now he Can't Pay $3,000,000 Short."* (25) In this devastating article, the Post had simply decided to vent its anger against Ponzi and, unable to pay his bail, he was told he would have to spend the night in East Cambridge Jail. However, he went on to spend three months there, which enabled Allen to turn the screws until federal charges could be brought. (26) Yes, the authorities simply wanted to have Ponzi 'stretchered off the playing field', and were prepared to use any tactics that were necessary.

During these weeks, Ponzi was inundated with federal and state indictments in probably the most complicated bankruptcy proceedings that had ever been seen in Massachusetts. In November, Ponzi now faced two counts of larceny, the second of which contained no less than 86 separate charges. At this time, it was unheard of that someone could face a federal and state court on the same facts, so Ponzi refused to cut a deal. (27) However, on 30th November 1920, Ponzi appeared in court and, following frantic persuasion from his lawyers, Dan Coakley and Daniel McIsaac, Ponzi submitted a guilty plea. Judge Clarence Hale promptly sentenced him to a five-year term in Plymouth County Jail.

The facts of the matter were quite simple. The Securities Exchange had been working towards extinction ever since it had attempted to trade International Reply Coupons the previous December. Ponzi himself, had simply taken an injudicious gamble with other people's money and, for survival, had resorted to 'robbing Peter to pay Paul'. During that halcyon day of 24th July 1920, when he had flashed his beaming smile to the onlookers before entering the Niles Building, Ponzi was already up to his neck in more problems than he would ever be able to handle – in spite of the millions of dollars he had been able to stash.

With Ponzi now out of the way, Allen's anticipated repercussions became reality.

(28) Some local banks now collapsed within days, in the proverbial 'pack of cards' scenario.

The president of Cosmopolitan Trust, Max Mitchell, and colleagues had been so dishonest with Bank funds that even Ponzi himself would have been ashamed. Unsurprisingly, Cosmopolitan Trust crashed and was followed shortly after by Fidelity Trust. A few months later, Simon Swig's Tremont Trust also failed. A terrible banking crisis now erupted which would, unfortunately, be repeated at the back end of the same feted 'Roaring Twenties' decade. Ponzi's scheme had attracted well over 20,000 clients, and some eventually received, after the Securities Exchange's failure, 37.5% of their original investment, but this was paid as late as 1930. (29)

A year after the arrest of Ponzi, his lawyer, Dan Coakley, and Suffolk District Attorney Joseph Pelletier, faced charges for their long-standing and lewd sexual extortion racket, but they were not alone. Alongside them was cohort Nathan Tufts, the Middlesex County District Attorney. In their devious scheme, they had created a position in which they could embarrass certain 'marks' all over Boston and beyond. But things were worse for Coakley. He faced further charges for selling soft pardons to known criminal and the authorities were determined to throw the book at him. (30)

Ponzi was released from Plymouth Jail in August 1924 for being well behaved, after serving four of his five-years. But, by that November, the State had Ponzi back on trial on the other five pending indictments, and the trial itself was eventually deadlocked. Seven months later, Ponzi was sentenced to seven to nine years in state prison as a 'common thief' but, with a modicum of relief for the little man, the sentence was stayed pending Ponzi's appeal.

Under the jurisdiction of the law, Charles Ponzi and Rose headed south to the sunny State of Florida in September 1925. However, prodded and prompted by the old demons, Ponzi could see that this beautiful place was also a haven where opportunities to make money in a property market boom were ready to be plucked like low hanging fruit – and this was irresistible. In an abbreviation of his own name, he set up 'Charpon Land Syndicate' offering investors 200% in 60 days based on his fantastically over-estimated ability to sell ten million lots of property around Jacksonville. (31)

He started on borrowed money from friends and bought 100 acres of desolate land for 40 dollars an acre, which was mostly waterlogged. It was named the 'Rose Marie Tract', but this was yet another Ponzi ruse as each acre was divided into twenty-three lots that were so cramped, the provision of adequate living quarters, with amenities, would have been almost impossible. Ponzi expected to sell the lots for $10 each to unsuspecting people, who would soon discover that they were owners of property in mosquito-ridden swampland. Yes, this would yield nearly 500% profit on his original investment. But extraordinary figures always attract exceptional attention, so the newsrooms were soon onto Ponzi, and CLS was promptly shut down. Ponzi was sentenced to a year in jail for violating Florida's security laws, but remained free pending an appeal.

It was now June 1926. With seven to nine years hanging over him in Massachusetts, and now one year in Florida, Ponzi decided to fake his own death. He left his clothes on a beach in Jacksonville and made it look as though he had disappeared into the white foam forever. However, even in disguise, the infamous Ponzi was soon identified. With a shaven head and sporting a moustache, he was working aboard a passenger vessel under yet another alias – Andrea Luciana. It seems that the impulsive psyche that was in control of Ponzi's very being had caused him to blab about his past exploits. His undoubted notoriety meant that the original spark of suspicion grew rapidly, and it was soon discovered that the man in disguise, was the much-maligned fugitive – Charles Ponzi.

When you don't know when to speak, and when to shut up, it simply makes you a fool. Yes, Ponzi was in huge trouble again, simply because he had an irresistible urge to seek self-justification in front of almost any willing audience. Ponzi was returned to Boston in February 1927 to begin his sentence in Massachusetts State Prison in Charlestown. He sought pardons on compassionate grounds in 1930, but failed. But this little man had a nature that would never allow him to yield. In 1934, he was released with another 'fortune' – $70 in prison earnings. But even with this token amount of money, the authorities knew that the indefatigable Ponzi was capable, from such a minuscule financial base, of attempting to launch yet another of his ground-breaking financial initiatives.

Unwilling to take the risk, all ties with the USA were well and truly cut on 7th October 1934, when Ponzi was deported to Italy as an undesirable alien. It was now America's Great Depression and during this period, 'The Gold Standard' introduced in 1879, came under a great deal of pressure in the 1930s.

Rose divorced Ponzi in 1936, which broke his heart. He had never been in a position to truly grant her the devotion she had craved, nor had he been able to amply demonstrate the sincere love he had in his heart for his beloved wife. The repercussions from the Securities Exchange, in fact, were a truly insurmountable obstacle in their relationship.

Notably, the Post published its very last edition on 4th August, 1956.

As for Ponzi – he had made a truly indelible mark during his era, and is still remembered extremely well by the financial commentators and historians of today.

This pint-sized con man's legacy was the term 'Ponzi Scheme' which was coined to describe his devious exploits. Almost inevitably, his name still seems to crop up whenever financial scams and under-hand dealings occur. The bankruptcy in 2001 of the corporate giant, Enron, led one senator to point an accusing finger at its chairman, Kenneth Lay. He was described as being the 'most accomplished confidence man since Charles Ponzi', after employees and investors lost billions of dollars when the business collapsed. (32) With a sense of irony, wildly optimistic or over-elaborate corporate propositions and 'upstarts', are still referred to as Ponzi Schemes. As we shall see in chapter eight, some of the companies that surfaced during the 'Dot.com Bubble' of the nineties would certainly fit the bill. We will also take a look at Bernie Madoff and his massive 'revolving door scam'. Many financial commentators soon likened this to a Ponzi Scheme, even though it was initiated around thirty years after Ponzi's death in a charity hospital in Rio de Janeiro on 18th January, 1949.

In his last interview with a reporter. Ponzi said, "I had given them the best show in their territory since the landing of the Pilgrims. It was easily worth fifteen million bucks to just to watch me put that thing over." (33)

The Roaring Twenties

In December 1928, the retiring President, Calvin Coolidge, delivered a positive speech to congress, which confirmed the healthy state of the Union. Indeed, his address epitomised the feeling of joy and contentment throughout its states, as the people were living life to the full. Financial optimism, exuberance, and glamour splendidly characterised this glorious period, which became known as the 'Roaring Twenties', or the 'Jazz Age'. With the American people in such a buoyant mood, there was not even an inkling that the nation had already set itself on a collision course with financial disaster. Worse still – this was a tragedy that would materialise during the next twelve months, and take the nation into a decade of depression.

A truly colourful decade!

Within a few years of the end of World War One (1914–1918), large American cities such as New York, Chicago and Los Angeles hosted a cultural renaissance and, as well as spreading throughout the United States, this ebullient air soon found its way to Europe and beyond. Cities like London, Paris and Sydney also started to heave with the new social ambiance when people were able to enjoy the trappings of a much better life. After the demoralising austerity suffered during the war years, most westernised nations wholeheartedly embraced the chance of a fresh start. (1)

Mass marketing campaigns and media advertising now escalated consumer demand to unprecedented levels. On the back of this wave, large movie theatres, clubs, sports stadia, vaudeville, shows, coffee shops, restaurants and other leisure venues were able to enjoy a stream of enthusiastic clientele. The lively street scene was further enhanced by the light blue and pink facades of Art Deco style buildings interspersed with bold innovative structures – and these landmark edifices were occasionally humbled by adjacent warehousing or small retail outlets clustered with goods. But then came the harsh pockets of dereliction, patiently waiting to make way for the inevitability of modernisation. America was certainly 'on the move', and anything seemed possible at this time.

The cultural surge of the twenties also brought new stars in the movie business, on stage and in the sports world. Naturally, fans were always eager to catch a glimpse of their latest heroes, and a vast majority of media advertising campaigns were smartly designed to fulfil their wishes. By January 1926, the most formidable marketing and advertising medium ever invented was unveiled by John Logie Baird – the world's first television.

Indeed, the rapid industrial and economic growth during this decade had turned America into the most prosperous nation in the world. The automobile industry now flourished, telephone lines formed a network in most of the big cities, aviation became a promising business, the chemical industry advanced, and millions of households were enthralled by the use of electrical appliances. In the film business, there were equally notable developments at the hands of Lee de Forest at Phonofilm, and the public now had the wonder of motion pictures with sound. Cinema going became a prominent feature of life during this era and, together with the expensive luxury of radio, it helped to provide society with what it craved most—entertainment. But as well as cinema and other social outlets, there was another huge passion at this time—jazz music. The swinging city of Charleston in South Carolina introduced a trendy new dance routine, aptly called the Charleston, and this would become a familiar jig in many of the vibrant ball rooms and dance clubs of the decade.

However, the 'prohibition era' ran throughout these times, and there was not a legal drop of alcohol to be found anywhere in the union.

This void provided an opportunity for bootleggers to smuggle illicit booze, which created very robust competition for turf between powerful criminal syndicates. To help sell their liquor, speakeasies were set-up in many of the large cities and towns, and these underground dens would pulsate, through to the early hours. The authorities mounted frequent raids, but as soon as they closed one hangout, another pre-planned venue would be opened within a matter of days. Indeed, illegal alcohol was big business in gangland and, together with gambling, it had been outlawed back in 1910. The exception to this rule was the state of Nevada, where casinos were still permitted to stay open. However, the syndicates quietly welcomed this law because it handed them, on a plate, exclusive control outside Nevada in both illegal liquor sales and gaming. This status quo remained until prohibition was lifted in 1933.

On the back of the cultural surge of the twenties, ex-banker and Vice President to Calvin Coolidge, Charles Gates Dawes, introduced the Dawes' Plan. (2) Within a few years of the end of World War One, Germany had declared that it was no longer able to pay war reparations to Great Britain, France and the other allied powers. This was hardly surprising as its cities, its industrial heartland, and the people's morale had been well and truly flattened. To help Germany pay its war reparations to the allied powers, Dawes instigated the rebuilding of this war-ravaged country through heavy Wall Street investment. In turn, the allied powers would then be in a position to repay the money they had borrowed from America to fund their participation in the Great War. This was an ambitious arrangement indeed, as it relied on a great deal of inter-dependency, as well as a very elusive time element – the length of time it would take to rebuild Germany and kick-start its economy.

Dawes' Vice Presidency ran from 1925 and ended at the pinnacle of the Great Wall Street Crash of 1929. It is doubtful that such a catastrophic meltdown ever came into consideration when Dawes conceived his elaborate plan, as all the nations he had intended to help were now embroiled in a global depression.

Chapter 6
The Great Crash of 1929

The stock market crash of October, 1929, also known as the 'Great Crash' and the 'Wall Street Crash', left a legacy that is still talked about by today's generations, and will certainly be on the lips of those to come. This was the most devastating crash of the securities markets in the history of the United States and was responsible for an economic slump that affected all the industrialised Western nations. With billions of dollars in wealth wiped out in just days, economies were soon gripped by the worst depression the world had ever seen. The austerity that followed did not show any signs of abating until the late thirties but, alas, the fresh shoots of economic recovery were abruptly squashed by the Second World War (1938–1945).

However, when America rolled into the Roaring Twenties, the nation had not fully recovered from the chronic after-effects of World War One. When hostilities finally ended, it was necessary for a number of large, industrialised countries to revamp their wartime economies so that they would be able to serve peacetime needs. This was a huge task because, in America alone, just under five million military personnel had returned from active duty and needed to be absorbed into civilian life.

Competition for employment thereby intensified significantly and, between January 1920 and July 1921, America suffered a short, but very severe recession. Economists believe that the main cause of this was the deflationary measures imposed by the Federal Reserve when attempts were made to abate the 9.8% average rate of inflation between 1913 and 1919 – a period which overlapped the Great War years. Nonetheless, these remedial steps were successful, and inflation was contained at around 0.4% throughout the remainder of the twenties. Farmers were particularly affected during this decade because the imposition of tight fiscal controls left their production costs very high and forced their sales values down, thereby reducing margins to almost unworkable proportions. (3)

In the early part of the twenties, stock market prices were quite low and didn't start to pick up until late 1924. But this was an indication that the effects of the industrial and economic reset during the immediate post-war years had started to accrue some benefit. Certain Americans were very receptive to the signs of a bull market phase, as this presented them with a means of bettering their post war status. This kind of materialistic credo was perhaps understandable during these times, as memories of the harsh war years still lingered.

Although gambling was outlawed throughout the twenties, playing the stock market was the next best thing for those who had a propensity for games of chance. Fortunately, this was the early stages of a good bull market and share prices were only going one way. The early participants therefore began to spread the word about this exciting opportunity and, fuelled by increasing media coverage, the curiosity of the wider public naturally grew. Being the odd one out in peer groups or in the workplace was often a reason to join in, but it would be wrong to say that everyone did. This new trend in the stock market was way beyond the comprehension of a vast proportion Americans, whilst many others chose to watch from afar and mull things over. As one would expect, those with an intrepid spirit jumped straight in, however, these parvenus had inadvertently pitched themselves against seasoned professionals in the finance world, (4) as well as erstwhile speculators from the public.

Of course, Wall Street did its best to accommodate anyone who was willing to take a chance, and more and more brokerage accounts were opened as the market activity gathered pace.

Throughout 1927, share prices continued to climb in a confident upward trend, thereby providing very hospitable conditions for retail traders and professionals alike. This was a time when the celebrations of those who were making money encouraged the participation of others who had taken refuge on the fence. As interest escalated still further, the nation's fascination with stock market banter became an unmistakeable feature of life in these times. Enthusiastic exchanges about promising new shares could be heard from the breakfast-table to the dinner-table, from the workplace to the leisure park, from the coffee shop to the speakeasy – where spirits were elevated to new levels by the prospect of making money.

By the late summer of 1928, in fact, the volume of shares traded had increased so dramatically, that this phase of the boom was often referred to as 'stock market fever'. As a result, the Times Industrial Average rose by 35% after new record volumes of shares had been traded by June that year. (5) With such a huge price rise in a relatively short space of time, this signalled that more and more bullish investors were now invading the market. As time would reveal, this mindset had inculcated a strong gambling ethos, where far too many of the people involved simply believed that everything they touched would continue to go up in value.

These were the good times my friend – we thought they'd never end!

This rapid increase in the number of market participants caused an escalation in the demand for brokers' loans – or margin. (6) This was usually made available after investors placed an amount of money in a trading account, which would be matched by the credit extended by the broker. This allowed clients to trade twice the volume of shares, but it also doubled their exposure. The stocks acquired in this manner were then deposited with the broker as collateral. This was routine procedure, and continued to be an adequate form of security, provided that the retained shares performed in a positive manner. However, if their value dropped to a level which wiped out the broker's margin, and then depleted the client's deposit, a margin call (*) would be made. This meant that the client would need to replenish his account so that the broker's security margin was re-established. Fortunately, American markets in 1927 were in a strong bullish trend, and margin calls were minimal – but as things developed, this would not be the case.

It was against this background, in fact, that investment trusts rapidly gained in popularity. (7) These alternative investment vehicles overcame the worries in this era about the shortage of common stocks and margin calls. These new funds aggregated their shareholders' investments to facilitate the purchase of a variety of securities, and thereby provided a much wider range of market opportunities for their clients. People with just a small amount of money now had a chance to participate and, through the pooling of resources, a diverse portfolio of shares could be acquired. Essentially, this spread the risk, but this consideration was immaterial to some credulous souls, as the notion of risk was not part of their psyche.

Such was the prestige of certain 1920s investment trusts, (*) like the Blue Ridge and Shenandoah Corporations, that the value of their own stock was sometimes much greater than the value of their underlying assets. Their underlying assets were the blocks of securities that had been bought in other companies on behalf of the trust's shareholders. The difference in value was created by the additional money that people were prepared to pay for the investment trust's shares, as this provided novices with the much-needed expertise of a fund manager. In recognition of their all-embracing service, the investment trusts would receive commission, fees and performance related bonuses.

In essence, all that some people really wanted during the 1920s was an open position (*) in what they regarded as a 'safe' market. However, the burden of paying over the odds to participate in the likes of Blue Ridge, Shenandoah or other individual stocks was not an ideal starting point for investors – albeit a sign of these times.

For investors who were willing and able to look with discerning eyes, this was already a heads-up that an unwieldy marketplace was starting to develop at this time. However, it certainly seems that very few people could understand that the overvaluation of so many different shares might sooner or later be problematic. But this may be considered a weak excuse for some of the top professionals who were unwittingly caught up in the dire events that eventually unfolded. (8) When shares are over-valued en-masse in a seemingly endless bull market, there is often trouble looming on a very large scale, and the 1920s would bear witness to this.

One of the biggest problems was that brokers' loans and investment trusts had significantly widened the scope of the public's involvement, and the attitude of many in the twenties was to jump on the band-waggon, and throw everything available at the opportunity. As a result, the extent of the stock market gambling became so extreme, that it eventually turned into self-delusion as people began to believe that they were simply pre-destined to enjoy good fortune and attendant riches. In many ways, this was no different to the earlier booms such as Tulip Mania and the South Sea Bubble.

However, certain adverse factors impacted the US economy during the twenties, and there is little doubt that these helped to shape the fate of the decade.

Quite some time before the fateful year of 1929, the American economy had already started to show signs of weakness. Both the industrial and factory production indexes began to decline and, in the aftermath of the war, it certainly appears that America had gained too much economic and industrial ground far too quickly. (9) Elsewhere, the 'Dawes Plan' had not delivered what it had promised, as some of the other nations involved in the war were still feeling its severe after-effects. We also noted earlier how difficulties in the agricultural sector persisted for a long time after the short recession of 1920 to 1921.

America's house building sector also experienced problems during the 1920s and this industry was a hugely important cog in the economy. (10) Following over enthusiastic speculation yet again, house values peaked in 1926 and were said to be declining between then and 1929. The dearth of buyers in this market by 1926 was both noticeable and worrying, particularly in Florida which had been the cradle of the boom. At its height, it became quite common for areas of land, sometimes of very poor quality, to be divided into tiny plots and then sold. In fact, this was a time when building plots were often perceived as tradable assets, rather than ground upon which houses were meant to be built. In any event, building houses on certain plots would have been very difficult indeed as they were in swampland. Carpetbaggers like Charles Ponzi had already been there and left their mark.

Florida – the land of opportunity for the likes of Ponzi!

The more recent 2007/8 housing boom was very similar, when a large proportion of real estate speculators simply wanted to turn their stake into a profit as quickly as possible, and then look for the next opportunity. However, this strategy created a host of problems. When properties had changed hands on several occasions, and in a relatively short space of time, asking prices eventually reached levels that were unsustainable. This was the point at which lower market values were created by receding numbers of buyers and, in this game of 'pass the parcel', far too many people were left holding overpriced pieces of real estate.

The Florida real estate boom of the 1920s certainly added to the nation's problems but, in terms of primacy, the stock market had reached an unprecedented and very uncomfortable position during the latter stages of its bullish phase. With many Americans still in a buoyant mood, there were certainly fears from those in authority that any negative commentary, or direct warning of danger, might be seen as an attempt to undermine stock market confidence. (11) Much worse, an orchestrated effort to break-up the boom could have triggered a frantic selling spree and a premature crash.

A laissez-faire policy was therefore adopted during the late phase of the trend by those in Congress, the Treasury and the Federal Reserve. As for the press, there were very few members at the time who did anything other than extol the virtues of speculation. Comments from a few sceptical economists were regarded as unimportant, simply because most people did not believe what they were saying. It was therefore plain to see that any effort to slow things down would have been most unwelcome. Besides, many of the influential incumbents of high office, well-known celebrities, and other high society figures were, of course, leading by example – they were speculating and enjoying life to the full at the same time.

With speculators in this frame of mind, it was clear that there was a serious conflict between the notion of regulation, sensible as it may sound, and people's right to free market enterprise. In the twenties, this conundrum would have placed those responsible for regulation between a rock and a hard place. Even when the state of affairs reached an unmistakeable crisis point, regulation, or rather, efforts to slow things down, were feeble at best. At this critical stage, some speculators had simply taken leave of their senses, and their lack of control escalated the recklessness of others. At least, the Federal Reserve could have restricted the use of margin, as this was still ladling a great deal of borrowed money into an already overbought market. Had this happened, it might have diffused what amounted to a ticking bomb but, instead, brokers were now lending investors and speculators two thirds of the face value of most stocks.

The estimated $8.5 billion that was out on loan was more than the entire amount of hard currency in circulation in the whole of the United States.

Looking back a couple of years, there had been a general strike in the UK in 1926 and, in the spring of 1927, the Bank of England urged the Federal Reserve to have an easy money policy in order to help the hard-pressed Europeans.

Life in the underworld – the Speakeasy

The Federal Reserve duly obliged and many economists believe that this was another factor that helped to escalate the stock market boom. However, restricting the money supply during the twenties surge would not have been an easy task. There were not only brokers' loans, but also loans from corporations and the banking industry. At this time, banks were borrowing money from the Federal Reserve at a rate of 5%, and re-loaning it to the call market at 12%. This was splendidly described as the best arbitrage game in town. (12)

The Federal Reserve could have increased interest rates but, in what would have been a vicious circle, this would have impacted straight away on the confidence and performance of the large corporations. This course of action was therefore resisted until the summer of 1929 – by which time, it was too late.

As the crisis point was approaching, the Harvard Economics Society announced that a recession was 'overdue', and other prophets of impending doom soon jumped on the band-waggon. On several occasions, the New York

Times had relayed quite sceptical narrative, and eventually announced that the day of reckoning had arrived, but this turned out to be premature. In February, 1929, the Federal Reserve dispatched an ambiguous letter to its member banks, which appeared to be sending out a warning about loaning money for speculation. The following month, Paul M. Warburg called for a stronger Federal Reserve Policy, suggesting that, otherwise, there would be a collapse. But, by this time, the position was just about irrecoverable.

As a result of the humongous scale of this boom, it has often been assumed that almost every adult in the nation was eventually engaged in speculation but, as indicated earlier, this notion would be quite misleading. (13) In 1920s America, speculation was way beyond the means of many, and far beyond the comprehension of others, but in this narrow field of play, those who actually took part did so with devastating vigour. During this period of time, America had a population of around 120 million, and it has been estimated that approximately 2%, at most, were speculating. But the definitive figure was secondary to other key issues. It was the amount of money that speculators had at their disposal, its origins, and their reckless use of it that mattered. After all, when these factors were combined, the 'cocktail' was sufficiently potent to tip the American economy over the edge, and hasten a global depression.

Immediately prior to the crash, it is perhaps ironic that blatant attempts were made to influence the course of events by confirming that prosperity would continue. Scholars and politicians often lent their names and blessings to certain glamour stocks and new promotions. It was common for values to be 'talked-up' by influential and articulate personalities of the time. (14) Certain self-serving individuals actually paid for favourable commentary on the market as a whole, as well as individual stocks. The Directors of the Federal Reserve Bank in New York were, themselves, engaged in the speculation, which indicates that the allure of this boom was irresistible – even for those who were at the source of the money supply.

Therefore, the old cliché that 'it had to end sometime' was a notion that most speculators had never contemplated – until it was too late. The frantic activity in the stock market culminated in a prodigious climb in stock prices in 1928, which peaked in the late summer 1929.

The markets then crashed in spectacular fashion!

'Black Thursday' dawned on 24th October 1929, and it certainly lived up to its name. The volume of shares sold on this particular day surpassed anything that the American stock market had ever seen in a single day's activity, when 12.9 million shares were traded. Instead of the euphoria that had been evident over the past number of months, there was now a dark atmosphere in which everyone was desperate to offload stock. Instead of the usual hordes of buyers, there were far too many frenetic sellers in the market – yet, some people were unaware, or refused to believe, that the stock markets had started to roll over. There can be no doubt that the ownership of shares on margin had simply disseminated the problems long before this fateful day. This meant that the blue-chip companies, and the banks and brokerages who had loaned money, were well and truly embroiled.

In the six years prior to 1929, the world had seen the Dow Jones industrial average increase fivefold in value, and prices peaked at 381.17 on September 3rd 1929. Over the next month however the market declined sharply, losing 17% of its value on the first correction. (*) Following a brief recovery, the downturn quickly resumed, and accelerated into 'Black Thursday's mass sell-off'. (15)

Total fear now gripped the markets so attempts were made on the floor of the Exchange to stem the tide of selling. During the lunchtime of that same day, several leading Wall Street bankers met to try and find a solution. They chose Richard Whitney, Vice President of the Exchange, to employ the financial resources at their disposal to place bids for large blocks of shares in certain blue-chip companies, at prices well above the current market. (16) This managed to slow down the rate of decline, but the respite was very brief and the markets continued to lose value at an alarming rate during Friday.

Over the weekend, these events were extensively covered by newspapers across the nation, thereby placing the current stock market problems within full public view. For half a decade, the same newspapers had highlighted the buoyancy of these markets, so some within the wider public now began to worry that the latest developments might have severe repercussions. Inevitably, the pressure built throughout Saturday and Sunday for speculators, as each one had little idea what others would do when the market action resumed on Monday.

Having to think in the dark caused panic, which led almost everyone to the same conclusion – to sell.

When the markets re-opened on 'Black Monday'—28th October, 1929—the frantic sell-off recommenced producing a record loss in the Dow of 13%. The following day, over 16 million shares were traded, a record that was not broken until 1968, which was nearly forty years later. (17) On this truly cataclysmic day for the American markets, the Dow declined by a further 12%. In monetary terms, this brought the total losses for the week to a staggering £30 billion.

Sadly, this did not prove to be the end of the decline. Following a putative bottom (*) in the markets in November, they attempted to rally over subsequent months, and reached 294.07 on April 30th, 1930. The markets then embarked on a steep decline which culminated in 1932 when the Dow closed at a low of 41.22 on 8th July. This concluded a financially shattering period in the US stock market, which had experienced a total loss in value from its peak, of 89%. This was the lowest the market had been since the eighteen hundreds but, fortunately, the Dow has never seen these price levels since. (18)

Of course, accusing fingers were pointed in several directions immediately after the crash.

Amongst the usual suspects, banks were particularly berated for being too eager to risk their deposits and lend money during what was latterly referred to as a catastrophic meltdown. As a result of this debacle, some 4,000 lenders failed, and vital industrial and commercial enterprises were now short of cash. This was an ironic twist as many of these same enterprises had been extremely willing to lend money during the boom – yet they were suddenly experiencing frightful liquidity problems. (19)

For public life in general, all of this would have dire knock-on effects. Head-first, the high life of the Roaring Twenties was about to run into the 1930s, and the worst depression the world had ever known.

The tentacles of blame for this cataclysmic event also reached Britain, Germany and France who had sought an easing of America's monetary policy during the twenties. But this was probably a secondary factor, or even a decoy, as other events had played a bigger part. Around this same time, the buying and selling of Government securities in America had increased significantly, and this had expanded the amount of cash available for speculation. This surfeit of ready money certainly helped to propel the markets towards their tipping point far more quickly.

As we have already learned, there was another significance source of impact. The 1920s had witnessed the final stages of the Florida property boom, and the escalation in stock market activity occurred straight after its decline in 1926. Many of those who had generated cash from the real-estate boom, were already on the lookout for their next opportunity.

Of course, the 1920s stock market boom provided an ideal platform – but one that eventually had to support an impossible burden.

Derivatives Became the
New Tools of the Trade

In several respects, the eighties proved to be a notable decade for the financial world, and Barings was certainly influenced by the course of events.

Between 1982 and 1985, derivatives (*) became the new-fangled 'tools of the trade', and these instruments were so called because their value derived from the price movement of an underlying asset – which was often a particular stock, commodity or currency. Innovative products such as futures contracts and options now took their place alongside warrants, which were already in use at the start of this era. To a large extent, Barings' earnings were underpinned by their trading in 'warrants' from 1985 to 1989, when Christopher Heath was CEO of the enormously successful Securities Division of the Bank. This kind of performance undoubtedly helped to maintain Barings' status as one of the most respected Banks in the City.

The Singapore Government opened the Singapore International Monetary Exchange in September 1984 and, during the early part of this same year, Barings had established a link to the far east by the acquisition of a small stockbroking company, Henderson Crosthwaite. This firm specialised in selling Japanese shares to British investors in what was quite a niche operation. In anticipation of a sea change towards the trading of derivatives, SIMEX launched the world's first Stock Index Futures in 1986, and this was based on the Japanese Nikkei 225. As a result of these developments, opportunity had knocked for Barings as it already had a foothold in the far east.

In order to keep the City of London up to speed with the other large financial centres, there was the 'Big Bang' on 17th October 1986. Under Margaret Thatcher and her Chancellor, Nigel Lawson, the government deregulated the London Stock Exchange. The LSE now became a private limited company which introduced an automated price quotation system to replace the 'open outcry' (*)

method. Stock-jobbing firms were no longer used as market makers on the Exchange, and fixed commission charges were removed. The LSE was now able to compete for turnover with the New York Stock Exchange, and the other large exchanges around the world.

Barings and its competitors now had to interface with these procedural changes, but plenty of notice had been provided by the government so that the process could be seamless. However, close on the heels of these major strides, another kind of 'big bang' rocked the finance world. Almost exactly one year after the overhaul of the LSE, the markets around the world crashed when, on 19th October 1987, there was 'Black Monday'. There has been a great deal of debate ever since about this fateful day, as so many bullish stock-market participants were caught in what turned out to be a frantic selling spree.

For many brokers, this activated real problems

In fact, just a few days before Big Bang, Nigel Lawson had said in an interview that 'the conditions for greater economic stability now exist'. At the beginning of October 1987, another important headline endorsed these sentiments when it was stated that "the leading US Government indicators are the main barometers of economic growth, and they have risen for seven consecutive months this year." The US Commerce Department postulated that this signalled 'continuing strength in the economy'. In the UK, the biggest order ever recorded had been placed for 20,000 lightweight cars and vans, the chemical industry had noted 'favourable conditions' and the overseas news was generally up-beat to bullish. As for Barings, it was reported that two thirds of the Bank's profits had come from securities dealing, so their forecasts for 1987 were positive. (1)

However, on Friday 16th October that same year, a ferocious storm hit the UK and closed the all the London markets. Throughout the 16th, there were large falls on the DJIA in America, as there were lingering concerns from the previous day about an Iranian missile strike on two oil tankers, one close to Kuwait's Mina Al Ahmadi Port. (2) In spite of the bullish outlook earlier in the month, sentiment suddenly changed, and it shook the markets violently.

Following that weekend, Monday the 19th October saw the Dow Jones Industrial Average lose 22.76% of its value, which was a record at that time. The S&P Futures dropped even further, and lost 33%. On Black Monday and Tuesday combined, the UK markets lost 26.45% in value and, in the southern hemisphere, the New Zealand markets plummeted by 60%, whilst Australia suffered a loss of 41.8%. Japan, however, was 'shaken but not stirred' by this crash. By 1988, it became the world's major creditor nation and was said to have the best stock market, the best financial institutions and corporations, which were also the best capitalised. These halcyon times were, however, short-lived and the Japanese bubble burst the following year. By 1990, stocks in this part of the world had lost 48% of their value.

Baring Securities under Heath had used a put option (*) to hedge against a possible fall in the Japanese markets, and had profited by £20 million in the process. (3)

In spite of Baring's sound judgement at this juncture, there were turbulent times ahead.

Chapter 7
Nick Leeson

In terms of tradition and prestige, there could be little doubt that Barings was pre-eminent within the banking industry. This famous old institution had competed for primacy alongside other family-controlled merchant banks such as the highly esteemed Rothschilds, Kleinwort Benson, Hambros and Schroeder. (4) Over in America, Merrill Lynch, Morgan Stanley and Salomon Brothers were comparable in stature. At its 1993 year-end, Barings certainly looked healthy when it reported that its total assets were just under £6 billion and its equity base was £309.4 million. By way of comparison, the much larger high street clearing house, Barclays, had reported assets worth £163 billion and equity of £5.98 billion. On a similar scale, NatWest had reported assets worth £152 billion and £5.89 billion in equity.

As we shall see shortly, some of the events that have been described so far became major factors in the shaping of Barings' destiny. If we use the once eminently successful Christopher Heath as an example, it seems that the Bank did not pay their financial traders for a service, they paid them for a result. As soon as Heath had a lean spell, his services were no longer required.

For me, personally, 1983–1986 was a glorious time as my property ventures finally started to reap rewards. In 1985, I managed to hit the higher end of a six figure profit for the first time ever, with the use of only 10% up-front capital. Having cash available for my projects became very important as lending had slowed down during this decade. The Bank of England is said to have secretly support around 40 small banks during the property collapse of 1991 of 1991/2.

In a cash-strapped market, 'cash is automatically king' as it not only makes you self-sufficient, it provides you with enormous opportunities – as long as you use it well.

After being detained at Frankfurt Airport on 6th March 1995, Nick Leeson was extradited to Singapore on Wednesday 22nd November 1995 to face trial. In early December that year, the headline in the Financial Times read – "Leeson in guilty plea as only two charges are pressed." Prosecutors in Singapore surprisingly announced that they had dropped nine of eleven charges after the rogue futures trader admitted to 'deceiving the auditors of Barings in a way that was likely to cause harm to their reputation, and cheating SIMEX'. According to reports, Nicholas William Leeson had singlehandedly brought about the collapse of Barings Bank and, on Saturday 2nd December 1995, he was sentenced to six and a half years in Tanah Merah Prison in Singapore. (5)

The lead prosecuting counsel, Mr Lawrence Ang, said that the decision to charge Leeson on just two counts had been made at the request of his attorney, and after matters had been considered by the Commercial Affairs Department, Singapore's financial police.

When the news of Barings' failure first broke on Sunday 26th February 1995, it seemed difficult to believe that just one man could have been responsible for accumulating a loss of S$1.4 billion, which was reported soon after to be S$2.2 billion (Singapore dollars). When the full force of the devastation became more apparent, the figure was calculated in sterling at £827 million. I was not the only one who wondered how regulators and senior bank officials failed, for any longer than hours or days, to detect that such enormous amounts of money had been placed at risk, or lost, during what was said to be a 'gambling spree'. By September 1992, Leeson was reportedly in the red to the tune of £2 million in a secret account. By August 1994, he is said to have been sitting on a deficit of around £80 million, which somehow escalated to £208 million by December that same year. It is worth noting, perhaps, that the figures seem to vary between Leeson's own version of events and others, but we must bear in mind that the actual balances would have been constantly changing with the market.

The man himself claimed that his unauthorised trading began when he tried to recover a loss of £20,000, incurred by a colleague in Singapore during the spring of 1992. (6) It was later revealed, however, that he had started his gambling spree some weeks before. This was a watershed moment for Leeson and he soon found himself chasing the recovery of mounting losses by placing even bigger bets.

However, during an interview with David Frost in Hochst Prison in Frankfurt, Leeson claimed that by mid-1993, he was almost back at break-even.

(7) Sadly, he continued to gamble, probably in the hope that he would be able to corroborate the winning streak that he had already reported. With his mind eventually in a fog of confusion and self-doubt, his financial position became irrecoverable but, somehow, he still managed to be a prominent figure on the SIMEX trading floor – until he reached the point of no return during the early part of 1995.

When life in the fast lane becomes tough!

How he survived for so long remains a mystery. On the eastern trading exchanges, such as SIMEX and Osaka, futures contracts lasted three months. (8) Formal settlements between trading institutions and the exchanges would usually take place within four weeks. However, the exchanges would tot up a bank's futures contracts on a daily basis and could ask for immediate cash payments if they felt that the losses were large enough to warrant this. These requests were known as 'margin-calls'. Sizeable drawdowns of this nature caught everyone's attention, so traders and officials usually made it their business to know who was involved except, it seems, Leeson's bosses.

After all, it transpired that their man in Singapore was responsible for taking the largest losing bet in the history of the Japanese stock market, with an exposure to £3 billion's worth of Japanese shares. (9) Leeson himself, in fact, placed the figure at nearly four times this amount. (10) It was claimed that none of the Barings' staff on the trading floor in Singapore, or in London, really knew that Leeson was involved in these humungous trades, until he disappeared and the story started to unravel. Leeson's counterpart at Barings Tokyo, Fernando Gueler, later said that he and others had wondered who the extremely large trader on the Nikkei could be, as they had worked out that he could be as much as S$250 million in the red.

As this chapter unfolds, we shall learn how senior figures at Barings had, in fact, received more than their fair share of margin calls as a direct result of Leeson's losing positions. But within this daunting context, it appears that those who met these calls, still allowed Leeson to return to the SIMEX trading floor with almost unlimited authority; but why would they do this? The clue might be found in Leeson's notable success when he first started life a 'rookie' trader. During this time, there had also been a change at the top, and Peter Norris had ousted Christopher Heath, who was one of the 'old guard'. Under Heath, Barings Securities had enjoyed enormous success between 1985 and 1989 in the Japanese warrant market. But when Securities lost £26 million in 1992, Norris took over as CEO and restructured the entire operation. In reality, this created a confusing overlap of management roles, and some felt that this made Securities vulnerable. It was therefore unclear who Leeson should report to and, operating within such blurred boundaries, he simply became a law unto himself.

Leeson's school years were nothing out of the ordinary, however, Barings certainly stirred his ambition. His goal from the early part of his career with the Bank was to get noticed, and elevate himself through the ranks. On 17th September 1986, he started as a settlement clerk at Baring Securities London but, during April 1992, he joined Baring Futures Singapore (BFS) as the manager of operations for derivatives. He was in charge of both the settlements office and trading floor. Within a very short space of time for such an inexperienced dealer, he became their 'star trader', principally by use of arbitrage techniques, also known as 'switching'. (*)

Did Barings therefore believe that they had unearthed a trading prodigy; one who they needed to cosset so that he wouldn't be poached by a competitor?

Only time would tell, but his early exploits certainly earned him an enviable reputation. Leeson revelled in this and was keen to underscore his standing, but this simply launched him on a trip of self-delusion and multiplied his problems. Somehow, he managed to continue as a rogue trader for around three years.

But what on earth were Barings' management doing during this time? Perhaps it might be reasonable to assume that those in charge of this old institution were in a prolonged state of slumber, because the Bank's fate had already been sealed when they were finally aroused by news that the 'rogue trader' had gone missing. The Singapore branch of Coopers and Lybrand, in fact, found a major discrepancy in the accounts of Barings Futures Singapore (BFS) as late as January 1995 but it is then reported that, by use of doctored paperwork, Leeson managed to convince them, and Barings' management, that everything was in order. It was probably at this stage that Leeson knew he had little choice but to flee, and on Thursday 23rd February 1995, he went onto the SIMEX trading floor for the last time. By the close of business that day, the Nikkei closed at 17,885 and Leeson is said to have been long 68,039 Nikkei 225 futures contracts, short 26,000 Japanese Government Bonds, and had a mixture of Euro yen and Nikkei option positions open – yet no one knew when this market would hit the bottom and start to rally. (11)

However, as history can most certainly testify, this was not the first time that this 233-year-old institution had found itself in difficulty.

The Barings family originated from the Netherlands and, after a spell in Germany, Johan Baring eventually found his way to London in 1717. (12) The great City had an unmistakeable air of excitement as a strong speculative mood was sweeping through daily life – for these were the heady days of the much-lauded South Sea Company. Sadly, however, it also proved to be an era when there was a great deal of political and commercial chicanery for which the nation would pay a heavy price. When the huge speculative bubble eventually burst in 1720, it left enormous difficulties in its wake. However, as the turbulent years melted away, Johan's three sons, led by the youngest and the boldest, Alexander, managed to launch a successful textile business. This 1762 enterprise, in fact, provided the bedrock upon which the Barings family were able to expand their operations into other areas and, by 1763, this included banking. (13)

The reputation of the Barings Brothers, and their many partnerships, grew rapidly. This thrusted the Bank into both the public and political spotlight and 'Barings Brothers' would eventually become bankers to the British Empire, making it one of the most powerful banking houses in Europe. In 1848, the Times reported that Barings held such great balances in American money, that their influence in New York was enormous, perhaps equivalent to that in Europe. (14) Personal accounts were also held for French emperor, Napoleon 3rd, and King Leopold of Belgium. However, the illustrious history of the bank was not entirely trouble free.

The Bank's earlier investments in Latin America had been a 'mixed bag' thereby producing some notable successes, together with certain setbacks, as this was an unpredictable part of the world for business and commerce at this time. In these emerging markets, due diligence, local connections and sound intelligence were paramount. However, in spite of the potential pitfalls, the adventurous Chairman, Edward Revelstoke, took the decision to involve Barings in a £95 million investment for overseas borrowers in the 1890s, with Argentina at the top of the list. The main attraction here was the flotation of the Buenos Aires Water Supply and Drainage Company; a huge infrastructure project that was much needed to remove the City's sewage, and deliver clean water. This time, the venture turned out be a disaster for the Bank. In the face of a political crisis and revolution, the Bank's position looked extremely tenuous when its liabilities amounted to £21 million, and there was no sign that this huge sum of money would ever be recovered.

It was vital to uphold the enviable reputation of the British banking industry so the Bank of England, as well as Barings' competitors in the City, rallied to support this distinguished old institution. The cost was £17.1 million, which would be around £450 million in today's money. (15) When the BOE and the utility industries were nationalised in 1946 by Clement Atlee's Labour Government, cavalier banking practices were most certainly frowned upon. However, Barings quickly paid off its creditors and, within four years, their huge debt was discharged with gratitude. Over the next decades, Barings went from strength to strength and at its 1993-year-end, it produced a very healthy set of figures. Within just fourteen months, however, Barings' halcyon days would change dramatically.

It was 4:00 pm on Thursday 23rd February, 1995. The Senior Settlements Director from Barings in London, Tony Gamby, visited the office of the Bank's

CEO, Peter Norris. (16) With a rather nervous demeanour, he did his best to deliver what appeared to be very disturbing news concerning their BFS Office in Singapore. Gamby explained that some alarming trading records had been discovered by Tony Railton, and he was worried that there could be an even bigger picture. Earlier, Railton had tried to confront Leeson in the Singapore trading pits to ask for an explanation, but Leeson had only been interested in buying and selling futures and proved to be very elusive. When the pit trading session closed, Tony Railton and Simon Jones, Operations Manager for South-East Asia, finally managed to sit Leeson down, but he seemed to be agitated and soon left the meeting. (17) With no other choice, Railton and Jones decided to pour over the trading figures themselves in an attempt to make further sense of a complex web of transactions. They soon realised, however, that only Leeson himself would be able to unravel the current mess.

But the concerns of these two executives eventually escalated to absolute horror – when Leeson failed to turn-up, or contact them thereafter. All attempts to get in touch with Leeson, or track him down, were unsuccessful so it was now apparent that he had fled. Sadly, it later transpired that Leeson's wife had recently had a miscarriage, and he had planned to take her to Phuket for the weekend to recuperate, and also celebrate his birthday. Whichever way it is viewed, Leeson's life was most certainly in a state of turmoil at this stage.

As the vital moments melted away CEO, Peter Norris, started to suspect that Barings could have been defrauded. With a cool head, he made the decision to assemble a team of senior Bank officials to look into the matter forthwith. One of the executives, Mary Walz, had already heard the news from Singapore earlier in the day, when she was informed that SIMEX had made a £45 million margin call. (18) As the executives assembled in the CEO's office, there was already a pungent atmosphere of despondency. For most, the word was already out about the gravity of the situation the Bank now faced. Everyone in attendance soon realised that they were dealing with an unknown quantity of moving parts, as Leeson had left his trading positions open, but no one could get a handle on the numbers involved, or the amount of damage that this could cause. An earthquake had struck Hanshin, Japan, on 17th January 1995, which was only a month earlier, and this had dramatically affected the exchanges that Leeson traded on.

Aftershocks!

While the shockwaves were still resonating in the London Office, news began to filter through from Singapore. Tony Hawes, the Barings' Group Treasurer, had started to unravel the convoluted mess that the rogue trader had left behind, and he was mortified. (19) The bad news kept coming through to the London executives in chunks, none of which were bite-sized or palatable. Inexplicably, it transpired that not a single one of Leeson's losing bets had been hedged, and this was a rapidly declining market as a result of the earthquake in Japan. (20) Then, the conspicuously numbered 88888 account was discovered, which was reported to be the main vehicle for Leeson's illegal futures trading. The Bank's exposure here was huge and, to make matters worse, it would move with the Japanese Nikkei 225. It was reported that this secret account had been opened 3rd July 1992, as an 'error account' on behalf of BFS.

As the picture continued to unfold in Singapore, the news was immediately dispatched to the group of executives in London. With Peter Norris pacing up and down, those present were frantically readjusting one set of figures after another – and then an update came in which floored everyone. Tony Hawes reported from Singapore that he had discovered that Leeson had been selling options on behalf of Barings in the 88888 account, and there were thousands of them. A vast number of these were 'short straddles'. (*) This involved selling a both a call option and a put option on the Nikkei Index, with the same strike price and expiration date.

Yes, this sounds rather complicated so let's try to make the language a little more friendly. As the option writers, Barings would have profited by keeping the premiums, provided that the Nikkei remained within a certain trading range of, say, 19,000 to 21,000 points. However, the earthquake in Hanshin had certainly affected the market as the Index had dropped down to the 17,700 mark. To make matters worse, no one in the meeting with Peter Norris, or elsewhere, had a clue when or where the market might hit the bottom. So, on the one hand, Barings had profited from the premiums but, on the other, they now faced almost unlimited trading losses.

At 5:30 am on Friday morning, Andrew Tuckey, Barings' Deputy Chairman, called Norris for an update. After a fitful night, Tuckey was hoping that someone had found the estimated £100 million that was reported missing late the previous day. Following a moment's hesitation, Norris informed him that the situation was, in fact, much worse than his team had feared, and he was unsure whether the Bank could be saved. They both realised therefore that there was a strong possibility that Barings could be trading whilst it was insolvent, and urgent advice was needed. During their conversation, they also contemplated the likelihood that the full extent of Leeson's gambling spree had not been uncovered, and this might add to an already devastating picture.

To cap it all, both men knew that when the markets resumed after the weekend, they might move against Leeson's open positions.

The Hanshin Earthquake certainly created a few rifts!

At 7:15 am that same Friday morning, Norris therefore had no choice but to pick up the telephone and speak to Peter Baring. The news didn't appear to ruffle the Chairman's customary demeanour; he was known to be a rather succinct but level-headed man by those who knew him. Baring immediately took the tube to the City, and met with his board members at 8:30 am that morning. Time was now precious and, following a relatively short meeting, Peter Baring walked straight from the Bank's offices in Bishopsgate, to Threadneedle Street, so that he could let the Governor of the Bank of England know about Barings' problem.

Eddie George had left for a skiing holiday and was just entering his chalet when his deputy, Rupert Pennant-Rea, contacted him on the telephone. Realising the gravity of the situation, George took a taxi back to Geneva and then flew to London. Later in the afternoon, the top brass of fourteen of the major British clearing and merchant banks were called to a meeting at the Bank of England, but were left in the dark about its purpose. A number of them were Barings' arch rivals and, on the merchant banking side, this included the likes of Schroeder, N. M. Rothchild and Sons, Hambros and Warburg. Executives from the two clearing giants, Barclays and NatWest, had also been summoned. Between them, they were vying for information so, as could be expected, speculation was rife. Someone must be in trouble – or could there possibly have been a serious clash between John Major and his Chancellor, Kenneth Clarke? Could a high-level resignation be imminent? Naturally, some of the contingent were extremely curious as it had crossed their minds that the wider industry might be impacted by some kind of shocking news.

At 5:30 pm that Friday, the elite of the City's banking world filed into the BOE's octagonally shaped Committee Room and, when seated en masse, they created a truly foreboding scene. They were soon joined by Pennant-Rea and Brian Quinn from the BOE who took no time at all to put the group in the picture about Barings' plight. In a very direct manner, they were informed that they would be called upon for assistance so, without further ado, Pennant-Rea asked them to leave their weekend contact numbers. The meeting was very brief and to the point and lasted no more than half an hour. Significantly, prior to this gathering, Peter Baring had been told by the BOE that public funds would not be available to assist with a bail out. The BOE did not want a repeat of the Johnson Mathey affair in 1984 when it had pledged bail out funds without consultation with those higher up. The BOE was under the control of the Treasury and its senior civil servant, Sir Terry Burns, who had been put in the picture earlier about Barings, by Pennant-Rea. (21) Burns had a close relationship with Kenneth Clarke, and therefore knew that he and the Prime Minister, John Major, must also be informed.

The BOE, affectionately known as the 'old lady of Threadneedle Street', Burns and Clarke were reasonably confident that the wider industry would not be affected if Barings failed – particularly when it became known that this was caused by a huge fraud committed by just one 'rogue trader'. Clearly, they were speculating on the sentiment of investors, depositors and the wider public, who were known to be rather unpredictable if bad news started to hit the fan. Other merchant bankers realised this and were most certainly concerned.

After weighing up the available options, and accepting that Barings would now lose its independence, Peter Baring and his deputy, Andrew Tuckey, decided to look for a buyer. They knew that they needed to have as many balls in the air as they could possibly juggle whilst they were waiting to see what their competitors might offer in bail out money. Their first port of call was the Dutch bank, ABN Amro and its Chairman, Jan Kalff, who they knew was interested in acquiring a merchant bank in the City. Next, they called two of the largest US investment banks, Smith Barney and Merrill Lynch but, as they had anticipated, it was Kalff who showed the most interest.

After a long and somewhat demoralising day, Baring and Tuckey set off home during the early hours of Saturday 25th so that they could rest, and then be ready for an 8:00 am start later that morning. When proceedings resumed, Schroeder were asked if they would act as advisors to Barings, and their head of corporate finance, Win Bischoff, was appointed. At 9:30 am, Bischof, Baring, Tuckey, Norris, Pennant-Rea and Eddie George, affectionately known as 'Hard Eddie', started their conference. At this stage, the losses were understated at around £385 million, but everyone knew that Leeson had abandoned his futures and option contracts, and prices would be on the move again by Monday. With a recapitalisation or sale of the Bank, this would pose an obvious problem, so they only had until Sunday night to strike a deal. The good news that morning was that staff from ABN Amro had already appeared, and were on the eighteenth floor reviewing information but, unfortunately, their interest was short-lived.

During Barings' conference with the BOE, there had been a ping-pong of ideas, and potential buyers were therefore suggested. The Quantum Fund run by Soros came into the picture and, in fact, interest from the Sultan of Brunei was soon confirmed. Eddie George felt that the Bank of Japan's governor could also be sounded out to see if he could organise a rescue through any of his contacts.

Credit Suisse Financial Products were approached to see if some sort of deal could be struck for them to take over Leeson's positions. Their CEO, Chris Goekjian, visited Barings' offices with a colleague at 6:00 pm that Saturday evening. Very highly regarded, Goekjian was a man who really knew the ropes, but when Norris presented him with the picture, he was simply in disbelief about the scale of the problem. He told Norris that he couldn't possibly fathom how Barings had let this happen. Goekjian and his colleague left through the rear doors of Barings' offices in Bishopsgate at 8:00 pm that evening, as members of the press had already started to gather at the front.

Meanwhile, Bischoff had been busy on the telephone asking for pledges from the bank officials who had left their telephone numbers the previous day. By mid-evening on Saturday, he was rather pleased that he had managed to raise around £400 million to cover Barings estimated exposure of £385 million.

However, he met with Peter Baring, Tuckey, Norris and Eddie George early the following morning for a quick review prior to their banking summit, and his sense of achievement soon wilted. He was given the news from Singapore that the Bank's losses were more likely to be around £600 million, which was a huge increase. All of a sudden, Bischoff became very apprehensive about passing this on to all those who had promised him money earlier, as they were bound to realise that, even with £600 million, this might not be the end of the matter. Bankers around the City, in fact, were already bracing themselves for the meeting that was scheduled for later that Sunday morning in the Committee Room of the BOE.

It started at 10:00 am and amongst those present was the distinguished looking Andrew Buxton, the Chairman of Barclays, which was then the country's largest bank. (22) He took his seat close to the head of the table, no doubt with a sense of primacy, and it was Buxton who would take a prominent role during the discussions that followed. There was also Peter Gillam, Chairman of Standard Chartered, who was in the company of around 25 other senior officials from merchant and clearing banks, all of whom had arrived through the back entrance to avoid the press.

Eddie George and Brian Quinn from the BOE, were followed into the meeting by Barings' executives, Peter Baring, Norris, Tuckey and Bolsover. Following a briefing from George on Barings' latest position, the level of concern deepened.

At the centre of this 'concern' was the requirement for a further £200 million, as there were unmistakeable risks involved in contributing any sum whatsoever. Funds could simply be swallowed when the markets opened the very next day so, as everyone realised, all the moving parts to the problem would need to be brought to a halt before a proper solution could be found. The futures contracts and options dumped by Leeson simply had to be dealt with.

David Brand, the CEO of Barclays de Zoette Wedd, was quick to point out what others in the room had already gathered. Anyone who took over Leeson's open positions would become a sitting duck for the hedge funds, who would simply pick them off. This was the harsh reality of the 'dog eat dog' environment in which the Bank was now trapped so, realising this could be an impasse, George stepped in to ask Peter Baring to make a statement. Anticipating a dignified display of humility, or perhaps an apology, those present bristled when Barings' Chairman merely went through his formalities, and then passed the buck to two of his senior executives to take the meeting forward. This was a bad move and did very little to engender the support of those present.

But things only got worse. Peter Norris had been given the task of outlining the Bank's corporate finance structure and stockbroking operations, and John Bolsover's job was to talk about Barings Asset Management (BAM). Instead of deference to those who had given their time to attend, there seemed to be a cold indifference. Barings' executives displayed charts showing that the Bank wanted to declare a pre-tax profit of £83 million and pay staff bonuses of £84 million. Sacrifices needed to be made and this display was simply taking liberties with the goodwill of those who had pledged support. This was much worse than simply 'ruffling feathers', so it was suggested that BAM should simply be 'snipped-off' to allow Barings to survive. Norris told those present that this could not be done because Barings had already met margin calls to the tune of £700 million. Now, there was a stone-cold silence in the room.

Here was a team of Barings' executives, claiming that they did not know anything about Leeson's illegal trading activity yet, they had already met margin calls of £700 million – which was almost double the amount of the Bank's equity. So where did the £700 million come from? Barings' fate was sealed when the Sultan of Brunei said that he would not purchase the Bank at such short notice as there was too much risk involved. Now Barings' faint hopes of a quick sale had gone, and all efforts to raise a bridging loan were therefore pointless.

Barings thereby went into administration and, as soon as the news reached employees, they raided the offices and started to seize files and documents as knee-jerk collateral. However, on 6th March 1995 the Dutch giant, ING, bought Barings for just £1.00, and then recapitalised it to the tune of £700 million. But there were repercussions, as this left very many unanswered questions and an open verdict.

Kenneth Clarke ordered the BOE to carry out an enquiry, which was published on 18th July, 1995. Barings' bond holders had lost around £100 million so this statement couldn't come soon enough, but it only served to disappoint those who had waited. Most thought that it was a whitewash, plain and simple, as it claimed that no evidence could be found of a conspiracy, or cover-up.

However, Richard Hu, Singapore's Minister of Finance, appointed inspectors to investigate the whole affair, and they were not nearly as kind as their UK counterparts. Norris was said to have been untruthful, and Bax was said to have given false evidence in material areas of the case. The inspectors pointed out that Norris had got rid of Christopher Heath when there had been losses in Barings' Securities, and therefore suggested that it was in his own interest to hide Leeson's much larger losses – just to save face. The Singapore authorities flatly refused to accept the claim that, for three years, Barings' executives were unaware of account 88888. They said that the Bank 'knew, or should have known' about its existence, as the investigation had already revealed that a number of the back-office staff, as well as members of the floor trading team, were aware of the five eights account. This was a devastating indictment of Barings' senior managers, who were said to have failed in their most basic duties.

Peter Baring and Andrew Tuckey resigned on 3rd May 1995 and, in a fresh start for Barings' new owners, ING, Peter Norris, Ron Baker, Simon Jones and James Bax departed. But it didn't end there. In January 1996, a number of the Bank's executives, including Bax, Jones and Norris, were summoned to a preliminary hearing in Singapore, to decide whether charges should be brought for breach of fiduciary duty – but the details from here appear to be cloudy. Perhaps Leeson summed it up best in his own words.

'I'd built up a massive exposure in Singapore. I was the only buyer in the market.

Everyone knew that this was ridiculous – everyone, that is, apart from the Barings' management, and they just didn't know anything. They could have found out in half an hour, if they'd done the most obvious check: looking at the positions I had reported to SIMEX, which included the 88888 account. They could have then compared this with the positions I had reported to London, which 'made no mention of it' – but Barings simply couldn't be 'bothered to check'.

A few months after Leeson had been caught, his illegal trading activity was trumped by Toshihide Iguchi in September 1995, who was accused by Daiwa Bank of hiding $1.1 billion in trading losses over a period of, no less than, eleven years. (23)

It certainly seems that if the management of a financial institution becomes dysfunctional or eccentric, there is always a danger that some egotistical whiz kid might sneak through the back door, and wreck the balance sheet.

Awash with New Ideas

Those who believed that valuable lessons had been learned from the frenetic stock market activity during the late eighties, which led to 'Black Monday', were wrong. Between 1995 and 2000, there was an exponential increase in the flotation of internet-based companies and, irrespective of fundamentals, almost anything that ended in 'dot-com' became fair game for speculators.

The world had now entered an exceptional commercial era when technical creativity would become synonymous with making losses.

Last Orders.com

A prelude to this was the release of the 'Mosaic Web Browser' in 1993, which made access to the world-wide web possible. (1) As a result, the application of information technology spread like wildfire. During this time, the value of many dot-com and technology companies reached ridiculous levels, and these startups now became the 'new tulips', as reckless buying and irrational behaviour swept the markets.

In this extremely bullish era, there is little doubt that a vast number of speculators abandoned traditional investment tenets, to simply 'go with the flow'. As well as the media and clever advertising, rumours and tips abounded and this brought an increasing number of buyers to the table. There was always a clamour for shares in the next start-up, and these were known as Initial Public Offerings (IPOs).

At this time, the abundance of opportunities served a few of my enthusiastic friends particularly well, even though they were anything but experts. Indeed, as the dot-com trend gathered momentum, it was difficult not to make money. By the latter stages of the nineties, it appeared that a fatal attraction had now developed between the 'obese bull markets', and those who were still willing to feed them.

Concerned that equities were hugely overbought, Alan Greenspan announced plans in February 2000, to aggressively increase interest rates in order to reign in prices. The prospect of higher company borrowing costs caused a significant change in market dynamics and traders were confronted with enormous volatility. Dell, Cisco and some of the big NASDAQ companies now placed huge sell orders on their own stock. A few weeks later, Japan declared that it was in recession, so it now became clear that precarious times were on the horizon for those who had shares in emerging companies, and other issues. Some of the major players, as well as those who had an inside track on what was taking place, now began to cash out as a new mood started to sweep the investment world. By 11th September 2001, and for the first time in 26 years, not a single Initial Public Offering (IPO) was brought to the market. (2)

Even the bellwether stocks such as Cisco and Intel had been carried along by the tremendous dot-com surge which, by the turn of the millennium, had propelled company valuations to unsustainable levels. The predominantly technology-based NASDAQ, in fact, increased from 1,000 points during the early months of 1995, and peaked at 5,048.62 on 10th March 2000.

This noteworthy bullish trend became known as the 'Dot-com Bubble', which led to one of the most devastating stock market crashes in modern times. In fact, by the late summer of 2002, the NASDAQ had returned to the same 1,250 mark as five years earlier. By October 1995, it reached its low of 1,114.10. (3)

The FTSE100 followed a very similar path. Just before Christmas in 1995, this index of the UK's top companies had reached 3,658.30. (4) A few days before Christmas 2000, it had climbed to 6,594, and this represented a staggering increase of 80% since 1995. By December 2002, the FTSE100 was down to 3,841.4, which was almost the same price as five years before.

Most of the leading indexes around the world were affected in some way or other, as they were moving parts within a nascent global system.

Chapter 8
The Dot-Com Bubble

This era of technical innovation and entrepreneurship had been enormously assisted by the lower interest rates of the mid-nineties, and the alacrity of venture capitalists to fund increasing numbers of new propositions to the IPO stage. It is reasonable to suspect that the extremely facile money supply was the main reason that certain capricious ideas ever got off the ground in the first place. The business models that launched some of these upstarts frequently fell somewhere between woolly, and wildly optimistic. There were even companies that were launched without a proper day to day business strategy, let alone the acumen that was necessary to project realistic long-term goals. Fortunes would often be spent on branding and advertising, then it was quite common for certain products to be sold at a loss in an attempt to increase market share. Although this 'loss-leader' (*) process was probably useful in the short-term, far too many dot-com companies were unable to turn the corner, and then move into profit.

It is unsurprising therefore that a number of tenuous upstarts only lasted days, weeks or months, and many others fell when the bubble burst. However, the venture capitalists were not unduly worried about the enormous failure rate as a successful IPO would usually provide them with an exit. This meant that they could continue with their rotation of funds, and look to profit from the next emerging prodigy. The losers were the public, who paid good money for shares when the venture capitalists cashed out. Nonetheless, anyone who had funding tied up when the bubble actually burst told a different story. It is reported that one venture capitalist, Fred Wilson, lost 90% of his net worth when the dot-com bubble burst after being heavily involved in the funding of new companies. (5) He quoted a friend when he said, "nothing important has ever been built without national exuberance." Most certainly, the technology boom had opened people's minds to a new world; one in which there was a dramatic upsurge in entrepreneurship, yet it was so often approached with 'rose tinted glasses'.

Even though the disaster stories were endless during the latter phase of this bubble, the cupidity was relentless. Members of the public were still aggressive investors at its very climax and, by the end of 2002, over 100 million people are said to have lost as much as $5 trillion in the stock market. (6)

Here is a random sample of the many company failures during this time.

The market capitalisation of a fibre optics company, '360 Networks', reached 13 billion dollars, but it filed for bankruptcy a few months later. (7) An online clothing retailer, Boo.com, spent $188 million in just six months, but filed for bankruptcy in May 2000. An online retailer of compact discs and music related products, CDNow, reached a valuation of $1 billion in April 1998. Two years later it was acquired by Bertelsmann Music Group for $117 million, and was later shut down. A telecommunications company founded in 1997, Global Crossing, reached a market capitalisation of no less than $47 billion in February 2000. By January 2002, the company filed for bankruptcy. Infoseek was acquired by Disney in 1999 and reached a valuation of $7 billion, but was eventually shut down. Within a few months, Looksmart's value rose from £23 million to $5 billion, and 98% of its market capitalisation was lost when the bubble burst.

The list of failures was so long, in fact, that people began to question the motives of many of the founders, who seemed to be more concerned about company valuations rather than the delivery of company profit. This 'back to front' way of thinking meant that a vast number of the new dot-coms had a fragile constitution, and this eventually led to their downfall.

Up to a certain point however, the flotation of many of these 'empty vessels' had been a bonanza for speculators who wanted to make rapid gains from hyped stocks, and then move onto the next upstart. Here is a sample of some of the 'early risers'.

Above Net's stock rose 32% on the day it announced a stock split. In July 2000, the stock price of wireless firm, Airspan Networks, doubled on its first day of trading. Covad's shares rose fivefold within months of its IPO (Initial Public Offering). The stock price of telecommunications software company, Interactive Intelligence, doubled on its first day of trading. The stock price of online conferencing company, Radvision, rose 150% on its first day of trading. The stock of Vignette Corporation rose 1,500% within days of its Initial Public Offering.

Empty Vessels—with zero returns—or prospects

This was, indeed, a frenetic stock market phase when almost everything was going up in price.

During this time, a very good Californian friend of mine was heavily involved in the early bonanza for quick returns, and he trawled the markets daily for emerging technology and dot-com stocks. He had a keen eye, and really did his homework before he would risk a single penny. In the first couple of years, he couldn't go wrong and, like many others, he reached the conclusion that the dot-com wave was such a great opportunity, he should simply 'go with the flow' and buy whatever he could. Unfortunately, this also meant that his level-headed approach had become a thing of the past. But little did he know that, within the next year or so, the generous mood of the market would also become a thing of the past.

He visited London in the late nineties, and we met in Woodstock on a lovely spring day. Over afternoon tea and scones, he told me that he sometimes returned to his Santa Monica home at lunch-time, just to marvel at his open positions. With a wry smile, and hoping to elicit a response, he dangled the prospect that most newcomers would be able to make money in this bull market. I nodded approvingly but had nagging doubts that it could be so easy. As his enthusiastic commentary persisted, I got the distinct impression that he had simply thrown caution to the wind and taken every single penny of his savings to the dot-com casino. But, in his next few words, I discovered that it was much worse. He was now using margin to leverage his bets, and he currently had a six-figure sum 'on the table' – which, in fact, was closer to the seven mark.

From this point, I wondered if there was something fundamentally wrong with the markets if speculators, such as my very intuitive friend, were simply taking it for granted that anything they touched would generate a profit. It occurred to me that this might be a dangerous game, but I wasn't nearly as clued-up as my companion on the dot-com topic, so maybe outsiders like me were missing out on something. In fact, Jed was still punting with an 'all-in mentality' when the markets pulled back sharply in the spring of 2000. Confident that it was just a correction, he simply hung on in there but, by 2002, he had lost all of his early gains, and more.

I'm still unsure if he received a margin call but, the next time I saw him, he was on Santa Monica beach selling iced-cream.

Joking aside, margin calls are a serious matter, as your broker demands money from you right away to mitigate exposure to losses. It is certain therefore that my friend would not have been alone on this by the end of 2002.

Of course, during our lively discussion that day in Woodstock, Jed was insistent that this was an opportunity too good to miss. I countered with my 'property developer's mindset' and told him that I wasn't particularly enthusiastic because the dot-com bull market was almost 'raging' – pointing out that it might be a bit late for me to chase the spoils. In fact, I was simply repeating the sentiments of someone I had listened to inside my law firm, who was also trying to make sense of the frenetic bull market.

Margin Call!

Anyway, I felt that I only had a scant amount of knowledge to call on – besides, I was just about to complete a real-estate development and needed to stay on top the closing phase. Yes, perhaps the mind does have a habit of fabricating its own obstacles once it departs from its comfort zone. However, Jed and the Dot-com boom had certainly stirred my curiosity.

I now started to wonder if I really did know enough to enter the game, as my limited knowledge had been shaped through property related business – as well as the very challenging climate that had ushered in the dot-com decade. So let's take a look at how events unfolded.

I had randomly bought and held a few stocks during the late eighties, but without any notable results. I had also been involved in foreign currency trading for several months during the early part of the nineties, and found that this was more interesting. In fact, it had been a preliminary learning exercise to help me get a handle on foreign currency mortgages, (*) which had become the 'new news' in the domestic and commercial property markets in the UK.

I opened accounts in 'a basket' of European Community currencies, and others in Japanese yen and US dollars, all of which were initially funded by nominal amounts of money. Alongside these, I kept the trading fund in a sterling account, and drew money from this to purchase other currencies, in lots, (*) whenever I felt there was a buying opportunity.

The buying signal would occur when one of the currencies in my group had weakened against the pound. By way of example, let's say that the exchange rate of £1:00 against the US dollar, had moved from 1.7000 to 1.7800. I would then be hoping that this foreign currency would strengthen against the pound and return to something like £1:00 = $1.7000. With a stake of £10,000, this meant that I would have bought $17,800 in the first part of the transaction, which I could then converted back to pounds at a rate of 1.7000. My sterling account would now have a credit of £10,470 (profit = £470).

All of this would seem to be plain sailing; however, any such notion would be quite misleading. I have provided an example of an extremely large move and, in the real world, these kind of moves only occur every so often. In addition, you would need to be on the 'right side' of such a move to benefit, and this happens to be the real crux of a speculator's trade to trade conundrum.

But let's hope that these figures have provided a basic picture of the strategy I was using at this time.

But the execution was very cumbersome and subject to slippage, as instructions were given over the telephone, or by fax, which would be regarded as primitive today. 'Intelligence' was usually gathered from newspapers, magazines, bank officials, and the regular bulletins provided by high street banks for their foreign currency mortgage holders or traders. The spot-prices of the currencies in the basket, and in general, could be reviewed throughout the day as various channels were available which provided this information – including Teletext.

Yes, you've got it. The dot-com boom made all of this redundant.

However, at the end of my exercise, there were some wins, some losses, and some punts that almost broke even. My £50,000 account was very slightly in front when I quit, so the 'risk to reward' ratios were not very impressive. However, I had worked out from the beginning that, should the exchange rate move against my position, the worst-case scenario would be that my pounds were 'trapped' in a foreign currency until the market moved in my favour or, at least, into a better position. I was fine with this, but these sentiments would not be shared by those operating on borrowed money. There was a time when I had to hold onto the Japanese yen for much longer than I wanted but, on a humorous note, I remember showing my yen account to a bank manager on a property deal. I'm sure he believed for a moment that I was a multi-millionaire – until he shook himself when I told him that the exchange rate at the time was around 270 yen to the pound.

I learnt two things from this experience. The first was that a speculative land and property deal with £50,000 capital, and no bank borrowing, would more than likely have delivered a better return. If the land had not sold, I would have simply held onto it because, as people say in the real-estate business, 'they're not making land anymore'. The second thing that dawned on me was the harsh reality that foreign currency mortgages could provide lower interest rates on the one hand, but pose an exchange rate risk on the other. In this game of swings and roundabouts, many people found that they eventually owed more 'pounds' on their currency mortgage, than when they started the exercise.

This is because currency fluctuations involving the pound had to remain within 6% on either side of the bilateral intervention rate, (*) otherwise the local bank manager would probably intercede. In addition, there was also the possibility of central bank intervention but, either way, the outcome could be costly. If we cast our minds back to 16th September 1992. This was 'Black Wednesday' when George Soros was said to have broken the pound, as well as severely testing the resolve of the UK Treasury at a cost of around £3.4 billion.

Chancellor, Norman Lamont issued an immediate threat to put up base rates to 15% in order to stop Soros's attack on our currency. These were undoubtedly hair-raising times for all of us but, prior to this, there had been a sustained period of high interest rates anyway, as 1991 had averaged 10.75%. However, Lamont took the decision to leave the European Exchange Rate Mechanism, and then he spiked interest rates at 12% against an annual average for 1992 of 6.875%. In 1993, base rates were back down to 5.375% but, as some will no doubt recall, the rapid fiscal spikes that occurred in 1992 were painful.

This was the early part of the dot-com decade, and many families in the UK were really feeling the pinch.

Around this time, one of my friends with a currency mortgage was taken out of his position by the bank, and back into pounds – thereby losing a large sum of money on the exchange rate. But this scenario had a knock-on effect for many. When mortgage 'loan' to 'value' ratios were out of kilter with banking covenants, some families had to find cash, or, in the worst case, sell their home. In certain instances, a re-mortgage provided a way out, but UK interest rates were still on the high side so affordability was yet another problem.

Ironically – even though a great deal of money was available at this time for new dot-com and technology companies, the banking world was far less hospitable with existing companies. So this is when the industry came up with other ways to deal with 'breaches of banking covenants' (BBCs) by small businesses.

The term, 'BBC', was an acronym created by lenders, which enabled them to hike interest rates, charge you exorbitant fees, increase your mortgage payments, or tinker with new ideas simply to – earn money. A corporate 'guru' would sometimes be appointed by the lender if banking covenants had been breached. Although his brief would be to assist with the day-to-day management of your business, his presence could sometimes be a source of discomfort. These 'experts' were not direct employees of the bank, so the burden of their fee was the responsibility of the enterprise they were meant to be helping.

During the dot-com era, I had the pleasure of meeting a corporate 'guru' when I was looking to conduct some business with a friend. He asked me to sit in on a meeting with his bank manager, some of the manager's team, and the 'guru'. In fact, we had any number of people seated within a space of around 400 square feet. This was simply overkill and probably intended to hype what was no more than a 'routine negotiation'. But the taut atmosphere got much worse. Straight after pleasantries had been exchanged, and coffee was in the process of being served, the 'guru' opened with a showstopping question: "Who is going out to fetch the bacon and egg butties?"

My friend simply lost his composure, as he was paying for this man's time and 'expertise'.

But this was an era in which traditional boundaries in commerce and finance were under severe pressure – where the 'unconventional' suddenly had an air of normality.

At last – a Corporate Guru with sound judgement!

As I was still working in the property markets, I took the easy way out and found a broker who offered to provide me with an advisory service. (*) At least, that was the idea. Just over eighteen months later, I was quite shocked; my initial stake of £20,000 was now down to £11,000. The account was probably saved because losing positions were quickly closed, and most of the stocks in the portfolio were in the 'quite conservative' category. This was rather fortunate because some of the dot-com and technology stocks were really tanking by this time. The priceless value of timing had always been paramount in my property ventures, but this was further confirmation that 'only fools rush in' to buy last minute stocks, or anything else, when the market has been massively overheated by a speculative frenzy. This would seem obvious yet, as we have seen in earlier chapters, it happens time and again, and this simply pumps too much air into the 'boom' and makes the 'bust' inevitable.

In all of these bubbles, we can now see that there is a very similar pattern. Common sense is often obscured by delusion and the 'herd mentality'.

During the tulip frenzy for example, speculators eventually woke up to the fact that the all-important price of certain tulip bulbs had massively outgrown their real value. We also know that share prices in the Mississippi and South Sea Companies had grown exponentially and, like tulip bulbs, were inflated to levels which could only bring a crash. In the furore of the dot-com era, it is perhaps unsurprising therefore that too many company values were driven dangerously higher than their fundamental worth. Hope and wishful thinking had descended on the markets and propelled prices to these levels but, unable to deliver the much-anticipated operating profit, or any profit at all, the majority of dot-com and upstart technology companies had little hope of long-term survival.

In spite of the loss of 45% of my account balance at the hands of an advisory service, I remained confident that I could get to know the ropes. During my early days in real-estate, I had learned that experience only comes with persistence, determination and the willingness to have a go – even by dropping one or two clangers. Right now, stock market speculation was on the agenda, and my earlier set-back didn't matter. I therefore started to absorb anything and everything to do with trading equities and, slowly but surely, a clearer picture began to emerge. From this point, it wasn't long before I developed an exploratory game plan, (*) so I put this to the test by conducting paper exercises for a while and looking back at the performance of stocks that would have matched my criteria.

In essence, I was trying to avoid the type of stocks in the dot-com era that had an ephemeral value, zero earnings, negligible assets, and inevitably consumed a large amount of the public's capital when they crashed. I referred to these earlier as 'empty vessels', launched on the back of boundless hope and wishful thinking. But, with that said, people can still make money on good new issues. I also wanted to be in a position where I could, at least, stop my loss (*) at a certain point if the trade went the wrong way and thereby retain most of my capital. For timely speculators, the bursting of the dot-com bubble, followed by the crash during 2001 and 2002, had really teed things up to have a punt as the markets had pulled-back from their highs, and some stocks by as much as 60–70%. To highlight my way of thinking, let's have a look at the following analogy.

I had always found that, in a property development scheme, the purchase price of the land was a critically important part of the development equation. As a result, I had a preference for undervalued plots that could be uplifted to a higher value by creative and cost-effective design, followed by planning permission. Therefore, I wanted to establish a similar procedure for locating under-valued stocks, which would have the potential to grow in price at a future date. Let's consider this further in relation to land acquisition.

Finding undervalued, off market, land became more difficult as competition increased throughout the nineties. By the late stages of this decade, it was quite frantic and prices were rising rapidly – as this was the prelude to the housing boom, which will be the subject of the next chapter. However, if a developer has to pay over the odds for land, this immediately places a burden on all the other development costs, as there is a notional ceiling to the overall equation. This is sales value of the houses. Simply put, the margin between the total development cost and the gross sales value is the developer's profit. Paying over the odds for the land can often mean that a sensible margin is therefore unachievable – and it's the same with stocks if the trader pays over the odds to acquire them.

The argument might be that sales values could be increased to re-set the figures in the development appraisal; however, this would be dangerous. As a general rule, the existing housing stock in the neighbourhood fixes the comparable values for any new scheme in that neighbourhood, as local market prices are considered to be fairly reliable. The stock market sets prices in a similar manner, but hidden within the vast number of stocks, there are still bargains to be found. And the same applies to development plots that are tucked away in existing urban and suburban areas.

I soon discovered that the cornerstone of a good solid share, which might also be undervalued, was the company's ability to grow its earnings. This would seem obvious, however, very many of the emerging companies during the dot-com boom had next to no earnings, yet their share price increased day after day. This was very similar to the 'bubble companies' formed during the South Sea Bubble.

To keep us on the right track therefore, we now need to refer to a new term, which is earnings per share (EPS). A company's ability to increase its EPS in the future, is the cog that really drives the price of good, solid stocks, and we will look more closely at this very shortly. As far as I was concerned therefore, only certain stocks would fit my criteria, so let's see how I drew conclusions about under-valued shares, and a company's future profitability.

To ease into this process, there are one or two key terms which will be explained as we move along.

A company's market capitalisation is something that we should certainly be aware of. In simple terms, this is calculated by multiplying the number of ordinary voting shares it has in issue, by their market price. When the share price moves at any time, the market capitalisation moves with it, along with the value of the company. Let's suppose that ABC company has 4,806,600 shares in issue, and its current share price is 150 pence (£1.50) –

Market capitalisation = 4,806,600 x 1.50 = £7,209,900.00

With a company valuation of this magnitude, and zero earnings, it becomes immediately clear why some of the companies with humungous valuations during the dot-com bubble were so dangerous.

As mentioned earlier, a company achieved a value of £47 billion – and was bankrupt less than two years later.

We can now move onto earnings per share (EPS). This is calculated very simply by dividing a company's profits (or earnings after tax), by the number of shares it has in issue. If, for example, ABD company had made £100,000 (or 10,000,000 pence) during the year, and had 500,000 shares in issue, then EPS would be calculated as follows –

$$\text{EPS} = \frac{10,000,000 \text{ pence}}{500 \text{ shares}} = 20 \text{ pence per share}$$

With this formula, at least, we are able to see that the company is making money, and the actual earnings for each share issued. In the dot-com era, I'm afraid that it would have been EPS = (Zero) in the profile of many companies.

Now we can move onto other key parts of a company's profile, which often come under the heading – fundamentals. (*) The price earnings ratio (PER) is sometimes called the multiple and is the ratio between the current market price of a company's share, to its earnings per share. This sounds like quite a mouthful, but the ratio is simply calculated by dividing the former by the latter, as we see below:

$$PER = \frac{PRICE}{EPS}$$

So, for example, if a company's shares were trading at 100 pence, and its earnings were 10 pence a share, then the PER would be as follows –

$$PER = \frac{100}{10} = 10$$

So why is PER important, and how do we use it? First, it is worthy of note that the majority of new companies during the dot-com boom had enormous PERs, and failed. The reason for this will become clear after we have worked through a few examples.

As a simple rule of thumb, the PER can be compared to the prospective growth rate in EPS. For example, if ABE company was growing at 10% per annum, it ought to be able to command a PER of at least 10, and a company with 15% growth rate should be able to command a PER rating of at least 15 (and so on). So let's have a look at how this works –

$$PER\ (Historically) = \frac{100\ pence\ share\ price}{10\ pence\ EPS} = 10$$

$$PER\ (Prospective) = \frac{225\ pence\ share\ price}{15\ pence\ EPS} = 15$$

In the second example, you will have noticed the word 'prospective' in brackets. This is simply the projected value of the PER for the next period.

Remember that the earnings per share (EPS) and the performance of the share price are inextricably linked. However, there may well be certain periods of time when a particular company's share price, and its earnings per share (EPS) are out of kilter, and this can present opportunities.

It is widely believed that the PER should only be used to compare companies in the same sector; for example, to measure one banking stock against another. The comparable values set by local housing, as a yardstick for new housing stock in the same area, is a very similar concept to PER.

The average PER for the market as a whole (the FTSE100 for instance) is widely available, and this can be used to provide the basis for broader comparison. This would enable you to determine whether your chosen FTSE100 company is performing better than average.

Let's assume that, through some extraordinary event, ABE's share price went up to 300 pence, but its earnings per share (EPS) were unable to climb above 3.5 pence. We would see a significant shift in the company's PER, as follows –

$$PER = \frac{300 \text{ pence share price}}{3.5 \text{ pence EPS}} = 85$$

It is quite easy to work out from the above that if the earnings per share (EPS) went down to a single penny, then the PER would shoot up from 85 to 300. Similarly, many of the stocks during the dot-com era had massive PERs, simply because they had next to no earnings. Large PERs occur when the market enters an extremely bullish phase, and share prices are driven upward in anticipation that substantial earnings will materialise.

In our quest to locate undervalued stocks, we are now going to learn about the PEG factor, (*) and this is where 'the rubber meets the road'. The PEG is simply the Price Earnings ratio divided by the Growth rate in EPS. It is important to note that the historical and current PEG values, will provide a good idea of how the share has performed up to that point. However, we are interested in the prospective PEG (projected PEG for the next period) to see how the share might grow in the future.

A great deal of the ground we have covered earlier in this section will, in fact, assist our understanding of the PEG calculation. In order to work this out, we simply divide the price earnings ratio (PER) by the estimated percentage growth rate for the next period in earnings per share (EPS). Let's look at some examples:

$$PEG = \frac{PER}{\text{Estimated percentage growth rate in EPS}} = x$$

Taking a hypothetical company, ABF, we could calculate and compare the PEG ratio of the current period with the prospective PEG ratio for the next period.

$$PEG \text{ (Historical)} = \frac{8}{10\%} = 0.8$$

$$PEG \text{ (Prospective)} = \frac{8}{12\%} = 0.66$$

As a benchmark, a stock with a prospective PEG ratio of 0.5 should certainly go to the top of your watch-list for undervalued stocks. It would mean that this company would have a price earnings ratio (PER) of 10, and prospective earnings per share (EPS) of 20%. The range for the prospective PEG ratio, if we are really looking for good, undervalued stocks, should be somewhere between 0.3 and 0.75. To back this up, we also need to ensure that there has been a steady growth in historical earnings.

Nowadays, it is unnecessary to go through all the previous exercises to find a company's PEG factor, (*) as good brokers provide this in a simple overview of the business in question. In many cases, this will include historical and prospective data. However, by working through the earlier calculations, at least we will know the significance of a 0.5 PEG factor when we come across one. We can also put the events of 1995 to 2001 into perspective. Anyone who had adopted the PEG (*) strategy during the dot-com boom, would have been unlikely to buy a single share in one of the upstarts. Almost without exception, they did not have the desired growth in historical earnings, or any prospect of improving this during the next period.

Of course, 'timing' your market entry is always a very important criterion to consider, so let's see how we might assist this process. Demonstration charting packages are widely available, should you wish to venture into technical analysis. If you had a stock with a prospective 0.5 PEG factor on your watchlist, you could set up a moving average (MA) cross-over (*) system to optimise the timing of your buy. To do this you could use a daily chart, with 20 and 50 period moving averages. Your signal to buy the stock would be when your 20 period MA crosses above the 50 period MA. Otherwise, you might commit your capital to an actual purchase, and then find yourself waiting longer than necessary for the price of the stock to gather momentum. Should the anticipated breakout fail to materialise, your capital would still be in your account.

On the other hand, when you set up your chart, you could find that the 20 period MA is already sitting above the 50 period MA, and the action is underway.

But this is not an easy game to play, so let's return to earth.

During the euphoric period between 1995 to 2000, a great deal of money was made by those who were prepared to buy and sell stocks in a timely manner.

For those who kept their 'chips on the table' at the dot-com casino, they would have lost very heavily when the bubble burst in 2001 – and reports suggest that the total figure was close to $5 trillion.

For many, reality eventually dawned!

However, the scale of the losses at the end of the dot-com era was well and truly over-shadowed by the 'housing boom', which is our next topic.

A Dangerous Upward Spiral

It was the spring of 2001, and I called into a coffee shop close to Sheffield's city centre, where I met two local estate agents for a catch-up. During that morning and lunchtime, they had carried out a reconnaissance mission on one of my developments just prior to work starting on site. This was a mid-range, suburban scheme for 28 newly built apartments with one and two bedrooms and secure basement car-parking. I was cautiously optimistic about the prospects of this project, simply because interest in the property markets seemed to be rising following the rapid decline of the technology bubble.

In the relaxed atmosphere of this popular town centre meeting spot, the two young sales-people had been showing potential buyers the layout drawings, a brochure with computer-aided-design images of the building, and the price list. When I sat down at their table, they both greeted me with beaming smiles, and then proceeded to explain that, over coffee and Danish pastries, they had received firm offers on 12 apartments earlier that day. Within just a few weeks of these pledges, legally binding contracts had been exchanged, bearing in mind that not a single brick had been laid. At this point, I realised that I had no choice but to pull the plug on any further sales so that I could re-evaluate my position, and this turned out to be a good decision.

Only a few days after these new property entrepreneurs had exchanged contracts with me, almost all of the apartments they had bought were placed back on the market. However, the new selling values had been marked-up, randomly, by around 10–12%. I was well into my second decade in the industry, and this was exceptional – in fact, this was the beginning of a marketplace in which more and more speculators, with bundles of money, continued to appear out of nowhere. Over the following months, it certainly crossed my mind that if this kind of trend continued, it might develop into something quite unwieldy.

As far back as the late nineties, certain property developers working in the UK could already sense that there was a tinge of something quite different in the air. After I had been involved in a number of bidding wars for certain sites, it occurred to me that development land, convertible buildings, and property related opportunities were attracting an unusual amount of interest. As the competition increased, prices naturally started to move with these strong signs of bullish sentiment. Between 2001 and 2003, the upward curve became so steep that it was difficult to find deals where the figures made sense. This bemused many developers and house builders, who would often have to revise their projected selling values well before they started building. There was simply no alternative because these industry professionals had to keep up with the changing market conditions in order to maintain viability. The rapidly rising prices of newly built dwellings now helped to drag the value of existing domestic property into unknown territory, and this escalated the tension in the wider market.

Those managing on-site building work after 2000, were severely impacted when it became increasingly common for sub-contractors and skilled labour teams to ignore existing contractual arrangements, and shift their services to the highest bidder. Even when the new work was out of town, some within the industry were prepared to follow the money. As a result, work in progress was constantly interrupted, and this meant that main contractors were penalised when their completion schedules had to be revised. Eventually, there were far too many developments and not nearly enough skilled workmen. As a result, labour rates reached astronomical levels by 2003, and this made building work far more expensive than it had ever been. There had to be a knock-on effect and, as the markets churned, domestic property prices were simply forced upwards and onwards – eventually reaching record levels.

At this point, we are all familiar with the term 'boom and bust', but when the property bubble burst in 2007/8, the magnitude of the event transcended anything the financial world had experienced since the 1929 crash. The severity of the inevitable 'credit crunch' that followed had far reaching implications. In the wake of this, many financial institutions went bankrupt or had to be 'bailed out' by the taxpayer, particularly in America as this was the epicentre. Here, the hugely inflated house prices had collapsed in truly unprecedented fashion. At the same time, the domestic property markets in the UK, Europe and other parts of the world were overwhelmed by similar devasting circumstances.

In these key global locations, delinquencies and repossessions were rife, ruining many family lives in the process. A large proportion of those who had entered the markets speculatively were also besieged by problems. Aspiring buy to let landlords, prospective and current owners of holiday homes, corporate entities and many opportunists decided to walk away from their contractual obligations, and their stake, in the face of increasingly austere market conditions.

The knock-on effect was devastating!

Certain coastal regions of Spain in particular felt the full weight of the crisis. The volume of units that had been sold 'off-plan' was enormous, as well as the sale of property that was still in the course of construction.

When buyers started to dwindle, and eventually became non-existent, some partially built developments became derelict as builders and developers found themselves in serious financial difficulty. The severity of the problems became so great that in certain American states, there were even instances of newly built houses being advertised – "two for the price of one." Friends of mine with a holiday home in a Florida beach community mentioned that they had seen desperate offers of this very nature close to their own home. Inevitably, the value of their property also plummeted to well below its purchase price but, fortunately for them, they had paid cash so they were not in the same predicament as some of the families whose lives were now in ruins. For a time, however, my friends decided against visiting their place in the sun, simply because it would have been too difficult to cope with the demoralising scene surrounding them.

The 'knock-on effect' of all of this was both predictable and catastrophic. Places as far away as Australia, China, Japan and Asia were unable to escape the widespread panic, and their stock markets went into a steep decline.

When the dust settled from the collapse, it was eventually estimated that around $3 trillion in asset value had evaporated including, amongst other things – pension money, real-estate values, investments and savings. (1) Bad news seems to be more palatable in small chunks, so estimates were frequently revised during the years that followed – which probably means today that the full extent of the catastrophe may never actually be known.

Between 2,000 and 2003, the number of mortgage loans in the US had quadrupled. By 2010, it was reported that there had been 6 million foreclosures in the US alone.

It was also reported that lenders had used extraordinary leverage of 33 – 1. Leverage is the ratio between borrowed money, and the bank's own money. In relation to the 33 – 1 ratio, a tiny 3% decrease in a bank's asset base would have made it insolvent.

In spite of this, some still managed to make billions out of this global collapse, and this is their story.

Chapter 9
Sub-Prime Mortgages and the Housing Bubble

During the 5–6 years leading up to the 2008 crisis, there had been a surge in the public domain for mortgages, as well as other financial products. This opened the door for home-owners with equity to take out second mortgages at far better interest rates than those they were paying on credit cards, car loans and other household debts. The message from banks and mortgage providers was simple and plausible – 'consolidate and pay less'.

In fact, the soaring house prices of the time even created opportunities for novice property speculators who, with the very willing assistance of lenders, were able to take out second mortgages against their domestic living quarters. For many of these new property entrepreneurs, this provided, in part or in full, the stake that was needed to participate in the new property boom. Predictably, certain problems soon began to surface. Most of these speculators and second mortgagors had more than one debt to service, and interest rate hikes fell due when low 'teaser' rates came to an end. This amplified problems in an already difficult market and, for countless borrowers, their financial circumstances became unmanageable. Even when tenants were able to pay their rent, some landlords failed to pay their mortgage.

As a result of the dangerous upward spiral of values in the wider marketplace, many innocent home-owners were affected by the huge downturn straight after the boom. This took tens of thousands of households into negative equity. At the same time, failure to maintain loan repayments led to widespread repossession of property. Now, rental values also started to plummet, as there were too many properties and not enough tenants. This classical supply and demand imbalance was compounded by another problem. The very willing and well-oiled mortgage machine in operation earlier, had now ground to a halt – so refinancing to generate cash was no longer an option.

In the US, many people had been sold on the idea of following the 'American dream' when they were offered the chance to take out their first mortgage. This included poor immigrant workers on low incomes, people who did not have any credit history, those with a poor credit history, and even people who were unemployed. Loans to people without income or job were referred to as NINJA loans, and the term 'sub-prime mortgage' therefore originated from the alacrity of the banks and lending institutions to provide loans for these and similar socioeconomic groups.

To make matters worse, some of the financial products on offer were well and truly lamentable.

This was a time when lending institutions were offering bespoke loans, which included 100% mortgages, high loan to value ratios, second mortgages on top of 100% mortgages, mortgages without a valuation, and even 'no document' lending facilities. In fact, the industry brazenly referred to these transactions as 'liars' loans'. In such cases, the broker would create a fictitious financial profile for the applicant, in full knowledge that the lender would agree to believe the paperwork. Between 2001 and 2005 the amount of reckless business that was written increased year upon year.

When an easily accessible money supply exists, certain dishonest individuals will always be willing to tap into it by whatever means possible. In fact, as early as 2004, the FBI warned of a growing epidemic of mortgage fraud, but the need to be more circumspect was largely disregarded by most mortgage providers. (2)

It seems that the addiction to making money had put the entire chain of command at certain banks and lending institutions into a state of paralysis. Here we are talking about Chairmen, CEO's, compliance managers, high ranking bankers, fund managers, department heads and team leaders. Of course, more lines could be added, but the message is already clear. On the other hand, the complete naivety of many of those who borrowed money made things much worse. For some, making regular repayments on their debt obligations became secondary to their overriding desire to have money in their pockets right there and then.

During the 1970s, Salomon Brothers was amongst the first banks to introduce the concept of Mortgage-Backed Securities – or tradeable mortgage bonds. The MBS was touted as an asset backed security which would provide a steadily rising yield. They were believed to be a sure bet, as they comprised mortgages that usually had a fixed rate for thirty years. This was backed by the questionable proposition that people would always pay their mortgage, but it failed to acknowledge that each MBS had thousands of mortgages in the mix, and was therefore a composite of different circumstances and conditions – as well as many unknowns. Nonetheless, the industry's positive views were shared by the big credit rating agencies, and these new financial instruments received AAA ratings from the likes of FICO, Moody and Fitch.

Unbeknown to everyone, a voracious financial tiger had just been let out of its cage – masquerading as a pet.

The revolving door just kept on turning!

By the late 1990s, a new trend had therefore developed in the financial markets. This was to provide mortgages across the entire spectrum of demand, simply because insufficient mortgages were being written through normal channels to satisfy the insatiable appetite of the industry.

Randomly, groups of mortgages were now being placed into bundles so that they could be securitised, and this created a marketable financial instrument which could be traded on an exchange. But there had been another twist by the

1990s. The product that had simply been known as a 'mortgage bond' back in the 1970s now assumed the rather swanky title of Collateralised Debt Obligation (CDO). Yes, this arcane term had appeared out of nowhere.

So, for those who had taken out a mortgage, what did this mean? In everyday language, this meant that a bank or financial institution somewhere, was able to use their mortgage to make money, without their knowledge or permission. At the very least, this was a crafty arrangement. Even though it did not directly affect mortgage repayments, it did impact very many people's financial position because eventually, almost everyone lost value on their property as a result of the reckless trading in the housing, mortgage and bond markets.

Until the end came in 2008, CDO's were considered by most of those in the financial services industry to be extremely safe, just like the 'tradable mortgage bonds' of the 1970s. After all, CDOs were often rated by the top rating agencies as 'AAA', 'AAB', and so on. As a result, the quality of these assets could hardly be questioned, or so it was believed before the crash. CDOs became so popular, in fact, that it wasn't long before institutional traders were considered to be outsiders within their own industry if they didn't trade these credit derivatives. (*) Of course, the enormous pressures within Wall Street had created this very competitive mindset, however, let's look at the position from another angle. Irrespective of the popularity of CDOs, it was impossible to escape the fact that these Wall Street institutions were really trading, in the form of asset backed securities, the mortgages of almost every Tom, Dick or 'Dirty Harry' who had turned up to the financial banquet. After all, this had been a sumptuous feast provided by the industry itself, for absolutely anyone who wanted to exercise their taste buds.

With such unfettered enthusiasm in both financial and consumer credit circles, it was only a matter of time before the asset backed securities (*) markets over extended, and then rolled over. Some of the mortgage bundles that were now being traded in the form of CDOs were extremely vulnerable. If the number of delinquent mortgages in the mix reached just 8%, this had the potential to place the whole of the CDO in jeopardy, even though it contained 1000s of mortgages. As a result, the AAA ratings that certain CDOs had been given did nothing to stave-off the problems that eventually followed from mass defaults. As we now know, a very large number of these delinquent mortgages (*) were 'sub-prime'.

When the thundering crash from the mortgage and property bubble finally came in 2008, some of the better known and more established institutions such as AIG, Merrill Lynch, Freddie Mac and Fannie Mae were bailed out by the US taxpayer. On the other hand, over 400 banks and credit institutions did not survive this financial apocalypse, including the well-known sub-prime mortgage lenders, New Century Financial, Countrywide, Lehman Brothers and Bear Stearns. (3) However, the latter of these two banks had also conducted a great deal of business with Madoff's 'elite hedge fund' and, with his arrest in December 2008, there was little chance of recovering any of the assets they had invested.

It has been reported that nine of America's largest banks eventually had no choice but to sell shares to the Government. After their initial refusal, a 'take it or leave it deal' was tabled in October 2008, which they reluctantly accepted. (4) This brought a hue and cry from various banking sources who now claimed that the government would be able to meddle whenever it pleased. However, from the perspective of the government, this was probably seen as a very good reason to intervene; one that was veiled in 'needs must' motives.

In the UK, large banking institutions such as RBS and Lloyds Banking Group received assistance in precisely the same way, with bailout funds of £22 billion and £17 billion respectively. For these loans, the UK Government took a stake in RBS of 70%, and 40% in Lloyds Banking Group. In 2008, the Northern Rock was nationalised by the Labour Government after it received critical support in September 2007 from the Bank of England. Just a year later, the Bradford and Bingley met a similar fate. Things were not much different elsewhere. On 30th September 2008, the German, Belgian and Luxemburg governments poured money into Dexia, which, prior to going into the boom, had been one of the financial powerhouses of Europe. (5) The Irish Government found that it had no choice but to Guarantee the deposits of all its banks, and Iceland went one step further by nationalising its entire banking system. (6)

Naturally, many of the innocent families who had suffered as a result of the 2008 debacle, questioned the role of regulators in the financial services industry, and even the position of their government. They wanted to know how a crisis of this magnitude could have possibly occurred in a modern global economy, under their very noses? It was clear that the usual safety-net measures in the finance world, such as risk management and sensible credit control, had failed. The valuation and rating agencies had also played their part, so how could this dangerous upward spiral in values have possibly escaped their attention?

The Bank of England (BOE), in fact, had been the body that was responsible for monitoring the health of the financial world in the UK until the late nineties. In 1997, the new Labour Government under Mr Blair stripped the BOE of its responsibility and handed the task of micro-management to the FSA. The BOE's main focus now became monetary policy. It has been suggested that, even if these changes had not taken place, it would have made next to no difference, because the 2008 crash was a global phenomenon, generated by the full force of human nature. In spite of this, one cannot help but wonder if more could have been done to stop this dangerous upward curve reaching its devastating climax.

Pyramid Alley

But the decades leading up to 2008 had certainly paved the way for problems.

During this period, the powerful Wall Street institutions had frequently resorted to experimentation, innovation, and taking risks, thereby generating periods of excessive enthusiasm in global markets. This was certainly the case between the late 1990s and 2007/8. From the standpoint of the various authorities, new wave banking initiatives had usually been met by a laissez-faire approach, sadly leaving critical historical events as a distant memory. As a result of this flawed short-termism, there was a failure to grasp that whenever cyclical trouble poked its nose through the surface, there could be a monster lurking beneath – and 2008 was the largest that had ever surfaced.

By 2008, there were far too many fragile financial institutions inextricably linked to the dangerous trend that had developed throughout the whole of the UK, Europe, and America. During the early part of its formation in the late 1990s, banks were hell bent on finding innovative ways to circumvent irritating obstacles, such as the rules imposed by the 1988 Basel Accord – overseen by the 'Basel Committee on Banking Supervision' (BCBS). (7) This demanded that all banks impose globally consistent standards for prudent banking, and maintain their reserves equivalent to 8% of their assets. This was certainly a modest sum in the ambitious times that were to follow so, by finding ways of holding less than 8% of assets in reserve, the Banks would have more capital available to conduct their affairs. In essence, less reserves meant more risk, but the bull was arrogantly strutting over the industry's trading floors, and through the corridors of power – but no one could control this huge and unruly beast.

As a result of institutional creativity, and flouting rules, the effects of the 1988 Basel Accord were subsequently negated, and the banks' responsibility to hold 8% in reserve became an irrelevance – thereby enabling financial institutions to trade in greater financial volume. This was a dangerous strategy but, for the majority of these multinationals, the idea of keeping up with the pack was always paramount in what was a fiercely competitive industry. With such a strong meeting of minds by so many global banks on policy matters, financial innovation provided the pathway to riches – for a time at least. This was beaten by a few in the late 1990s, and followed by the whole industry later. By 2008, the critical point in the journey had actually been reached by the time the regulatory bodies caught up with the pack, and then it was too late for the leash.

The mortgage and property markets had started the rush, but this had led to something much bigger. This was a humongous growth in the derivatives and commercial paper markets which eventually overstretched certain banks to breaking point. The enthusiastic innovation that had helped to shape these new products, really amounted to the conception of a financial time-bomb. The very earliest whispers of distress and fatigue, in fact, emanated from IKB in Germany when it demurely reported a liquidity problem. (8) As more and more distress signals came in, other institutions were hit like dominos and the crisis that took hold didn't let go until it had shaken the whole of the financial system to its foundations. This was unavoidable because the nexus between global financial institutions had been created by generation-to-generation inter-bank lending and trading relationships. The property and mortgage bubble simply became the accelerator for the production of many of the esoteric products that were employed during this trend, and these were instrumental in its collapse.

In spite of this, a few people were actually able to profit when the mortgage and property bubble eventually burst in 2008, although any such notion may seem unfitting, or even impossible, following a global collapse. Yes, whichever way we look at it, someone will always make money when others lose heavily – so let's pick-up the trail that led to their success.

Between 2007 and 2008, a small group of Wall Street professionals eventually reached the conclusion that the housing, mortgage and bond markets were almost certainly beginning to sag under the burden of an increasingly unwelcome load. Day after day, more pressure was being exerted by the exuberance and recklessness of market speculators, mortgage lenders and the big financial institutions. Those who held a pessimistic view of these markets were known as 'contrarians'. However, this particular group was made up of very perceptive individuals who, through their background, were instinctively wired into the machinations of Wall Street and the wider trading community. Some were of the opinion that the situation was so dire, that a market collapse might even be imminent. If they were correct, a huge opportunity to make money was staring them in the face, albeit, they were considered to have taken leave of their senses by those who were still riding the industry's high wave of bullish sentiment.

One of the contrarians was Michael Burry who formed Scion Capital back in 2001. (9) From inception, Scion had consistently delivered good returns for its investors, and Burry himself was a very well respected professional. However, unlike many of the flamboyant asset managers of the day, Burry was hardly the loquacious type and was even quite awkward when it came to social interaction and relationships. This occasionally put a strain on his client liaison as the humble Burry always preferred his own private space to the limelight. As a result, he was more comfortable emailing his clients rather than speaking to them in person or on the phone. In spite of this, Burry's results had certainly kept his clients happy, and this in itself spoke volumes.

However, when Burry reported to some of his most influential clients that he was convinced that Scion should place a bet against the bullish position taken by almost all of those working on Wall Street, and beyond, quite a few of his devotees panicked – and some even rebelled by withdrawing their funds. Nonetheless, Burry was sure that he was right, so he quickly started to carry out further analysis so that he could convert the sceptics. In order to follow through with his bet, Burry had estimated that Scion would have to commit around $80 to $90 million in capital, but he believed that the returns could be somewhere up to 20 times the capital invested. (10)

To provide a picture of how the contrarians' belief had taken seed, it is necessary to understand what they had gleaned from the mortgage and bond markets, to lead them to their conclusion. To assist, let us summarise some of the important financial instruments and other key elements in play at this time, as most are specific to this chapter and may not appear in the glossary at the end of this book.

AIG – global insurance provider, and writer of Credit Default Swaps which were used to short the market.

Asset Backed Security – a mortgage bond for example.

Aspiring Property Entrepreneurs – often 'newbies' and second mortgagors.

Bond Traders – those working in the specialised trading departments in firms on Wall Street, London, Europe and globally – who were buying as many CDOs as the market could provide.

Contrarian: one who has an opposing view.

Credit Derivative – a CDO or Collateralised Debt Obligation.

Delinquent Mortgage – one that is in arrears.

Derivative – A financial instrument such as a CDO, a futures contract or an option, the value of which has a strong relationship with an underlying asset. For example, the underlying asset could be a share, a currency or a commodity.

Estate Agents – those selling domestic properties.

FICO – Credit scoring agency for mortgage applicants (USA).

Financial Instrument – CDO – Collateralized Debt Obligation – in easy language, a bond comprising bundles of mortgages – introduced in during the 1990s.

House builders – those involved in development and the real estate business.

Insurance Policy or 'Swap' – CDS – Credit Default Swap used by those who wanted to sell the market, or short the market, because they believed it would fall – like Michael Burry.

Long Position – a position held in derivatives, securities, currencies or commodities, such that a rise in the market increases the value of the position.

Mortgage-Backed Securities (MBS) – a 1970s version of a tradeable mortgage bond – or asset backed security – or a bond simply made up of mortgages.

NINJA Loans – loans to applicants with no income, no job and no assets.

Securitised Mortgage – is one that does not belong to a single lender as it is part of a pool of mortgages sold to an investor. The mortgage service company is responsible for collecting payments and sending them through to the pool. The investor may trade the group of mortgages as a bond on an exchange.

Short Position – a position held in derivatives, securities, currencies or commodities, such that a fall in the market increases the value of the position.

Teaser Rates – usually the introductory rate offered to new borrowers, which is much lower than the general market rate.

The banks and lending institutions – the mortgage and loan providers.

The public – the borrowers/mortgagors.

The rating and valuation agencies – Moody's, Standard & Poor, Fitch, and others.

Wall Street – simply a street (USA) where large banks and financial institutions are domiciled.

Yes, a great deal of the above summary will have been difficult to digest, but complex terminology is not unusual in the banking and finance industry. On this same subject, one commentator wrote: "It has been in the interests of money mandarins to convince the public that these issues are too complicated for novices. Through the use of technical jargon, and by hiding reality inside a maze of bewildering procedures, they have caused an understanding of the nature of money to fade from public consciousness. It is generally regarded as beyond the understanding of mere mortals." (11)

The confusing world of finance!

In order to back-up their suspicions about the frailty of the housing, mortgage and bond markets, Burry and the other contrarians decided to take a close look at the way in which some of the CDOs had actually been packaged. First of all, they noticed that during the early part of the trend, the number of sub-prime mortgages in the overall spectrum was relatively small but, in comparison to this, the current number was enormous. However, alarm bells were well and truly activated when they discovered that certain CDOs with 'AAA' ratings were made up almost entirely of sub-prime mortgages. (12)

The composition of CDOs with 'AAA' ratings, in fact, should have only consisted of mortgages written for borrowers with high FICO scores and prime credit ratings. However, with the kind of mortgage packaging that had taken place, the CDOs themselves were only as good as the risky mortgages in the bundle. This had exposed a potentially disastrous situation because, as we have already learnt, if delinquent mortgages in the mix reached just 8%, the CDO was finished. (13) As a result, it was now clear to Burry and the others that, with any more pressure, the mortgage and housing bubble would burst into vapour before everyone's eyes. In spite of this, those in the wider financial marketplace simply continued to exert this pressure, in their relentless drive to make money in what were now – raging bull markets.

Burry and company realised that the CDO writers had cleverly tried to overcome the truly dire sub-prime problem by manipulating the rate of interest that they were prepared to pay, which was supposedly commensurate to the risk involved. However, this manoeuvre was never equitable because the writers had created a derivative that was extremely fragile. Let us remember that, during the late 1990s, simple 'mortgage bonds' had assumed the rather arcane title of 'Collateralised Debt Obligations' and by 2005, these novel financial instruments had already started to develop problems. After all, in spite of their pretentious title, CDOs were still bonds made up of mortgages and, by 2008, a dangerous quantity were toxic.

It remains a mystery to this day why these problems were not obvious to the whole of Wall Street and beyond. At the very least, traders and top banking officials themselves should have had an inkling that far too many of the AAA rated CDOs were in trouble, and that most of those with lesser ratings were in an even worse state. The credit scoring agencies for mortgage applicants had simply allowed a very large number of 'sub-prime' applicants to slip through the net. When challenged later however, their attitude was that if their own firms hadn't underwritten these ratings, other firms would have.

However, it transpired in the aftermath of the boom that mortgage providers were not overly concerned about the status of the borrowers because they were able to sell their mortgages to someone else, often abroad, within a matter of days.

So many large institutions had been making such huge profits out of this boom that they simply turned the other cheek, and continued to 'follow the money'. As a result, the industry and beyond failed to even consider the possibility that CDO ratings could be unreliable.

"Buy your own property and fulfil the American Dream." Yes, this was a time when people had to be fast asleep to believe it.

The composition of the CDOs that Burry and the contrarians examined, finally convinced them to make their move as they were now sure that the housing bubble would burst at any moment, and the mortgage and CDO markets would plummet at the same time. To enable them to profit from the inevitable crash, they took a short position (*) in the CDO market, and some took the same position against the stock of certain banks, mortgage lenders and large house builders. With heads in the sand, many of Wall Street's big players were still buying and keeping the markets high, as they had never considered that a short selling programme (*) of this scale could be initiated without them knowing about it – but how wrong they were.

Bury, and the other short-sellers had decided to adopt a rather unorthodox method to execute their trade, and this is when the Credit Default Swap (CDS), or simply 'Swap', came into play. In reality, a Swap was a kind of insurance policy used to insure against defaults on certain financial instruments (*) – and defaults were now inevitable in the mortgage and bond markets, as they were not just overheating, they were white hot. The Swap provided a perfect way to be positioned, quietly, on the opposite side of the trade to almost all of those on Wall Street who still had long positions (*) in the mortgage bond markets.

Burry and the others started to buy their Swaps from large Wall Street firms who, with a degree of irony, snatched their hands off. However, this sale of Swaps, in itself, had the potential to create problems further down the road for Burry and the short sellers. If the markets crashed, what would happen to the institutions that had sold them the Swaps? After all, many of these same firms were also involved in the heavy trading of mortgage bonds. Essentially, those who had sold swaps had placed bets on both sides of the market, both of which could lose at the same time. If the bond markets crashed, these firms could lose very heavily but, in this event, they would still be legally bound to pay to Burry and the other short sellers. What a predicament. Naturally, Burry and the rest now wondered if these same Wall Street firms would still be around to meet their obligations.

Once again, Wall Street had played both ends against the middle, and this was a tricky dilemma for Burry and company, so they decided that it would be better if they spread the risk. This is where the insurance giant, AIG, came into the picture, and this conglomerate would become the biggest insurer of Swaps in the marketplace. In view of the magnitude of the losses that AIG eventually reported, it would seem feasible that this corporate powerhouse had taken the brunt from the other Wall Street firms, who had jumped at the chance of selling Swaps to anyone who wanted to take a short position. This was a marketplace where 'pass the parcel' was a real game, provided that those who passed it on, had taken their cut of the spoils beforehand. Although relatively few traders had taken short positions, those who placed these bets had used huge amounts of money.

All that Burry and the contrarians now had to do was maintain the payment of their Swap insurance premiums, and then wait for the crash. This in itself was not an easy matter as no one actually knew when the markets would roll over whilst, at the same time, insurance premiums were adding up day by day. In the meantime, more people panicked at Scion Capital and withdrew their money, until Burry drew a line in the sand which emphasised that no more capital withdrawals would be permitted. Threats of law-suits now followed, but the resilient Burry simply stuck to his guns.

Of course, he was right and the markets rolled over very soon after.

This created one of the most devastating financial disasters in living memory. Michael Burry, and the contrarians, had correctly interpreted the writing on the wall during the financial free for all that led up to the crisis, but these intuitive professionals had been ridiculed earlier by whoever sold them Swaps. There can be no doubt that other big players in Wall Street, and the wider industry, should have tuned into the increasingly corrosive events well before the thunderous crash in 2008, but they were too busy elsewhere.

Michael Burry is said to have made around $100 million personally, whilst Scion's investors raked in around $700 million from his resilience, although this was not quite the return he had estimated. Burry was certainly good with his projections, so it seems possible that some of the Wall Street firms had become insolvent in 2008, and were therefore unable to pay Scion what it was owed on the Swaps. However, Michael Burry departed from Scion Capital straight after, leaving a legacy of 489.34% returns for investors (net of expenses) between November 2000 and June 2008. (14)

According to the Wall Street Journal on 17th September 2018, John Paulson's hedge fund firm, Paulson and Company, was said to have made $12 billion on their short position between 2007 and 2009, driven by bets against sub-prime mortgage products. (15) If this was insured by AIG, it would have accounted for a very large proportion of their loss on Credit Default Swaps.

As a result of failing to be sufficiently diligent during these dangerous times, AIG had almost drawn its last breath by the time pay-outs fell due on the business it had underwritten. To prevent its collapse, the Federal Reserve loaned this global giant $85 billion, and took a 79.9% stake. It has even been suggested that AIG might have been holding as much as $560 billion in 'super senior risk'. (16) It was later reported that AIG's liabilities could have included up to $150 billion against Credit Default Swaps, however, figures were updated and revised on a number of occasions thereafter.

By September 2008, the International Monetary Fund estimated that the total losses from this catastrophe could possibly reach $1000 billion. (17) A year later, the situation became so grave that economists estimated that losses could be close to $3 trillion. In the next revision, the figure went up to $5 trillion. The public were outraged when they were made fully aware of the scale of this catastrophe, as were most politicians on both sides of the Atlantic and beyond. Only one trader—Kareem Serageldin of Credit Suisse—was prosecuted and sent to prison for 30 months in 2012. (18) He was convicted of artificially inflating the value of CDOs which were made up of sub-prime mortgages, and this caused losses for the bank of several billion dollars. However, leading up to 2008, cheating and unethical behaviour had been endemic at almost every level of the industry, and the public felt that it was the heads of the people in charge that should have rolled.

During the confusion that ensued, many obvious questions were raised by consumer groups, high ranking politicians, together with any number of those in minor positions who were trying to make political capital from a world disaster – but the reality was simply this:

During this boom, extraordinary pressure had been exerted on two fronts.

The first was a combination of the public's robust desire to take out mortgages, irrespective of cost or consequence, and the lenders' willingness to meet this demand. This drove the domestic property markets to unsustainable levels.

Secondly, and at the same time, there had been extraordinary activity in the derivatives markets by global financial institutions. A very large proportion of these derivatives were CDOs, and they were made up of the mortgages supplied by the mortgage lending market. Some of the mortgages in the supply chain were sub-prime and defaulted.

The 'cocktail' described above eventually became so effervescent that it could not be contained, and this was enough to collapse the property and mortgage markets for years to come.

In the face of all of this, it is worth noting that JP Morgan emerged as the largest Bank in the world with a market capitalisation in 2009 of $170 billion, and amongst its celebrated advisors were personalities like Al Gore and Tony Blair. (19) Unsurprisingly, the banks and lending institutions had gone full-circle by 2015, when they started to sell 'Bespoke Tranche Opportunities'. According to Bloomberg News, these new financial instruments were re-branded Credit Default Obligations (CDOs). Lest we should ever forget, CDOs were at the epicentre of the 2008 crash of the mortgage and property markets.

A well-worn cliché says that history always repeats itself. One can't help but notice that, every 10–12 years or so, the financial markets have a very strong affinity with this same old chestnut.

A Meteoric Rise to Fame

There are a number of instances in which bogus financial gains in Wall Street have created serious financial pains in Main Street – but this time, the severity was unprecedented.

"Uneasy lies the head of he who wears the crown."

Bernard Lawrence Madoff was born on 29th April 1938 and spent his early years living in middle class Laurelton, Queens, with his parents, Ralph and

Sylvia, and his older sister and younger brother, Sondra and Peter. After working as lifeguard on $8.78 a day 'Bernie', as he was known to family and friends, entered the world of business and finance at the age of 23. From this point in his life, he was able to enjoy a truly meteoric rise to fame which started when he and his brother created one of the most successful broker-dealer firms in New York, where millions of shares were traded every day.

The Madoff brothers soon realised that there was an enormous need to speed up the execution of buy and sell orders, so they turned to computerised trading very early on to improve the efficiency of their operation. The NASDAQ, which was founded in February 1971, had led by example and Bernard L. Madoff Investment Securities was one of the first five broker-dealer firms to join. By 1983, Bernie had become a member of the Board of Governors at the National Association of Securities Dealers, which was a self-regulatory securities industry organisation.

Following this, he served as non-executive Chairman of the NASDAQ in 1990, 1991, and 1993. During this time, he became a founding member of the International Securities Clearing Corporation in London. In 1996, he accepted a position on the board of trustees of Yeshiva University, and provided this service alongside his involvement in a number of charitable posts.

However, Bernie gained his enviable reputation from the truly mouth-watering returns he had purportedly delivered to his clients over a number of years. With such impressive credentials, Madoff was understandably regarded as a Wall Street icon who was lauded by governments, global banks, rival fund managers and almost everyone within his industry. He thereby attracted pension funds, charities, university endowments, banks, and some of the highest-profile clientele on the planet. Madoff was also well known in Washington D. C. and, significantly, on Capitol Hill where he was a donor to both the Republican and Democrat campaigns.

Yet, with such a distinguished background, he was found to have taken part in one of the biggest financial frauds in America's history. With apparently so many positives at Madoff's finger-tips, it would seem impossible that he could have fallen into such dishonest ways and, once revered, was now reviled by his investors. Others were left in a state of shock when the news broke, including long-time friends and associates, the industry in general, and most of his 180 employees – some of whom were family members.

Bernard L. Madoff Investment Securities Company (BLMIS), which had been founded in 1960 by Madoff and other family members, was a legitimate business. However, there was also an investment management advisory division, which unofficially became known as Madoff's 'elite hedge fund', and this was not publicised. This part of the business eventually became Madoff's prime focus and was used as a cash-cow to fulfil his colossal ambitions in the trading world. However, he would eventually discover that when ambitious plans wildly exceed reasonable odds for success, they are no more than illusions.

To put the scale of Madoff's scam into a meaningful perspective, it has been pointed out by one commentator that his $65 billion loss exceeded, at the time, the combined fortunes of 'Bill Gates, Tiger Woods and Roman Abramovich'. (1) The WorldCom and Enron corporate scandals were said to have both incurred losses in the tens of billions of dollars. The Bank of Credit and Commerce's collapse in 1991, due to its alleged 'extraordinary affairs', gave rise to claims of wildly fluctuating amounts, but it certainly seems that they were also in the tens of billions. (2)

The term 'hedge fund' had been coined back in 1949 by Alfred Jones. (3) He would buy and hold stocks he thought would go up in price, then 'hedge' his long positions with stocks he thought would fall in price. During the sixties and seventies, most within the industry believed that this posed a high level of risk, whilst a few intuitive traders recognised that the potential rewards from this set-up could be much greater than those produced by the more traditional techniques of the day.

As many as 4000 clients are said to have been ensnared in the staggering $65 billion loss incurred by Madoff's 'elite hedge fund'. This would have meant there was an average loss of no less than $16.25 million per client, with varying sums invested by larger and smaller players. But when Madoff appeared in court, it became apparent that no one would ever know what the true extent of the losses actually were, where the money had gone, or the names of everyone involved.

After being arrested by the FBI in December 2008, the seventy-year-old Madoff found himself in front of Judge Denny Chin on 12th March 2009, in the downtown Manhattan court-house.

Underneath his charcoal-grey suit, Madoff was wearing a bullet-proof vest. He was facing eleven criminal counts, including securities fraud, mail fraud, wire fraud, money laundering, making false statements, and perjury. (4) There was a determination amongst a few of his clients to simply absorb their losses quietly, particularly with money laundering on the charges sheet. On that day though, several investors had hauled themselves to the court-room to vent their anger and bay for Madoff's blood – but this once legendary pillar within his community simply hung his head.

Madoff had promised returns of anything between 12 and 20%, but asked his clients not tell anyone who was managing their money, or what the terms were. This highly suspicious arrangement, under the guise of confidentiality, played perfectly into Madoff's hands. It thereby enabled him to proliferate his corrupt scheme, unquestioned by investors old and new, and their timely receipt of dividend cheques and withdrawals certainly upheld their faith. At the same time, it also helped to maintain his 'enviable reputation', as well as his tenuous hold on the affairs of a slowly decaying empire. In fact, the rot had started to set in on the very day he crossed the line between honesty and dishonesty.

Then came the devastating stock market and property crash in 2008, which caused a banking crisis, a credit crunch, raging unemployment and a large number of bankruptcies. As a result, it left many of Madoff's investors so cash poor that they had no choice but to ask for their money back, and this placed Madoff in his own private hell. He needed to find new investment to repay the old, but this was most certainly not a good time as markets around the world were crashing – thereby severing his supply lines from feeder-funds.

Madoff went on to plead guilty to all eleven criminal counts that day in the Manhattan court, thereby giving up his right to a trial, and refusing to implicate anyone else. This meant that he would not have to disclose any of the details of how his crimes had been committed. A trial would have required the likes of J. P. Morgan Chase, HSBC, Swiss Bank and other high-profile institutions and personalities, to appear on the witness stand, and this was simply not going to happen.

Three of Madoff's victims had made statements in front of Judge Chin. George Nierenberg, a filmmaker whose family had lost everything, asked why conspiracy charges had not been brought by the Government, which would have opened up an investigation on other suspects such as Madoff's wife, Ruth, sons Andrew and Mark, and his brother, Peter. (5)

After all, it was Andrew and Mark who had given up their father to the FBI after being tipped-off by Peter the previous day. But, naively, the two sons had never questioned their recent payments totalling $31.5 million, which had been written up as loans from their parents. The day before Madoff's arrest, his wife withdrew $10 million from an account at Cohmad Securities Corporation, a firm that was jointly owned by Madoff and long-time friend, Maurice Cohn. Cohmad was used by Madoff as though it was a family-owned bank, which conveniently shared office space with BLMIS. As the evidence unfolded, a vast number of investors also discovered that they had been introduced to the very same accountancy firm—Sosnik, Bell and Company—who were mentioned over 900 times in a 162-page legal document. (6)

There can be no doubt that conspiracy charges would have created a legal environment in which there were far better prospects of unravelling the financial web that Madoff had left behind – and who had truly woven it. The proceedings revealed that the Madoffs had enjoyed such an extravagant lifestyle, no less than five people within their organisation had been given the task of keeping track of their personal affairs.

Upon the company's crash, the unpicking of Madoff's crooked accountancy procedures therefore proved to be an onerous task. His high-tech set-up on the 18th and 19th floors of the Lipstick Building, allegedly managed under the pretext of efficacy and providence, was yet another guise. The real centre of operations was the office that was hidden on the 17th floor below, and this was a highly regulated domain, designed to confine the true nature of Madoff's fraudulent activity to within just a small group of people.

With such a tight knit operation, it made it very difficult to determine the precise number of clients involved in this catastrophic loss, where their money had gone, or if $65 billion was the whole of the iceberg, or if the losses were, indeed, much less.

Centre of operations hidden on 17th floor

This humungous scam eventually became a global talking point with widespread disparagement aimed at Madoff and his operations, Wall Street, the USA's regulatory services and the industry in general. In fact, there had been a number of earlier warnings from well-informed sources that Madoff needed to be investigated, or even given a red card. Financial analyst, Harry Markopolos, had persistently said that Madoff's 'split strike conversion' strategy could not produce the returns claimed by Madoff. (7) However, both the Securities Exchange Commission, and the Financial Industry Regulation Authority, failed to lift a finger. This provided the opportunity as late as May 2006, for Madoff to lie under oath about the way he ran his businesses.

Over a period of more than twenty years, and by falsified figures and lies, Madoff had successfully convinced almost everyone that he had been running a world-renowned, and very exclusive investment operation. In reality, Madoff was not a master of trading the financial markets – he was simply a master of deceit, and manipulating the government. This allowed the theft of investors' money by means of 'a revolving door scam'—which is paying one man with another man's money—also known as 'robbing Peter to pay Paul'. In fact, it was this very same ploy that gave Charles Ponzi his notoriety and, as a result, Madoff's scam is always referred to as a gigantic Ponzi Scheme.

Like Ponzi, Madoff had a well-honed network of feeder funds, agents, subagents and introducers, some at the very highest level of society, business, banking, the world of showbiz, and even high-ranking public figures. Simply for commission and kick-backs, they kept the money flowing into Madoff's coffers. To pull this off, he needed unquestioning loyalty from those within his network, but he kept his closest secrets on 'the 17th floor' of the Lipstick building and, it is suspected, within family ranks. As for the commission agents, perhaps it would be wrong to suggest that they all fully understood the extent of the crooked game that Madoff was playing, but it might also be appropriate to suggest that their servile attitude and blind faith, for back-handers, meant that they were quite willing to turn a blind eye and deaf ear. For sure, if you don't start using your own mind, someone else will – and Madoff happened to be an expert at it.

If we give or take a billion or two on the Madoff's scam of around $65 billion, it makes Ponzi's insolvency almost ninety years earlier for $3 million look like small change, yet Ponzi is arguably more notorious than Madoff – but why? This is because Ponzi was larger than life, and revelled in the publicity he received. He therefore clung onto the misguided belief that he was held in high esteem throughout Bostonian society, and the US in general. In reality, people were simply in love with his promise of a miraculous but impossible 50% – 100% return, making Madoff's promise of 12–20% return look far less inviting. This championed Ponzi's persona during his day, and has helped to transport his name into modern day narrative as the king of the scam artists. On the other hand, Madoff was far more cunning, and had a preference for the shadows instead of the lime-light. This retiring approach enabled Madoff to perpetuate his scam for well over two decades whilst Ponzi was only able to sustain his scheme for just over twelve months.

The very same question has always lingered. Were the original plans of Ponzi and Madoff above board, whereupon their aspirations became too big and ran out of control, or did they both have devious intentions up their sleeve from the very beginning?

The king of the con-artists?

In Ponzi's case, there is a belief that he probably set out with decent intentions, however, he naively immersed himself into chaos simply because of his half-baked scheme.

So, had Madoff's plans also been derailed by a downturn at some point, and had he then tried to patch things up with more cash from his feeder funds? Perhaps the distress within his operation is revealed by his eventual decision to simply bank incoming money rather than invest it with confidence. The fact that Madoff had been given up by his two sons on the same day as his arrest also arouses some suspicion. It seems quite possible that this was a pre-arranged ploy to save his family, and this notion would be supported by Madoff's refusal to give evidence in court. After all, this more or less led the investigation into a dead-end, as it was Madoff alone who had cut most of the deals with his larger clients, and his promise of 12–20% return certainly gave him plenty of leverage.

David Friehling, Madoff's long-standing accountant, was eventually indicted. (8) Someone else simply had to know something, and he must have been a prime witness to the rollercoaster of inflows and outflows of cash, and the company's dire financial state throughout the operation of this giant Ponzi Scheme. But Friehling pleaded not guilty to securities fraud, aiding and abetting investment advisor fraud, and four counts of filing false audit reports with the Securities Exchange Commission. Friehling decided to stick to his story which, once again, left Madoff in the frame – all alone.

With so many ponderables, could it ever be stated with some degree of certainty that the whole of the $65 billion in purported losses ever existed – except within Madoff's own falsified paperwork?

Chapter 10
Bernie Madoff

In the courtroom on 12th March 2009, the US Attorney, Lee Dassin, addressed the court. He expressly pointed out that the charges reflected the truly extraordinary array of crimes committed by Madoff, which had continued for over twenty years. Some observers believed, however, that this time-frame was based on speculation, because no one really knew when Madoff had first gone astray – and the man himself wasn't giving anything away. The US Assistant Attorney, Mark Litt, who was the chief prosecutor on the case, then stood up and announced to the court that Madoff could face a term of up to 150 years behind bars, under the current federal sentencing guidelines.

Then it was Madoff's turn. He said, "When I began my Ponzi Scheme, I believed that I would end it shortly, and I would be able to extricate myself and my clients from this scheme. When I didn't, I always knew that this day would one day come. I never invested the money; I just deposited it into a Chase Manhattan bank." (9) The evidence would later reveal that incoming money was placed in a Chase account numbered: 140081703, and that Madoff's illegal scheme had started after just one year's bad results. This is when Madoff started doubling down (*) to recover the earlier losses.

This astonishing statement from Madoff undoubtedly left an open verdict on several burning questions. "What had really led him to this point in his life? The extent of his crimes indicated that there were no bounds to his dishonesty, and this was surely a sign of some sort of underlying personality disorder – one which Madoff had managed to keep hidden. His ice-cold persona had simply provided the mask, and this enabled him to filch money from all and sundry, including his sister and her husband. Elie Wiesel, who had survived Hitler's death camps and was a Nobel Peace Prize laureate, was truly appalled at Madoff's fraud." (10)

Wiesel had lost his life savings, and the Elie Wiesel Foundation for Humanity had lost all of its $15.2 million.

So was Madoff's mind a product of twisted family roots, and could this have created a moral compass that mis-directed his behaviour in adult life? After all, so many people had trusted him, and claimed to know him well.

Towards the end of the 'Roaring Twenties', the Wall Street crash of 1929 brought the Great Depression during the thirties which, to everyone's relief, had started to abate by the middle of the decade. However, by 1939, Hitler had unleashed his terrifying war-machine in Europe, and word-wide tension was escalated when America went to war with Japan in December, 1941. Bernie was born in Brooklyn a year before the start of World War Two, as the second child of Ralph and Sylvia Madoff. Bernie's older sister, Sondra 'Sonnie' Madoff, had arrived during the depression in 1934. By the early forties, the family was able to move from their less than humble tenement in Brooklyn, and step-up to a three bedroomed house in middle class Laurelton, Queens. The Madoff's youngest child, Peter, was born during 1945 – the final year of the war.

Bernie was always pressed by his parents to concentrate his mind on ways to make money. (11) This was quite a burden to place on a young boy who had responsibilities at school, and no doubt the desire to be involved in normal childhood pursuits. Ralph and Sylvia, it seems, were trying to turn the young Bernie into an adult before he had grown up, and this was undue pressure on a formative young mind.

Yes, Bernie soon developed into a street-smart kid, who knew what he wanted and who he should hang out with. He was quite popular with some of his schoolmates, whilst others had mixed feelings. Bernie naturally gravitated towards the kids from wealthier backgrounds but, at the centre of the peer group was Bernie's best chum, the good-looking Elliott Olin. Other companions often remarked that it was as though Bernie and Olin were joined at the hip, as they did almost everything together. Wherever Olin was, there were girls, and this was a good incentive for Bernie to keep close ties with him.

In high school, Bernie liked competitive sports and was involved with Olin on the soft-ball team, as well as the 8th grade team that won the school basketball championship. Bernie's father always demanded a winning attitude and his son always tried to deliver, but he certainly wasn't one of the best players on these teams. His image seemed to be more important to him than his performance, as the self-conscious Bernie always wanted to wear the same top of the range sportswear as some of his team-mates, but such accoutrements were always considered excessive by his parents.

Academically, Bernie was anything but brilliant and, when the collapse of BLMIS became world news, one ex-school chum jested that someone else simply had to be involved as Madoff would have been incapable of going it alone. (12) In spite of his apparent lack of academic talent, Bernie always seemed to be one step ahead in other ways. One of Bernie's class-mates in the sophomore year at Far Rockaway High School, Jay Portnoy, recalled that the English class had been given a reading assignment, which required the students to read a book of their choice and deliver an oral book-summary to the class. (13)

Priorities!

Bernie told Jay and best friend, Elliott Olin, that he couldn't be bothered with such a boring chore as he had better things to do with his time.

On the day, Bernie was chosen straight away by his teacher to stand up and deliver his report, and the street-smart side of Bernie's personality soon took over. He strode confidently to the front of the class, and words began to roll off his tongue – but there were several giggles from around the room. Bernie had simply made up a story about fishing and hunting by Peter Gunn, who happened to be a suave television detective. For around ten minutes, Bernie delivered what appeared to be a plausible book summary, but it was based on a book that didn't exist, so the suspicious teacher asked to see the book. Instinctively, Bernie blurted that he had already taken it back to the library. For a brief moment, you could have heard a pin drop, then the fraught atmosphere was pierced by nervous and irritating giggles in different parts of the room. However, Bernie's willingness to lie and cheat in front of his friends and classmates caused some to have doubts about him – and friends can sometimes make the worst enemies. Had this incident revealed early flaws in Bernie's character, or had it just been a cheeky schoolboy prank, carried out by a street-smart lad?

In Bernie's case, it seems that his true nature was a lifetime's work, but his childhood influences certainly affected the rudder that steered his future path.

With Elliott Olin, Bernie was a member of the Boy Scouts of America throughout his high school years. The first Scout law Bernie promised to uphold was – "A Scout tells the truth. (14) He keeps his promises. Honesty is part of his code of conduct. People can depend on him." Unfortunately, young Bernie's allegiance to these codes wasn't always upheld as his mindset had been influenced from an early age – by his parents' obsession with making money by any means. In fact, the noble scout laws he had promised to uphold would turn out to be unwanted baggage on this journey.

Father, Ralph Madoff, was the self-proclaimed local plumber, but he was never available to carry out any work, nor had anyone seen him on the job. He was regarded by many in his local community as a hard-boiled individual with an intimidating demeanour who certainly wasn't the receptive type. People were naturally wary of him and preferred to steer clear. He was often seen walking through the neighbourhood wearing a pin-striped suit following regular visits to the city, as Laurelton had a station on the commuter line.

Ralph Madoff's materialistic credo soon clicked into gear when the fifteen-year-old Bernie let on that two of his schoolmates were making good money between semesters by installing sprinkler systems for new homeowners in the suburbs of Nassau County. (15) Eddie Heiberger and Sheldon Fogel were paid a visit by Bernie and his father, who tried to prise their way into the business by asking for a three-way split. The enterprise was known as the Shedwin Company and Heiberger and Fogel later said that Ralph Madoff was particularly aggressive and quite scary. Nonetheless, the two young founders of Shedwin stood their ground and refused to accept the proposition put forward by the Madoffs. As a result, Bernie simply pirated Shedwin's set-up and, with a better financed operation, plus much stealthier sales techniques, he managed to continue his business throughout his time at college.

Like many Americans during this era, Ralph Madoff was looking for opportunities to make his fortune by some means or other, but it certainly wasn't in the plumbing trade. Ralph's real Christian name was Zookan, and he was born in Scranton, Pennsylvania, on June 8th 1910. His future wife, Sylvia Munter, was born in Brooklyn in December 1911 and, during the Great Depression in 1932, they were married. The couple's roots went back into Eastern Europe, Poland, Romania and Austria. Interestingly, on their marriage license, Ralph's occupation was recorded as 'Credit' and Sylvia's as 'None'. (16)

It certainly seemed, therefore, that Ralph's purported livelihood from plumbing was a front for something else. In fact, quite a few people in the local community suspected that Bernie's parents could be up to something and they were not trustworthy. What's more, the parents of some of Bernie's friends didn't like their kids hanging out with him, or going into the Madoff's residence, so perhaps young Bernie had clung onto the coat tails of the popular Elliot Olin simply to gain acceptance within his peer group. Olin's mother had heard whispers that the Madoffs were running some sort of share dealing operation from their home across the street. (17) Ralph Madoff and Saul Alpern met quite regularly and their favourite topic of discussion was always making money in the stock market. It was through this relationship that Bernie first became acquainted with Saul's daughter, Ruth Alpern, who would later become his wife.

It was confirmed that a shifty broker-dealer firm had been operating in the Madoff residence when Bernie was already running Bernard L. Madoff Investment Securities as an over-the-counter Penny stock trading business. For a twenty-five-year-old, he was doing quite well for himself, however, in August 1963, his mother was investigated by the SEC, as she was the registered owner of Gibraltar Securities at the family home address.

It was strongly suspected that Sylvia Madoff was acting as a front for her husband and, in 1964, Gibraltar Securities was closed down by mutual agreement between the Madoffs and the SEC. This staved off the pending legal action against Sylvia, which brought a sigh of relief from the up-and-coming Bernie, but it cast a long shadow over the name of his parents. In fact, Ralph Madoff was immersed in financial difficulties, including serious tax problems, and these issues had been long-standing. (18) The family home in Laurelton had liens against it dating back to 1956 for unpaid federal income taxes amounting to $13,245.28. This would be around $121,000 in 2020. But, as a front for her husband once again, it was Bernie's mother who took the fall, as it was her name on the tax demands.

The extremely elusive Ralph Madoff was conveniently said to have been working alongside Bernie at BLMIS during the 1963 incident with the SEC, whilst allowing his wife's reputation to be well and truly tarnished by that very same incident. Sylvia Madoff's problems with the federal income tax authorities told a similar story. Ralph Madoff had simply hovered in the background as the furtive captain of the ship—the one that inevitably sank—but he always refused to go down with it. Clearly, Madoff senior was an imposing figure to his wife, his children, and others who knew him. To say the least, his paternal influences were massively out of kilter with the norm, and this particularly affected Bernie.

Back in September 1956, the eighteen-year-old Bernie had enrolled at the University of Alabama, which was embroiled in acrid racial hostility around this time. A black graduate, Autherine Juanita Lucy, had just been employed by the university's administration department, and the whole campus was soon locked down by a seething student mob. Bernie didn't feel that this was much of a reception party, so he quickly joined a fraternity known as Sigma Alpha Mu. (19) This was an exclusive frat for Jewish students, where Bernie felt some degree of comfort amid ongoing racial tension. He had enrolled at the Alabama University simply because there were no other alternatives, however, Bernie only managed to complete his freshman year, and the end of term party was his grand finale.

His room-mate, Marty Schrager, couldn't help but remember a very cute 16 year-old accompanying Bernie during this weekend, and this was Ruth Alpern who would become Bernie's wife in November, 1959. (20) In some ways, Ruth was quite different to Bernie as she was extremely extrovert, and exuded natural style and self-confidence. Like Bernie, she certainly knew what she wanted, and she preferred to keep company with influential young people.

On the outside looking in – an uncomfortable position for Bernie!

Whilst at the university of Alabama, Bernie had missed his hometown of Laurelton and decided to transfer his scholarship so that he could be closer to Ruth and his family.

In September 1957, Bernie enrolled as a sophomore at Hofstra College on Long Island, which was a short commute from his home. His plan was to slip through to graduation with minimum effort and fuss, then set up a neat little stock brokerage firm, as Bernie's father and Saul Alpern had greatly influenced his way of thinking. In the meantime, he offered hot tips on penny stocks to Hofstra students, which were quickly seized upon by those who thought they might earn a few extra bucks. Their buy orders were often placed with Gibraltar Securities or Lou Lieberbaum. Lou's son, 'Shelly', had financed Bernie's sprinkler operation in and around the gardens of Nassau County to the tune of $10,000, as the Lieberbaums saw potential in Bernie's ability to spot good opportunities.

Bernie was eventually said to be netting $2,000 a week from his sprinkler business, which continued throughout his college days. In a seemingly endless network of friends, acquaintances, contacts and hangers on, Lieberbaum and Company would, a few years hence, send Bernie an enormous amount of business to his stock-broking firm, Bernard L. Madoff Investment Securities. There is certainly a belief therefore that BLMIS could have simply risen from the vestiges of Gibraltar Securities, and Ralph and Sylvia Madoff.

It was now a case of the anxious mother and father clinging onto their son's coat tails, as Bernie Madoff had qualified as a general securities representative, and a general securities principal on 29th March 1960. In the same year, he also graduated from Hofstra College with a degree in political science, and then set up Bernard L. Madoff Investment Securities (BLMIS). In 1965, the federal income tax was paid off by BLMIS and the liens on the Madoff residence were lifted. Bernie would later claim that he had bankrolled BLMIS through his sprinkler system enterprise at college, which turned to be another of his myths.

In 1967, the very well-educated Peter Madoff joined the firm and, alongside Bernie, he was instrumental in its development over the next few years. Although Peter chose to be the one who avoided the limelight, he was much the brighter of the two brothers and was the inspiration behind a great deal of what was happening day to day. This continued to be a source of irritation for Bernie, who frequently felt that he should demonstrate who was boss. But he sometimes climbed onto his high horse in front of BLMIS staff, which would always sour the atmosphere as Peter was popular amongst his colleagues.

In the beginning, BLMIS created a niche for itself by providing a service in a tiny segment of the market. This was where many of the smaller public companies did not meet the trading requirements for either the New York Stock Exchange (NYSE) or the American Stock Exchange (AMEX). As it turned out, this specialised sector was very popular and the public companies classified in this domain were listed on what were known as 'pink sheets'. They were so called simply because of the colour of the paper upon which the companies were listed, and their shares were known as 'over the counter stocks'. (*) Little gems, emerging prodigies and a number of good penny-shares could often be found within the lists. BLMIS, and just a handful of other brokers, provided services in this niche market, where a firm's brokerage income was usually supplemented by a proprietary trading account. (*) Of course, through the brokerage, Madoff had a wonderful inside track on what people were buying or selling – and when.

To the credit of the two brothers, they eventually managed to establish one of the busiest broker-dealer firms in New York, which effectively provided a 'third market', behind the New York Stock Exchange (NYSE) and the American Stock Exchange (AMEX). The volume of shares traded on a daily basis at BLMIS was in the millions which, in turn, generated excellent returns by way of a constant flow of commission. The BLMIS set-up was popular because it made trading cheaper and faster for brokers and investors alike.

Carl Shapiro was certainly a man of substance, and one of the first clients of BLMIS in the 1960s. (21) Under the brand name of Kay Windsor, Shapiro had made a fortune in the ladies' clothing business and opened a $100,000 account with the Madoffs. In order to retain this account, Bernie promised to clear Shapiro's trades in three days instead of the industry's average of five to eight days, and often longer. This appealed to Shapiro because he had realised that he could make money by arbitraging (*) the market with quick 'in and out' transactions on price differentials. By 1969, in fact, the National Association of Securities Dealers made it a rule that all securities sold to clients had to be delivered within five days. (22)

The Madoffs had already spotted where the need was, and real time quotations together with the speed of execution of buy and sell orders was the name of the game. They knew that this would be an excellent marketing tool per se, simply because the existing quotation and execution system was very cumbersome, which offered distinct advantages to those who could be nimble. From the 1960s into the early 1970s, transactions on Wall Street were carried out on the telephone, person to person, and the conversation was then transcribed onto a trade ticket. Next, the broker would hand this piece of paper to a young runner who would take it to the office where the stock certificates were issued. However, brokers for pink-sheet stocks could take several weeks just to find buyers and sellers and, as well as the chore of filling out paperwork, this kind of time-frame was wide open to abuse. Before many others, the Madoffs therefore recognised that there was a need for a better world, and this would involve electronic stock market operations via computers.

In 1971, the NASDAQ introduced a computerised communications web which was capable of competing against the NYSE and the AMEX, thereby providing cutting edge facilities for a network of broker dealers. (23) It quoted the bid and ask prices, as well as the daily volume, for stocks traded by the tiny public companies not listed on either of these exchanges. The Madoffs welcomed this quantum leap and soon embraced the NASDAQ technology, as it would greatly assist their trading of the stocks listed on the pink sheets. Contrary to popular belief, the Madoffs did not invent the NASDAQ, but BLMIS was one of the five broker dealer firms that set it off in the early 1970s. It was Gordon Macklin (24) who had devoted himself to the creation of the NASDAQ, and he was a central figure on most of the committees during the 1960s.

During 1975, the Securities Exchange Commission was now pressed by Congress to introduce a National Market System (NMS) which would improve the efficiency of the marketplace. (25) The subsequent changes meant that prices would be quoted from several different sources in real time, thereby providing much better opportunities for broker-dealers and their clients. Madoff believed that this was a chance to challenge the monopoly enjoyed by NYSE and AMEX on exchange listed public companies. He tried to persuade the SEC that it was now opportune to introduce a third market by bypassing these major exchanges.

The SCC concurred, so it was now believed that this would be the beginning of the end for AMEX.

The winds of change were now blowing over the industry and in Madoff's favour, so he took another huge step when he became a regional specialist through his connection with the Cincinnati Stock Exchange. This had been established back in 1885 and was hopelessly out of date, but Madoff believed that it had the potential to compete with the NYSE and AMEX. (26) He was willing to put his money where his mouth was so he decided to outlay $250,000 to update operations and set his own agenda. During the early 1980s, those who ran the Cincinnati Exchange had the foresight to close its trading floor, and deal through a computer. Madoff had certainly made his mark, and as a result of this advanced set-up, he managed to persuade 48 Wall Street firms to use its services. Meanwhile, over at the NASDAQ, the shares of over 3,000 companies were listed on its exchange by 1981, as compared to 2,500 quoted on NYSE and AMEX. (27)

However, the late seventies and early eighties had witnessed a terrible recession which was considered by many to be the worst since World War Two. High interest rates and tight fiscal policy were responsible for falling output and rising unemployment, thereby causing an enormous slowdown in the manufacturing sector. This financial turbulence had been compounded by the overthrow of the Shah of Iran in February 1979, which had caused an energy crisis. There were also serious banking problems and 1,043 out of 3,243 US loan and saving institutions failed between 1986 and 1995. With inflation raging, the average yield on Federal Reserve funds reached 22% during 1980. In 1986, however, Bernie's name appeared in the 'Financial World magazine, which described him as one of the top one hundred earners on Wall Street – having made $6 million that same year'.

In spite of the austerity of the eighties, the Madoff's took very positive steps. First, Madoff Securities International Limited was opened in London in 1983, and its sole purpose was propriety trading. Next, they hired the formidable Neil Yelsey from Solomon Brothers in 1986, (28) who was an expert in the field of statistical arbitrage. (*) With Yelsey's knowledge, the Madoffs believed that their trading model would become leading edge, and recognition as an industry pacemaker in this field would do their brand no harm at all. By the late nineties, Yelsey had created an automated trading programme which had the capacity to oversee a portfolio of up to $750 million. The trades were taken without manual intervention, and it was possible to trade up to 3,000 stocks at a time. To begin with, the programme returned as much as 20% but, when the market environment later changed, profitability dropped to 2–3%.

For the Madoffs, and all those working in the financial markets, the eighties proved to be particularly eventful. A notable mile-stone in this decade was 'Black Monday' – so let us briefly pick up the trail from Chapter 7 in order to see how this crash might well have been precipitated.

Nature takes its toll on fragile markets!

We have seen how chaos reigned within the markets when record losses were suffered as the Dow Jones Industrial Average plummeted 22.76%, accompanied by a 33% drop in the Standard and Poor's Futures. An Estimated $500 billion in capital was lost during this single day yet, very few traders anticipated this huge sell-off. However, the extratropical cyclone that savaged the UK and parts of northern Europe on the 15th and 16th October 1987, brought power cables down and interrupted communications. As a result, very many speculators panicked, as they were now holding positions 'in the dark'.

But as well as the cyclone, and the attendant communication problems, other critical developments around this time may have helped to paint the backdrop for Black Monday's sell-off.

Although the eighties began in deep recession, technological advancement in the financial trading world had already started to define an exciting new era of opportunity. There was the 'Big Bang' in October 1986 when the London

Stock Exchange made a quantum leap by introducing an automated price quotation system. In 1987, NASDAQ workstation software enabled any PC to become a work terminal, and computerised dealing and automated quotation systems were readily adopted by most of the world's major financial centres. As a result, the markets were facing something quite different. A myriad of fledgling pairs of eyes were now able to interpret live price action, and each speculator had the ability to place an order at will, by the mere press of a button. With an online presence of this kind, even a flicker of panic would have had the potential to escalate into a melt-down of epic proportions.

However, Madoff managed to weather the storm, and BLMIS was one of the few broker-dealer firms that was able to stay open afterwards – but at what cost?

But, irrespective of events during 1987, Madoff was more determined than ever to forge ahead, as he believed that this was a good opportunity to leave the competition behind. His brother now designed a computer software programme by the name of 'Madoff Integrated Support System' which was built by TCAM Systems Group. (29) It could execute trades at the best bid and ask prices (*) in the market in just four seconds, and was completed in 1988. It also helped traders to mitigate risk by hedging, and was far more advanced than anything used by other market specialists.

The Madoffs intended to make money on all the trades they executed, so they bought shares at one price and always tried to sell them at a better price. As market-makers, they were able to execute either the buying or selling of up to 2000 shares in any one transaction. They were perfectly positioned to complete the round trip by repurchasing what they had sold, and reselling what they had bought. By 1989, BLMIS's handled 5% of all the trades on NYSE listed stocks and, just four years later, increased its buy or sell limit to 5,000 shares on the S&P 500. By agreement with the other Cincinnati members in 1995, it was decided to move the black-box (*) to Chicago, which was the home of the Chicago Board of Options Exchange. (30) Although Bernie himself was a little awkward around computers, he had wholeheartedly embraced the idea of electronic trading as he was the one who had the eye for spotting opportunities, and an uncanny ability to manoeuvre people into his way of thinking.

The broker dealer part of BLMIS was now highly successful, so the Madoffs felt that they could take a step back, and gradually hand over the operation to Bernie's two sons, Mark and Andrew. This was a convenient transition because Bernie had already established a number of important relationships which he knew he would have to service. Almost as soon as he had started to make a name for himself back in the 1960s, he had begun to build up a secret 'advisory service', which was also described as an 'elite hedge fund'.

Initially, Bernie had opened brokerage accounts for family and friends, who allowed him to trade on their behalf. This soon became a regenerative operation, as existing clients recommended their friends and other potential clients. As well as the promise of good returns, existing clients were paid to introduce others. Bernie would always emphasise the 'long game' to his clients because he wanted to hang onto their money, and he therefore vilified 'get rich quick' schemes. But Bernie was just a market maker so his advisory service was illegal, simply because he was not a registered provider, however, he was never one to allow rules and regulations to litter his future pathway, as he had developed a knack of tip-toeing around unwelcome regulatory obstacles.

Word of the returns from Madoff's advisory service soon spread – from one excited client to a number of prospective clients, from one avid Madoff fan to members of his family, from one wealthy person to others within his circle, from one industry professional to his counterparts, from one investment fund manager to the next, from one bank's trading arm to a rival's – and so the Madoff feeder network was born. However, it eventually became so extensive and complex that a large number of innocent souls would, unwittingly, find themselves tangled in its web. Professor Leon Metzer, who delivered lectures on alternative investment management firms at Columbia and Yale Universities, would eventually say in his congressional testimony that hedge fund registration would not have prevented Madoff's setting up this kind of pyramid scheme network. (31)

The reality was that, in spite of the expertise and cutting-edge technology within Madoff's office, he didn't really have a trading strategy capable of consistently generating the 12–20% returns he had promised, and nor did anyone else in the whole of the industry for that matter. There would always be a hiatus with incoming investment at certain junctures, and no one could predict when there might be a spate of withdrawals. When Madoff's cash-flow was exacerbated at times like these, he found himself between a rock and a hard place, as he always needed that mountain of cash in the bank to perpetuate his charade.

Had Madoff therefore survived the eighties recession, the devastating Black Monday crash of 1987, and the impact of a number of ground-breaking industry changes, simply because he had generated enough cash from an already existing Ponzi Scheme?

Or did he have to resort to a Ponzi Scheme after incurring big losses during these seminal events, just to enable him to stay open for business?

As we are about to see, Madoff would have to endure financial crises that were much worse.

Chapter 11
The Fall of Madoff's Gigantic
Ponzi Scheme

In the eyes of the outside world, Bernard L. Madoff Investment Securities had certainly emerged from the turbulence of the eighties and early nineties in a favourable position, as the business had honoured its commitments and remained unscathed, whereas a number of other firms in the industry had not. But what had really taken place behind the scenes at BMLIS, Cohmad Securities and, in particular, on the 17th floor of the Lipstick Building during these difficult times?

Between 1962 and 1992, a large number of investors had been referred to Madoff by his father-in-law, Saul Alpern, who had also loaned him $50,000 to open his broker-dealer business. Alpern brought Frank Avelino and Michael Bienes into the picture as 'introducers', as they had access to an extensive client list. They worked at the firm of accountants retained by Alpern and, from the 1960s onwards, Avelino and Bienes raked-in enormous amounts of commission from their fund-raising activities on behalf of Madoff's hedge fund. In 1992, however, the SEC decided to close their operation down, thereby severing a very productive relationship for all concerned. (1) Avelino and Bienes were fined a joint total of $700,000 for selling illegal notes to investors, which were backed by the promise of Madoff's trade-mark yield of up to 20% annually. Their scam had unlawfully raised a sum of $440,000,000 for the hedge fund, but Madoff himself was somehow spared by the SEC, and this raised eyebrows far and wide.

Madoff's operation was boosted again when Sandra Manzke opened Tremont Capital Management in 1984, after receiving the backing of the charismatic Mario Gabelli. Within no time at all, Manzke had beaten a pathway to Madoff's door, and this was the beginning of what would become a long-standing and mutually beneficial relationship. By 1987, Tremont had raised funds of over $650 million, a great deal of which was placed with Madoff.

In 1985, Maurice 'Sonny' Cohn and Alvin Delaire had decided to leave the trading floor at AMEX and, furnished with a large number of contacts, became fund raisers for Madoff. In February that same year, Cohn formed Cohmad Securities with Madoff, and their new enterprise eventually shared office space with BLMIS. (2) Delaire was placed on the payroll at Cohmad as the principal facilitator for incoming investments, and was also responsible for the onerous task of overseeing account information and withdrawals. The firm started with six principal employees, but it would become a vital cog in the operation of Madoff's hedge fund for the rest of its existence. Whenever the roller coaster of inflows and out flows of cash swung downward, many of his primary fund raisers would be incentivised to bring in more investment, and some were paid as much as $500,000 a month. (3) The early team of Avelino, Bienes, Jaffe, Delaire and the Lieberbaums provided the fuel that set Madoff's roller coaster in motion.

Their corny old sales pitch worked like a charm. New clients would have to audition for Madoff and not the other way round, as 'the elite hedge fund' was usually closed to new investment. However, members of his team would suggest to hopefuls that there might be a back-door to this exclusive club if they pulled a few strings. This well-worn ruse created the perception of a very privileged opportunity which, for good measure, would be sweetened further by the suggestion of double-digit returns of up to 20%. At this point, the rational instincts of most aspiring clients were sedated by overdoses of euphoria, yet, an old maxim should have prevailed – 'if it smells like fish, it usually is'.

By the eighties, Madoff was able to move his rapidly expanding operations to the colourfully named Lipstick Building at 885, Third Avenue in Manhattan. Here, he decided to settle his proprietary traders on the 19th floor, and the broker dealer side of the firm on the 18th – whilst also renting space on the floor below. The mysterious 17th was quietly occupied by around eight carefully selected employees, and was off-limits to staff from the other two floors. With this small group, Madoff ran his illegal hedge fund which handled billions of dollars in client funds. This part of the operation was so secretive that the entrance to its offices was cleverly obscured within a dark mahogany wooden wall. (4) The SEC belatedly claimed that they never knew that this office space existed.

In charge on the remote 17th was the rather abrupt and sometimes rude Frank DiPascali, who joined Madoff in 1975. He bore the title of 'director of operations' and liaised directly with Madoff and his brother. Next in line was Madoff's personal assistant, Annette Bongiorno, who also worked closely with

DiPascali. Under them were Jo Ann Cupri who processed client requests, Eric Reardon who was the first point of contact for clients, and Eric Lipkin who handled the payroll for all the employees. (5) Another important figure in the inner sanctum was the trusty Robert Cardile, who worked for the firm for 24 years, through to its closure in 2008.

The offices on the 18th and 19th floors always looked immaculate, whereas those on the floor below had a dysfunctional appearance, as they were littered with a confusion of printouts, paperwork, files and boxes. Madoff had insisted that all emails should be printed and then deleted, thereby adding to this problem daily.

Centre of operations

But Madoff knew that if he tried to restore order out of this chaos, he would need to hire more people—which meant that there would be new eyes and ears—and this he could not afford. Instead, he relied on just one IBM AS/400 to silently run his multi-billion-dollar fraud, which only he himself had access to, and this was probably a critical factor in the investigations that were to follow. (6)

Robert M. Jaffe managed Cohmad's Boston office from 1989, and was said to have earned roughly $100 million in fees and performance related payments during just over a decade. (7) The industry standard for hedge funds, was a fee of up to 2% on the assets introduced, and a cut of any profit margin realised, usually up to 25%. With Madoff's Ponzi Scheme, profits were simply invented so there could not have been a performance related incentive for Jaffe, yet, he is said to have earned his astronomical nine-figure sum. It is highly likely that many investors failed to understand, or were never told, how their money would be divvied up behind the scenes by Madoff and his fund-raising crews. It was discovered, in fact, that Cohmad had paid out, from the year 2000, no less than $67 million for professional services, and 85% of Cohmad's total investment income had derived from fund raisers. (8) Of course, a large proportion of this money eventually found its way into Madoff's 'elite hedge fund'.

On paper, Bernie owned 15% of Cohmad, Peter Madoff owned 9%, Maurice 'Sonny' Cohn had 50% and Robert Jaffe had the remainder. However, it was later revealed that proxies and other arrangements (*) were in place, and it was really Bernie who had the biggest stake. It is ironic, however, that Madoff would audaciously testify at his hearing on 12th March 2009 that only he was involved in the huge $65 billion fraud, as the shareholding in Cohmad clearly indicated that a number of others were working with him – hand in glove.

Whenever the question of investment returns cropped up, figures inevitably varied from investor to investor, conversation to conversation, one sales pitch to another – or from one desperate moment to the next. However, many rivals within the industry were well aware of Madoff's promise of a consistent flow of low volatility returns, well into double figures. Although some fund managers felt that this was impossible, others were willing to take a chance on Madoff, just to have an easy life. As hedge funds and private equity firms became increasingly popular, the rate of investment into Madoff's coffers therefore increased but, before an investor's money arrived, introducers wanted a slice of the cake. Madoff had let his feeder funds know that he would only charge commission on the transactions he carried out on a client's behalf but, as well as providing excellent cash-flow, it also created its fair share of red flags.

A number of industry professionals were keen to get a handle on Madoff's game-plan, as it didn't seem plausible that he would forgo a cut of tens of millions of dollars in easy money – just for commission. However, Madoff knew that if fund raisers kept the initial up-front fee and other payments, still more money would be introduced, and this was really the essence of his closely guarded strategy. In order to maintain the charade, Madoff would have to pay introducers a performance fee, profits or no profits, and this was a real chunk of money to cover. However, Bernie's mentality was simply to grab the money first, and then sort the problems out later. So, whilst some harboured doubts about Madoff's 'elite hedge fund', others liked the fee arrangements and were eager to fill its coffers.

One fund that charged excessive fees was run by a French aristocrat, and was called Access International Advisors. (9) Rene-Thierry Magon de la Villehuchet had so much faith in Madoff, that he put all of his clients' eggs into his basket. Before Madoff received a dime, Rene's clients were charged a 5% fee up front, followed by a 0.8% yearly management fee, and a 16% performance fee based on profits generated. It seems that this 'Dick Turpin' of the investment world was clever enough to filch people's money and make it painless, however, he was a calamitous investment strategist as he'd dumped all his clients' money into the biggest Ponzi Scheme in history.

Another firm that invested heavily with Madoff was FIM Advisors LLP, whose Kingate Europe and Kingate Global Funds managed $3.5 billion. The two Italians who ran these funds also collected a huge 5% entrance fee, as well as an annual 1.5% management fee. (10) The 1.5% management fee was seemingly small change yet it was a clever ploy as it would have to be paid win, lose or draw, whereas performance related payments were dependent on those who were responsible for making trading decisions. In this case, it was Madoff – who preferred to outlay these fees so that he could have a buffer between him and the source of the money.

The Fairfield Greenwich Group was established in 1983 but, like many asset management firms, it really came into the picture in the mid-nineties. (11) It was run by former attorney with the Securities Exchange Commission, Walter Noel, and partner, Jeffrey Tucker. They established Fairfield Sentry for the sole purpose of fund raising and, as well as sending hundreds of millions of dollars through to the elite hedge fund each year, it gave Madoff a degree of legitimacy. The difference was that Fairfield actually told its clients that it was investing with Madoff – whereas many who had invested through other feeder funds didn't have a clue who was actually running their money.

A fund comprising various hedge funds by the name of Gabriel, Ariel and Ascot was set up by J. Ezra Merkin, which had $2.4 billion in assets under management. Unbeknown to his clients, Merkin simply sent hundreds of millions of dollars through to Madoff and, in an exercise akin to the 'blind leading the blind', allowed Madoff to take the lead. As well as ordinary people, some of Hollywood's elite became ensnared by the tentacles of this unholy alliance. Actor Kevin Bacon and his wife had fallen into Merkin's hands after being referred by another family member – and they eventually lost everything. One of the industry moguls who controlled the 'Dream Works' animation studio, Jeffrey Katzenberg, placed funds with Madoff, and suffered a similar fate.

Having been open with his clients, however, Walter Noel decided to push the boat out with Fairfield Sentry, and Madoff's hedge fund. Four of his five daughters married promising young men, who were soon groomed to achieve bigger things on behalf of the family business. Three of his sons-in-law set up offices in Lugano, Switzerland, London and Madrid, which dealt with the European, Latin American, Brazilian and Middle Eastern markets. Incentivised by the fact that Madoff did not take a slice of the fee income, these particular feeder funds would eventually rake in annual payments of $135 million and, by 2004, Fairfield had placed 85% of its assets with Madoff. (12)

Edgar de Picciotto had formed the Geneva based bank, Union Bancaire Privee in 1969. As a result of an extraordinary expansion programme, it had a global presence by the early seventies and, today, this powerhouse has $140.3 billion in assets under its management. (13) However, against the opinion of some of his key employees, the decision was taken by Picciotto to invest with Madoff, and the amount eventually reached $700 million. When he was later asked about the bank's due diligence, (*) Picciotto explained that he himself had dealt with this. He pointed out that the relationship dated back to the seventies, when men were taken at their word – so 'gut feeling' was the due diligence he had used to make the call. By the early nineties, UBP had opened an internal analysis department, but the bank was already on Madoff's hook.

With 12–20% returns as bait, Madoff was able to land some 'big catches'!

The Berlin wall had been demolished in 1989, and the newly freed eastern bloc suddenly became prime territory for money scouts – including the New York based Sonja Cohn. This elderly Jewish grandma had first met Madoff in 1990 and, that same year, opened the Eurovaleur Fund which was managed by the well-known Felix Zulauf. (14) In line with its designation, the fund's main focus was European clients, who required a minimum of $5 million to gain access to its services. In return, Kohn promised an upward curve of 10% annually. Cohn was exceptionally ambitious and, with the help of her husband, who was a director of Commerzbank, she incorporated the Bank of Medici in Vienna, Austria, in 1994. Using this as a networking platform to attract other banks and hedge funds, she would go on to raise $3 billion from investors in the former Soviet countries. All of this money was placed with Madoff through her Primeo, Herald and Thelma funds – assisted by a web of inter-connected operations.

The Medici family had become powerful during the Renaissance, and their name has since been regarded as a bastion of trust and solidity. Having borrowed this legacy, Kohn went on to obtain a full banking license for Medici Bank in 2003, by courtesy of the Austrian authorities. In a meeting with the Gibraltar government in 2005, Cohn claimed that her returns during the previous decade had averaged 12.01%, but she conveniently failed to explain that the whole of this amount had been invented (15) in order to sustain a massive revolving door scam. (*) Austrian prosecutors eventually said that she could have channelled, overall, as much as $8billion to Madoff. As a result, Medici's banking license was summarily revoked, and Kohn went into hiding after being accused of procuring millions in kick-backs from Madoff – which he brazenly called brokerage fees.

The marketing of hedge funds became big business and eventually extended to the brokerage divisions of a number of Wall Street banks, including the likes Barclays, Bank of America, Bear Sterns and Goldman Sachs. (16) They started to offer what became known as 'prime brokerage services', which included a general fund-raising initiative targeted at their clients, or even loans for the purpose of speculation. This was the mid-nineties, and prime-time, as the markets were red hot with the 'Dot-com Bubble'. However, Madoff was unable to tap into this new source of funding, as he was extremely afraid that his books would be scrutinised – and his illicit scheme would unravel.

As well as these new opportunities, there were omens as it had been discovered in 1994 that Steven Hoffenberg was involved in a gigantic Ponzi Scheme after his Towers Financial Corporation had collapsed just one year earlier. He was sentenced to 20 years in prison and ordered to pay a $1 million fine, plus $463 million in restitution to his investors. Some within the industry believed that such enormous investment into a mere 'debt collection operation' was bold to say the least but, perhaps, a sign of the times.

The Nick Leeson affair came to a head on 22nd November 1995, when he was extradited from Frankfurt to stand trial in Singapore for 'rogue trading', which precipitated the downfall of the UK's prestigious bank, Barings. Then, in 1998, news broke that 'Long Term Capital Management' was on the brink of collapse, after taking highly leveraged bets to the tune of $120 billion. (17) This was simply unthinkable, and the stock market quickly answered by another sell-off. In 2000, there was the curious case of Michael Berger and his Manhattan Investment Fund, which he had maintained from 1996 on the back of falsified account information. During the dot.com bubble, he had traded against the stocks he believed were overvalued, which reflected the status of the vast majority. Even though he had read the situation correctly, his scam stood in the way of him benefitting from their eventual crash – and his fund incurred losses of $400 million.

In spite of Madoff's avoidance of the new 'prime brokerage service', he had already established relationships with banking industry giants such as Bear Sterns, Lehman Brothers, Charles Schwab and over a dozen Swiss and French Banks. These European banks had invested in Madoff without demur, as they had always received preferential treatment, as well as lucrative and very easy fee income. One of these was the influential Notz Stucki, which controlled a huge $16 billion in their fund of funds. Another was Spain's largest bank, Santander, which invested with Madoff through a subsidiary, Optimal Strategic United States Equity Fund. It was connections such as these that gave Madoff's 'elite hedge fund' plenty of kudos and credibility. However, some within the industry could never quite rid themselves of nagging doubts about the man, and his operation.

In 1997, Rob Picard of Royal Bank of Canada, together with a group of his executives, flew into New York to meet Madoff as they wanted to find out how he would deliver his consistent flow of low volatility returns in markets that were often random or extremely volatile. Picard had done his homework and knew that Madoff was not mentioned in lists of Wall Street's major players compiled by the 'Institutional Investor' magazine, or in data bases created by the likes of MARH Hedge and TASS. The top performing funds around the world included the likes of Renaissance Technologies on Long Island, Citadel in Chicago, Farallon in San Francisco, Julian Roberts' Tiger, Lon Cooperman's Omega, and Highfields in Boston. (18) The sceptical Picard had wondered why Madoff's operation was not featured, as he knew that some of his own clients had invested with him through feeder funds.

This time, Madoff was facing intuitive industry professionals who were asking leading questions, and he was uncomfortable. With only a glimmer of a strategy to offer, the Royal Bank of Canada team could sense that Madoff's words were running faster and starting to trip over each other – something was amiss. A bemused Rob Picard left this awkward meeting in New York, unimpressed and harbouring serious doubts – but others would soon share this view.

After doing some digging at Fairfield Greenwich in 1998, Ken Nakayama of Deutsche Bank began to wonder how Madoff was really making the returns he claimed. (19) Madoff's 'split strike conversion strategy', also known as 'reverse conversion', had just about reached its heyday during the middle of the nineties, when option volume (*) peaked, and started to decline. After probing further with industry contacts, he decided to give Madoff a wide-berth, as no one had noticed the presence of this 'maestro' anywhere in the marketplace.

Picard would later conclude that hedge funds were not about technical indicators, investment strategies or expert advisors. They were about access to people, thereby alluding that more people would simply equate to more money invested, which would generate more fee income, and the creators of these funds would reap rich rewards. Picard's main concern with Madoff was the shabby pieces of paper upon which account information was recorded, as the returns simply did not correlate with market action. (20) The word of RBC's negative perception of Madoff soon spread, and a number of the bank's clients withdrew money from certain feeder funds, particularly Tremont Capital Management, which was very heavily invested with the 'elite hedge fund'.

Losing these clients soon made Sandra Manzke and Bob Schulman realise that doubt and confusion about Tremont would reign within the marketplace unless something was done. They needed to redirect investors' focus back on their organisation and, by 1998, they had developed the first hedge fund index Known as CSFB/Tremont Hedge Fund Index, which functioned in a similar fashion to the Dow Jones, or the S&P 500. Their new system was able to track the performance of the leading hedge funds against returns in other investments, and would become a standard benchmark of hedge fund performance on Wall Street. Three years later the big investment bank and insurance conglomerate, Oppenheimer, bought Tremont at $19 a share, not knowing that it was Madoff's phony profits that were behind its remarkable and consistent rise in stature. (21) It was now Manzke and Schulman who were on the tread mill of Tremont's new owners, as they desperately needed Madoff to maintain his huge profit margins, even though they had never bothered to question how these had been duly delivered.

Caught in his own elaborate network!

At this time, Madoff's 'magic wand' was now acting in a similar fashion to a clothes prop—as it was propping up the whole of his intricate web of deceit—and Tremont was just one strand of a huge network. Madoff's nexus now included Cohmad's clients, funds made up of hedge funds, exclusive hedge funds, alternative investment funds, brokers, global banks, high profile figures, pension funds, charities, trusts and, not least amongst others, ordinary people. Inexplicably, those involved had adhered to a strict code of silence, which had given Madoff's elite hedge fund such an extraordinary air of exclusivity that investors old and new believed it would be an affront to ask too many questions. It was as though Madoff's entire client base had been hypnotised by the promise of easy money, and those involved felt that they would have too much to lose if they were shut-out of this elite investment cult.

Some within the industry began to reason that, if Madoff was a confidence trickster, he simply had to be working with a number of kindred spirits. At the very least, the new electronic communications era of the nineties should have provided an online presence between feeder funds and Madoff, which would have enabled the verification of account information and up to date performance. This access could then have been extended to clients, to enable them to prudently monitor their own affairs. In view of the appalling failure of 'feeders' and 'money scouts' to provide such a basic service, it would not be unreasonable to suggest that many were, themselves, equally culpable in Madoff's giant Ponzi scheme.

Rob Picard of RBC was now convinced that Madoff could have escalated his scam straight after the 1987 crash – an event which had caught a vast number of market participants completely off guard. In an ideal world, Madoff would have hedged his positions to mitigate any losses on the long side, but his operation was shrouded in so much secrecy that no one could be really sure how he had played his hand during this crisis. Picard's view was shared by Doug Tass at the Sea-Breeze Hedge Fund. Tass claimed that, by late 1998, Madoff was frantically patching up his operation by selling illegal notes to investors, in a fashion that was reminiscent of the old Avelino Bienes affair back in the sixties and seventies – but his elite hedge fund was also under pressure in other ways.

The 'dot-com bubble' had now peaked and, with so many overvalued stocks in the marketplace, the boon was destined to wane over the following months. By 1999, Congress decided to repeal parts of the Glass-Steagall act which had been introduced during the Great Depression of the thirties in order to keep commercial depositor banks and investment banks separate. This reversion simply brought a fresh wave of opportunities for hedge funds, as the revamped institutions proved to be extremely willing lenders. However, the hiatus came in February 2000 when Federal Reserve Chairman, Alan Greenspan, announced plans to aggressively increase interest rates to curb the enormous folly in the equities sector. It worked and by 11th September 2001, not a single IPO was brought into the marketplace. (22)

Many of the smaller broker dealers also realised that their ability to make easy money had been negated at the stroke of a legislative pen when, on 9th April 2001, the decimalisation of stock prices was introduced. (23) In the preceding system, prices usually ticked (*) in increments of 12.5 cents, with a spread (∗) of 25 cents, however, the new system ticked in increments of just one cent with a spread of around two cents. This left broker-dealers very little room to make their usual 'easy money' on the spreads, (*) so even though the new system was loathed by many, they had to keep in step with the times in order to survive.

In spite of the ground-breaking regulatory changes sweeping through the industry, there proved to be a lingering taste for speculation when a new-fangled trend tip-toed stealthily into the trading world. Financial instruments known as derivatives, (*) and in particular, 'credit default swaps' (*) now began to establish their presence in the marketplace, particularly when the post dot-com bear market ended in 2004. These financial novelties with weird sounding names heralded a new wave of optimism which would lead Wall Street, and the industry, into the biggest spate of gambling the planet had ever witnessed. Fully immersed in the pretence of a successful hedge fund, Madoff's operation was eventually bounced around in the turbulence this created.

Madoff's enormously important feeder, Fairfield Greenwich, was placed on the market by its owners in 2004. Discerning purchasers would now need to run the rule over its affairs, and take a close look at Fairfield's relationship with Madoff. The value of this organisation was inextricably linked to his performance, and this was common knowledge throughout the asset management industry. One interested party appointed a very shrewd banking official to do its due diligence, and he was alarmed by what he found. During a meeting with Jeffrey Tucker, the banker asked him to run through the firm's basic investment strategy, and back the results up by paperwork. This seemed a reasonable starting point, but Tucker flatly refused. After pressing harder, the banker was eventually allowed to look at—what was claimed to be—the firm's trading logbook. As presented, it would have meant that Madoff's trades accounted for an impossible 82% of all the volume in the S&P 100 Options Index. (24) It was obvious that Tucker knew what was going on, but he chose to maintain his charade.

By 2004, hedge funds had become very popular investment vehicles for pension funds, and this is hardly surprising as the likes of Fairfield Sentry had somehow been churning out 12–15% returns, year after year, even in bad markets. (25) By 2005, an estimated 8,000 hedge funds were overseeing assets of around one trillion dollars whereas, only fifteen years earlier, there had been around 1,100 hedge funds managing around fifty billion. The explosive action continued into 2006, when some hedge funds did initial public offerings – or IPOs. At the same time, the property markets and mortgage lending markets were in an upward spiral day after day, and something had to give sooner or later.

Although 2007 was a decent year for Madoff, storm clouds were gathering in anger over the housing sector, as well as the mortgage lending markets. By now, two trillion dollars had found its way into hedge funds. (26) During the fateful months that followed, Madoff had slowly depleting cash balances at JPMorgan Chase and, with a financial storm on the horizon, his bankers were closely monitoring his account activity. They had placed $250 million with the Sentry fund, and they knew that this firm relied on Madoff for its results. (27) This was a time when stock markets around the world had already plummeted by as much as 30%, but Fairfield Sentry still reported gains of 5% – and this did not add up. During the months leading to September 2008, Chase discreetly closed its position with Sentry, and this was a big blow to Madoff.

Throughout 2008, and in the face of a deteriorating economy, Madoff had to deal with $7 billion in redemption demands, which took his account at Chase into the red. In the wider hedge fund industry itself, over a dozen fund managers had made at least one billion up to this point, but this year saw the end of these halcyon times. The bubble in the housing sector evaporated in a blink, credit became tighter than people could ever remember, banks and other financial institutions begged for money from the government or went to the wall, unemployment spiralled, families suffered, and big corporations were either strapped for cash or fighting for their lives. Up to the final month of 2008, Madoff's legitimate broker-dealer side of the operation had been making money, but not enough to support his scam on the 17th floor. Madoff had always repaid investors quickly, and this had kept him going – but he was no longer able to do so.

After confessing his sins to his brother, Madoff was given up to the authorities by his two sons, Mark and Andrew. FBI agent, Theodore Cacioppi and partner, arrested Madoff at his apartment building at 133, East 64th Street, at 9.00 am on 11th December 2008.

In the most devastating financial crisis ever known, stock markets eventually went down by 47%, and around 75 hedge funds had to be liquidated, whilst others suspended client withdrawals. Sandra Manzke at Tremont Capital now claimed that she was 'disgusted with hedge funds' and declared that she had lost her $280 million fortune with Madoff. (28) At the same time, however, she had also fed $6 billion in client funds to his Ponzi Scheme.

When the investigation began, it was discovered that Madoff's 'elite hedge fund' had not made a trade for at least thirteen years, and possibly as long as two decades, so the inspectors were unable to pin-point a definitive starting date for his scam. But to pull this off for so long, Madoff had relied on a clever ploy. He had asked a couple of his 17th floor employees to back-test (*) for profitable stock price trends in blue chip companies, so that he could fabricate phony trading records for his clients. In spite of this, no one on the 17th floor was charged. Investigators found that, by 2008, he had used Madoff Securities International Limited to launder a personal fortune of $113 million and, amongst his trophies, was a $7 million leopard yacht ironically called – 'The Bull'.

The SEC had received quarterly statements from BLMIS and other operations, which purportedly disclosed facts and figures about all of Madoff's affairs, and these were signed off by his brother, Peter. Had this same information been checked with discerning eyes, the SEC might have realised that Madoff had insufficient stock holdings to support the billions of dollars under his management. The industry professionals knew that electronic trading on the scale alleged by Madoff, should have left visible footprints, but the likes of Deutsche Bank, Salomon-Smith-Barney, Goldman-Sachs, Merrill-Lynch and others on Wall Street reported that they couldn't remember seeing any signs of his trades. In a self-protective stance, the SEC would later assert that they had been deceived by Madoff, claiming that he had used figures from the legitimate broker-dealer side of the operation—BLMIS—to lead them to believe he was taking real market positions. (29) In addition, the SEC said that Madoff had boosted his figures by manufacturing trade tickets for 'ghost trades'.

The President of Cohmad Securities, Marcia Cohn, would later be sued by the SEC for having ignored 'many suspicious practices which clearly indicated that Madoff was engaged in fraud'. (30)

'The Bull' was heading for the rocks!

Throughout the duration of this huge Ponzi Scheme, no one in Madoff's operation was out to connect the dots, as too much money was being made by all and sundry. In addition to this, client and other payment obligations were consistently met on time, thereby maintaining the charade. What is clear though is that Madoff went to great lengths to carefully ring fence each part of his operation, so that no one part would be duly concerned about what another part was up to. This is clearly highlighted by his secret hiding place on the 17th floor, and his old-fashioned IBM AS/400 computer, which he was unable to update because it stored the secrets of his huge Ponzi Scheme. However, some within the industry had flagged their suspicions—in particular Harry Markopolos, Ken Nakayama, Doug Tass, and Rob Picard of Royal Bank of Canada—but to no avail.

As always, the industry marched on—albeit lame for a few years—but every lie that Madoff told, also incurred a huge debt for its integrity.

Global Financial System or International Casino?

Perhaps similar questions sprang to mind whilst reading some of the earlier chapters, so let's start by refreshing the picture.

Up to this point, we have reviewed the effects of a number of prominent boom-and-bust scenarios dating back to the 17th century, through to present day. In further chapters, we have covered the injudicious dealings of a few notorious individuals who, with an abundance of money at their fingertips, shot for the stars and fell way short. Unsurprisingly, the common thread throughout these destructive events was the enormous financial loss incurred by certain sectors of the general public and beyond.

However, there were other interesting factors to consider. The early 1900s saw a drive towards universal programming of financial procedure through a central banking mechanism. At the time, it was believed that these changes were made to stem operational difficulties within the system, but the real objective was to take control of the money supply. Despite this radical shift in strategy, an epidemic of financial crises still plagued western economies for many years thereafter, and this continued into the last two decades of this modern era.

With this in mind, let us quickly remind ourselves of some of the key events before and after 1900 – with a keen eye on the interval between each one.

Tulip Mania came to an end in 1637, and this was followed in the early 1700s by the collapse of an enterprise hosted by France – John Law's Mississippi Scheme. Sadly, this imprudent excursion also devastated the country's economy. Almost at the same time, the South Sea Bubble in England ended abruptly – again, leaving another fragile economy in tatters.

A little earlier in this era (1694), the Bank of England had been established under William of Orange and became the world's first central bank. However, still in a period of stagnation after the South Sea Bubble, it suffered its first real crisis in the 1730s. Unable to cope with a rising tide of demand for its banknotes to be redeemed in gold, local goldsmiths and merchants rallied and provided guarantees so that the bank could stay afloat.

The American financial system searched for ways to find its feet during a long period of experimentation. It was unfortunate that banking emergencies in 1873, 1884, 1893 and 1907, continued to blight progress. Yet again, heady speculation was partly to blame for these panics and, as a result, there was a loss of confidence in what had become an unwieldy system. Nonetheless, it was caried forward by the invisible will of progress, and this heralded the formation of the Federal Reserve in 1913. Interestingly, America's new central bank was modelled on the Bank of England, which had been formed well over two centuries earlier. (1)

However, America's bold modernisation of a dysfunctional banking system gave rise to further woes when another financial crisis surfaced at the turn of 1920. This happened to coincide with the collapse of Charles Ponzi's 'get rich quick scheme' when, during the melee, still more financial institutions were ruined.

But the winds of good fortune started to blow, and these problems dissipated relatively quickly. This enabled America and other westernised nations to saunter into a period of exuberance and excess during what became known as the Roaring Twenties. Alas, spirits were then shattered by the Great Wall Street Crash of 1929, which suffused the 1930s with massive economic problems. The Great Depression of this decade strangled global economies until 1939 and the outbreak of the Second World War. When it ended, the UK urgently needed an injection of funds to assist its recovery. In 1946, the government negotiated a $3.75 billion loan agreement with America, and one of $1.19 billion with Canada, also denominated in US dollars.

This economic ebb and flow continued when it's unconscionable swell took the UK into recession in 1953. A few years later—and just over a decade after the end of World War Two—the country entangled itself in the Suez Canal crisis in 1956. This resulted in acute shortages of petrol, food and other staples after President Nasser of Egypt attempted to nationalise the canal by use of force. After furtive talks with the UK and France, Israel mobilised in opposition, thereby saddling the world with another impending crisis. Under enormous pressure from America's indignation, as well as fervent local unrest, Prime Minister, Anthony Eden was forced to resign.

Soon after the 1956 Suez predicament, the ten-year purge struck again. In 1965, America responded positively to desperate pleas from the UK government for a bailout. Despite this lifeline, the country remained close to the fiscal brink through to 1968. Dockworker strikes, oil embargoes and a hefty trade deficit of £800 million were blamed. Under huge pressure, Harold Wilson's government had to devalue the pound from an exchange rate of around $2.8 to $2.4. But this sequence of problems didn't yield when still more recessions disrupted economic stability in 1975 and 1981. (2)

It would seem likely therefore that some of the more recent events are already etched into the public's consciousness as, unforgettably, they followed the same destructive pattern as those that preceded them. However, in order to bring matters up to date, let's take a brief look at some of these.

In 1987—on a day now known as Black Monday—stock markets crashed around the globe, when the majority of participants failed to see essential weaknesses in world markets. George Soros then mounted an attack on the pound in 1992, followed by the Nick Leeson affair in 1995, precipitating the collapse of Barings Bank later in the year. The dot-com bubble inflated between 1995 and 2000 – and then burst in 2001. Less than a decade later, the subprime mortgage and housing boom crashed spectacularly in 2008, and this put an end to Bernie Madoff's giant Ponzi Scheme. During the latter stages of that same year, he was arrested and later sent to prison. The reality of this scandal eventually exceeded worst fears, and it turned out to be one of the biggest frauds in modern times with losses to investors of no less than $56 billion.

The last two of these destructive episodes helped to herald the most recent downturns of the economic roller-coaster, bringing us to within two decades of today. We will also recollect that reference was made earlier in this passage to the interval between the 'upswing' and the 'downturn' in economic affairs. From our review of past events, it is eminently noticeable that a change of sentiment occurs, on average, once every ten to twelve years.

This leads us to a significant question. What has been at the heart of these persistent problems, and why have remedial measures been elusive for so long? Could it be that the rubrics of modern-day finance are so indeterminate that they are actually beyond the comprehension of monetary mavens and theoreticians, as well as the custodians of the financial system? This is certainly an interesting possibility and one that cannot be discounted.

In his 2010 book, 'Creature from Jekyll Island', Edward Griffin referred to a recent letter circulated by a group of experts who, for years, had conducted an ongoing exchange of ideas regarding monetary reform. The editor said: "It is fascinating that we cannot find more agreement amongst ourselves on this vital issue. We seem to differ so much on definitions and on, really, an unbiased, frank, honest, correct understanding of how our monetary system really does function." (3)

Tacitly, this could mean that it is expedient for certain aspects of the financial system to dwell beneath a blanket of fog – simply because it suits some other agenda. This brings us onto the forthcoming chapter where we will try to disperse with the unwelcome haze and shed light on the roots of the boom-and-bust cycle and other destructive episodes.

Before we turn the page, I would ask the reader to note – not all the historical peaks and troughs have been highlighted since Tulip Mania occurred in 1637, but hopefully enough to make the last part of the journey enlightening.

The Topics Covered in Chapter 12

Ancient money; its transition into different forms; the development of the early banking system; the financial instruments used at this time; the gold exchange standard; the abandonment of the gold exchange standard; fiat money; the rubrics of modern banking; the ratcheting of the money supply; a lingering problem, and the boom-and-bust phenomenon.

Chapter 12
Crazy Money and the
Boom-and-Bust Phenomenon

Section One

Ancient money; its transition into different forms; the development of the early banking system; the financial instruments used at this time; the gold exchange standard:

Money may be broadly defined as a medium of exchange for goods and services, which would seem to be a simple enough starting point.

However, it is not nearly as easy to establish the precise point at which money was first used for this purpose, or where it occurred. Modern historians tend to differ on these two salient issues, and this probably stems from the lack of written evidence available today. Inferences may have been drawn in the past from the discovery of artefacts such as tally sticks, which suggest that prehistoric accounting records were kept for different modes of trade in the early commodities markets. (4) But this alone is not enough. As a result, we have chosen our own starting point, simply because 'when and where' the money trail actually began is perhaps less important to this passage than the milestones reached in more recent times.

Our trail begins with Croesus, the last king of Lydia (c 560–546 BC) who, during his fourteen-year reign, conquered the ancient Greeks of mainland Ionia. Known for his enormous wealth and temerity, Croesus introduced a monetary system based on the circulation of gold and silver coins, which later proliferated throughout the whole of ancient Greece. (5) Because of its very high gold content, the drachma was eventually adopted during this evolutionary phase, and it became the standard currency unit for Greece and Asia Minor.

Despite prolonged periods of tension between Athens and Sparta, including the Peloponnesian War between 431 and 404 BC, the stability of the monetary system in this part of the world ensured that trade abounded, communities flourished, and large cities were built on solid foundations. Byzantium (now, modern-day Istanbul) was one such ancient Greek city, and its development began on the banks of the Bosphorus about 660 years BC. Greatly assisted by the ascendency of Greece's coin based monetary system, as well as its strategic location, it soon started to grow in prominence.

Byzantium was renamed Constantinople in 330 AD by its Emperor, Constantine the Great, who introduced a gold coin called the 'solidus' and one in silver named the 'miliarense'. (6) This rapidly expanding metropolis eventually became a world trading centre and cultural powerhouse, which extended its influence in visual arts and architecture to Italy, throughout the Balkans, and into Russia. Constantinople became the capital of the Eastern Roman Empire in 395 AD and replaced its earlier coins with one known as the 'bezant'. The new tender was soon recognised for its reliability and was accepted in China, Europe, and parts of Africa.

As more and more coins went into circulation in different parts of the world, old modes of trade melted into new. The trading of fungibles had been customary throughout the ages when items of the same perceived value were willingly exchanged without the use of money. But sometimes, it was necessary to barter in order to reach agreement on value, and this was all so often a frantic process. However, by use of a coin-based system, it was soon recognised that transactions could be concluded within a much more reliable context. Acceptance thereby continued to grow until the exchange of coins for goods and services became the de facto monetary system throughout the advanced civilisations of the world.

For many centuries thereafter, the principles of this early coin-based system were a symbol of stability, prosperity, and cultural progress.

In 1119, Pope Honorius 2nd granted recognition to a Christian military order in Jerusalem – the Knights Templar. They played a prominent part in the Crusades of the 12th and 13th centuries and, although they took vows of chastity and poverty, they accrued enormous wealth in gold, silver, artefacts, and coins. The Templar's failure to follow their sacred vows incurred the wrath of French King Philip 4th who charged them with heresy. Resentment against this secret order of knights therefore grew, and between 1308–1312, they were suppressed at the behest of the French monarchy. But by this time, the Templars had already created one of the world's most advanced monetary systems, which had a network of temple churches as its branches. The work of the Templars had a profound impact on the rubrics of modern-day banking, as we shall see later in this chapter.

Frederick 2nd (1194–1250), who was also the Holy Roman Emperor from 1152, started to mint gold coins during his Crusades and recovered Jerusalem in 1228. Notably, this was achieved by a negotiated treaty instead of war. (7) In 13th century England, gold coins were minted during the reign of Henry 3rd (1207–1272) and, by the 14th century, production gathered pace in Europe, where Vienna was the principal casting centre. Back in England circa 1670, the gold guinea coin began to circulate alongside the silver crown and during this same period, the Bank of England was formed in 1694. At this important juncture, the monetary system had experienced significant change, particularly through '*the transition of money into different forms*'.

The categories of money that emerged, may be defined (8) as follows:

1. Commodity money
2. Receipt money
3. Fractional money
4. Fiat money (evolved by the 20th century)

Commodity money: At first glance, this designation for a category of money might seem a little strange, as we naturally reflect on the legal tender known today. However, before the coinage system came into being, commodities such as—livestock, grain, other staple foods, metal tools and weapons, pottery and eating utensils, trinkets, ornamental goods, and amulets—all had an intrinsic value to the early civilisations that used them, and they were traded as 'fungibles' or through 'barter'.

Even without the use of coins, the notion of a 'profitable outcome' would have brought a satisfactory conclusion to these negotiation.

When we relate the trading of these commodities to our introductory definition of money, it is possible to see that there is a great deal of alignment. We broadly defined money as '*a medium of exchange for goods and services*'. These early commodities were a medium of exchange for other goods, at an agreed value. When viewed in this context, we are able see why '*commodity money*' is acknowledged as one of the earliest known categories.

Receipt Money: Although coin-based monetary systems created stability, and provided a reliable means of financial settlement, a couple of crucial issues lingered. These were highlighted in Chapter 3 when we said: "The problem with coins was that they were often 'clipped', thereby losing some of their weight and value. In addition, they were extremely cumbersome in large quantities, so the transportation of chests of money posed obvious risks."

This same security problem was also highlighted by Venetian traveller, Marco Polo, in the 13th century. Following his visit to China between 1271–1275, he reported the use of rudimentary promissory notes, which were carried as an alternative to the transportation of large chests of coins. However, this system had not been adopted universally, so reports of theft, robbery and dangerous encounters were still rife in certain locations. A group of goldsmiths latched onto the idea that this could be an opportunity to make a profit, so they started to offer their vaults for the safe storage of coins. The response was so enthusiastic that they were able to earn a steady stream of fees for providing a much-needed service.

In order to record the number and type of coins stored, the goldsmith would issue a receipt to each depositor. However, it was soon recognised that the paper notes themselves could be traded for goods and services, as they were backed by the surety of the coins lodged with the goldsmith.

As the trading of receipts increased, it is believed that some individuals requested theirs in batches. This meant that, instead of receiving one receipt for thirty coins, a depositor might have been issued with five separate receipts, each for six coins. At any time, the bearer of the receipt would be able to redeem it for the stated number of coins held by the goldsmith – or use it to buy goods and services. As a result, the circulation of receipts proliferated, and the term '*receipt money*' was thereby created – but a much greater concept had now dawned. The provision of vault-deposit facilities for the storage of money was an important stage in '*the development of the early banking system*'.

So, who were the first bankers?

The fine monetary system devised by the Templars started around 1120–1125, but it is believed that goldsmiths' guilds were already providing vault storage facilities for coins and other valuables at this time. Therefore, receipts would have been issued and eventually circulated as money. Within these broad parameters, it would be reasonable to assume that goldsmiths were the earliest known bankers. What is certain though is that both goldsmiths' guilds and the

Knights Templar made significant contributions to the creation of the early banking system.

Continue to next page...

Fractional Money: In an upward spiral of change, new categories of money rendered others obsolete.

The transition to '*fractional money*' was made when another money-making scheme was conceived by the goldsmiths' guild – and this was both daring and ground-breaking.

The 'smiths recognised that they were jointly harbouring a large proportion of the public's wealth – yet all this money was sitting idle. The measly fee they charged their depositors was all they had to show for shouldering this huge responsibility, and it became a source of irritation. Silently in the beginning, a few crafty goldsmiths went into the business of moneylending but, instead of using their own funds, they made loans from the coins deposited by the public. Even worse, the interest paid on these loans was credited to their own accounts, as they believed no one would be any the wiser.

This secret use of someone else's money was clearly a breach of trust and also illegal. However, as word began to spread through black-market channels, the public got wind of these furtive loans. Unsurprisingly, the idea of making easy money from idle funds was too much of a temptation, so the majority of depositors opted to join in.

With the support of their clients, goldsmiths could now market their scheme openly. As a result, both parties were able to share the benefit of an increasing flow of interest from the monies out on loan. In what seems to have been an arbitrary calculation, the smiths decided they could lend up to 85% of the coins in their vaults, and hold *'a fraction'* of 15% in reserve. Quite boldly, they gambled that this residual amount would be quite enough to service a steady flow of repayment demands from their clients.

However, they were really working in unchartered waters. Anything more than just a 'steady flow' might have escalated into a run on their reserves, but it is unclear today whether the 'smiths had taken this into account. However, as most readers will realise, a 'run on reserves' would have simply been an early take on a modern banking theme. Nonetheless, *'fractional money'* had arrived on the scene, and this was another step closer to the transfer of affairs from goldsmiths to the early banking system. But, during this process, these two entities remained synonymous for quite a while.

One of the earliest banking centres was established in Florence under the Medici dynasty, with Giovani Medici (1360–1429) as the founder. Round about this time, Venice joined the nascent monetary scene, and became a rival to the esteemed Medici empire. The Bank of Amsterdam was known to be in operation by the 1630s, and Sweden and Genoa were also providing banking services during this same era. The Bank of England was opened in 1694 and, inspired by John Law, France's Banque Générale followed in 1716.

Financial Instruments Used at This Time: In terms of broad definition, the proximity of *'receipts'* to *'IOUs'*—and *'promissory notes'* to *'letters of credit'*—was very close. For example, the goldsmith issued an IOU, and the depositor kept this as a receipt for his coins. During the 13th century, Marco Polo reported that a similar system was in operation in China where promissory notes were in circulation. Instead of transporting coins, the bearer of one of these notes was carrying a contract to pay a specific number and type of coin, at an agreed future date.

However, the Knights Templar managed to come up with a clever twist on this arrangement. During the 13th century, travellers, pilgrims, wealthy merchants, and moneyed men were able to leave their stashes of coin at a Templar church in one city, and carry *'a letter of credit'* to a different Templar refuge, where they could exchange the letter for their money. (9) A letter of credit was almost the same as carrying a modern-day cashier's cheque and this simple but very effective procedure was used to obviate the expense of an armed security detail. The promissory notes reported by Marko Polo served a similar purpose to the letters of credit issued by the Templars.

The use of hazel-wood tally sticks for accounting purposes was, perhaps, a good measure of how the industry had lingered in the distant past in a few areas whilst making notable progress in others. In this accounting method, which had prehistoric roots, tally sticks were notched on two sides and then split down the middle – the depositor retaining one strip and the bank the other. This procedure was called into question during the South Sea Bubble (c. 1710) when the Chancellor of the Exchequer, Robert Harley, discovered several discrepancies in the records kept by the Treasury. As a result, tally sticks were eventually phased out in favour of written records of account.

With the cogs of the banking industry now turning in several strategic locations, it wasn't long before banknotes were issued instead of receipts. We will recall from Chapter 3 that Scotsman, John Law, was a strong supporter. He was aware that some of Europe's leading banks had started to issue notes, so he persuaded the French Regent to adopt this process around 1716. However, the Regent failed to abide by Law's strict parameters for the production of the new paper money – and we described the dire after-effects as the 'Paris Flood'.

Since the metrics of this event are a central theme from this point onward, our understanding of the following scenario is essential.

John Law had insisted that the total face value of all the banknotes produced, should be identical to the total value of the specie (coins) lodged at the bank. He also believed that a fractional reserve system—similar in nature to the one introduced by goldsmiths—would not have been suitable at that time. But through lamentable ignorance, or dogged determination, the Regent decided to instruct the printing of banknotes, almost without limit. The consequences of this may be described as follows:

"The first exhilarating effect of this flood of new money was the flush of apparent prosperity, but that was soon followed by raging inflation." (10) As exhilaration turned into desperation, hordes of French citizens tried to redeem their banknotes for coins, but there were too few coins to cover the face value of the paper. The dire effects of this critical imbalance plunged the French economy into depression for years thereafter. But this was a crisis that had certainly been avoidable. Even though Law's initial instructions to the Regent were based on solid banking principles—namely, 'a value ratio of one to one' for paper money and coins—the printing press continued to turn. Hence, the excessive production of money 'out of thin air' created an uncontrollable boom, which was followed by inflation, and then an economic crash.

England's financial system was also harbouring a number of complex issues at this time, and these needed to be addressed. The Warden of the Royal Mint, Sir Isaac Newton, was commissioned in 1717 to produce a report on 'The State of Gold and Silver Coins' relative to their purity and weight. Coin clipping had been rife for some years, and this had an impact on their value, thereby creating wider problems in the economy. As well as fixing the value of the guinea at twenty-one shillings, Newton's account is said to have paved the way for a much-needed benchmark system for monetary control – and this was 'the gold exchange standard'. (11)

In this process, the value of paper currency was now defined in terms of gold, for which it could be exchanged, and these principles were universally applied between 1870 and 1914.

MARCO POLO
1271-1275 CHINA

EARLY BANKING
1360-1429 - MEDICI DYNASTY

BANK OF ENGLAND
1694

JOHN LAW / PARIS FLOOD
C. 1717-1718

GOLD STANDARD
1870-1914

Continue to next page...

President William McKinley had reinforced the system's value in 1900 when the Gold Standard Act of the United States was passed on the 14th of March that year. This established gold as the only standard permissible for redeeming paper money, as the other metals used for this purpose had devalued the exchange mechanism. (12) Between 1900 and 1910, the benefits of this economic strategy started to kick-in, and many of the larger corporations were able to grow independently of banks. With the surety of stockpiles of gold, and a stable and balanced monetary system, the Federal Government was able to reduce national debt rapidly, as well as redeem the money issued during the Civil War.

However, the gold standard operated on the premise that there would always be sufficient gold resources to service the needs of the system – but this required the custodians of the banking industry to adhere to the optimal ratios between gold reserves and money creation. But, as we are about to see, this critical relationship was abandoned so that more money could be created and loaned.

One of the most significant junctures in the evolution of a universal monetary system was the year 1910, when a meeting took place on Jekyll Island, Georgia, between certain prominent members of the banking fraternity and politicians.

Amongst those present was Nelson W. Aldrich, Republican whip in the Senate, Chairman of the National Monetary Commission, business associate of J. P. Morgan and Father-in-law to John D. Rockefeller Junior. The United States Treasury was represented by Abraham Piat Andrew, who was the agency's Assistant Secretary. Frank A. Vanderlip was at the table on behalf of the National City Bank of New York, which was one of the most powerful banks in America at that time. Henry P. Davison was there to act for another giant, J. P. Morgan. A very prominent member of the forum was Paul M. Warburg, a partner in Kuhn, Loeb, and Company, who was also the delegate for the Rothschild banking dynasty in England and France. (13) At this time, the powerful Jekyll Island contingent jointly controlled around one sixth of the world's total wealth, as later reported by New York Times 3rd May 1931.

The Jekyll Island forum was responsible for the conception of the Federal Reserve Bank, which was signed-off by President Woodrow Wilson's Federal Reserve Act on 23rd December 1913. But this was not an agency of the United States – rather, it was a private central bank, modelled on the Bank of England.

The objective of this nascent giant was primacy, and there were reasons. By 1910, the number of banks in the US had grown to around 20,000, which represented a wide spectrum of competition. In addition, all US banks had been national banks back in the 1880s, which were chartered by the Federal Government. However, 'by 1896, the number of non-national banks had grown to 61% and they held 54% of the total banking deposits. At the point at which the Federal Reserve Act was passed, the number of non-national banks had increased to 71%, holding well-over 54% of the deposits – and the Jekyll Islanders wanted to reverse this trend'. (14)

Crazy Money and The
Boom-And-Bust Phenomenon

Section Two

The abandonment of the gold exchange standard; fiat money; the rubrics of modern banking; the ratcheting of the money supply; a lingering problem, and the boom-and-bust phenomenon:

During the two decades that followed its inception, the Federal Reserve did very little to stem the problems within the financial system, and it presided over the crashes of 1921 and 1929, as well as the Great Depression of 1929–1939. (15)

Over the other side of the Atlantic, some notable events also unfolded around this time. By 1914, Treasury Notes (informally known as Bradburys), were issued by the UK in place of gold coins, and were amalgamated with Bank of England Notes by 1928. This was probably a precursor to the United Kingdom's *'abandonment of the gold exchange standard'* in 1931 under Labour Prime Minister, Ramsay MacDonald. Although he claimed to be a keen supporter of this mechanism, he took the decision to dispense with it during the Invergordon incident, when about 1000 sailors in the British Atlantic Fleet mutinied, thereby causing panic at the London Stock Exchange, and a run on the pound.

Mr MacDonald's actions provided the temporary respite the UK needed but, in reality, he had discarded an invaluable benchmark system, where values were set by the strict laws of supply and demand. This offered a great deal of protection against manipulation, whereas a paper monetary standard meant that currency could be created at will. (16)

As a result of the UK's abolition of the gold exchange standard, our final, and current, category of money arrived on the scene.

Fiat Money: *'The Oxford Dictionary for the Business World (1993)'* defines fiat money as: "Money (especially paper money) that the government has declared to be legal tender, although it has no intrinsic value and is not backed by (gold) reserves." It goes on to say: "Most of the world's paper money is now fiat money."

The United Kingdom's abandonment of the gold exchanged standard soon sparked equivalent sentiments in the United States. Immediately after taking office in 1933, President Theodore Roosevelt declared a nationwide banking moratorium in order to prevent a run on the banks by those customers who were lacking confidence in the system. He also forbade banks to pay out gold or export it – effectively replicating the UK's decision to disconnect gold from its money supply two years earlier. "But only a couple of months after the presidential mandate, a joint resolution of Congress repealed the gold clause' and, for a time at least, the much-needed benchmark monetary system managed to survive in the United States. (17)

"However, this was an uncomfortable position for those who were driving towards the universal programming of financial procedure through a central banking mechanism. It transpired therefore that there was a summit in Bretton Woods, New Hampshire, in 1944 involving some of the world's most prominent socialists, financiers, politicians, and theoreticians. The meeting was held at the Mount Washington Hotel under the designation of the United Nations Monetary and Financial Conference. The principal outcome was the establishment of the International Monetary Fund (IMF) and the World Bank. It was agreed that the IMF would be funded on a quota basis by its member nations – and almost two hundred countries were soon co-opted.

"Purportedly, the principal role of the IMF was to promote monetary cooperation between nations by maintaining certain parameters for currency exchange. The second purpose of the IMF was to make loans to war torn, underdeveloped nations so they could build stronger economies. In spite of this, the IMF was soon utilised by its custodians as a means through which gold could be eliminated from world finance." (18) This also meant that the main monetary pipeline would now go from the Fed, through to the IMF and the World Bank. The ultimate goal was to extend the powers of the Fed's two protégés, so that they could provide worldwide central banking services – and therefore create fiat money globally.

While ever there are monopolies, markets can be moved.

In 1966, Alan Greenspan wrote: "The abandonment of the gold standard made it possible for the welfare statists to use the banking system as a means to an unlimited expansion of credit. In the absence of the gold standard, there is no way to protect savings from confiscation through inflation." (19) At this juncture, the UK had already disconnected gold from its money supply (1931), and the US was now making plans to follow suit.

Twenty-seven years after the Bretton Woods forum, the lobbyists managed to bring this about. They had argued that a more flexible money supply was needed to accommodate the changeable demands of modern commerce. But, in real terms, their eventual victory enabled them to create money as and when they wanted. On 15th August 1971, President, Richard Nixon, finally announced that the United States would no longer convert dollars to gold at a fixed value. At this pivotal moment, the world central banking mechanism had taken charge of the global money supply.

The Rubrics of Modern Banking: The disconnection of gold from the money supply created a fiat banking system for all nations – and this is the monetary policy that is still in operation today. The monetisation of government issued treasury bonds is the first step in this process.

A treasury bond is simply defined as: '*A bond issued by the US Government*' whilst, in the UK, it is referred to as a *'Gilt-Edged Security'* or *'gilt'*. Treasury bonds and gilts are fixed interest securities, which are widely regarded as very safe investments by the public as they are effectively government IOUs. They are redeemable between 5–15 years in the longer term, or up to 5 years in the shorter term. In today's fiat monetary system, the issuing of government treasury bonds is the starting point for almost all of the nation's supply of new money.

So, let's take a closer look at how this works.

When the government decides that it needs to raise funds, it issues treasury bonds for sale to the public. Public subscribers are thereby lending money to the government, and charging interest on their investment at a pre-agreed rate. The Federal Reserve for example (the Fed), purchases the bonds that have not been sold to the public, as well as the other debt obligations in the government's inventory. In order to make this purchase, the Fed is able to create fiat money on the spot, as there is no longer any need to hold gold reserves in order to produce new currency. As we have just seen, the new currency is actually created out of government debt.

However, the Fed now refers to the government bonds it has acquired as 'reserves', and it uses them to create 9 additional dollars for every dollar that it was obliged to return to the government when it purchased the bonds.

Via this process, the government can happily spend the money it has received from its bond issue, whilst 9 times this amount becomes the birthplace of all bank loans made to the nation's businesses and individuals – and this never-ending *'ratcheting of the money supply'* is the key to the whole of the fiat monetary process. 'Quantitative easing' is the euphemism that is widely used to describe the production of new money.

Walter Wriston, the chairman of Citicorp Bank, alluded to a 'revolving door process' when he pointed out that 'treasury notes are redeemed with the proceeds of identical notes, which are sold to the public when existing ones become due'. (20) However, it is unlikely that the purchasers of these bills even have an inkling that theirs will be repaid at maturity by the government selling a new bill of a like amount.

We have seen how the Fed creates new money in a $9 to $1 ratio, from which $1 is returned to the government – so let's see how the $9 quotient is moved into the economy. It is circulated through various banks, a complex structure of government organisations, foreign aid, and by the direct financial backing of institutions. Once again, we must remember that all of the money out on loan was created when the government incurred the original debt from its bond issue. The new currency now merges with, and starts to dilute, the money that is already in the system – but this has consequences. Prices now start to rise, and the value of existing money is lowered.

But the monetary production line does not end there.

Banks borrow money from the Federal Reserve at one interest rate, and make a profit by lending it to the nation's businesses and the public at a higher rate. Based on monetary reserves of around 10%, a bank is able to lend money at a ratio of $9 for every $1 borrowed from the Fed. The bank's so called 'reserves', are created by simply retaining the Fed's original loan.

Let's take a look at a quick example of the metrics. To illustrate this, we will assume that the bank receives $10 million from the Fed at a rate of 3%. The total annual cost to the bank is therefore $300,000 (.03 x $10,000,000). The bank treats the $10 million loan from the Fed as a cash deposit (as its 'reserves'), which means that it becomes the basis for the manufacture of another $90,000,000 (9 x $10 million) and this is added to the nation's money supply.

The bank will mark-up the original 3% interest rate from the Fed to say 5%, thereby creating a profit margin of 2%. Annually, the bank would therefore make $180,000, plus fees, on its original loan from the Fed – but, over a longer term, this amount would increase significantly.

The total fiat money jointly created by the Fed and other large commercial banks, is up to 10 times the amount of the original government debt.

We now know that all of this money emanates from the government IOUs (bonds) that are issued at the very beginning of the production-line. But the effect is that prices rise because the comparative value of money goes down. However, it seems that this stark reality is not widely understood. Earlier, we subscribed to the idea that a reasonable understanding of the financial system is hampered by a muddle of highly specialised jargon and complex procedure. It is quite refreshing therefore to consider the following commentary, as it clearly highlights some of the salient features of the system just a couple of decades after the Federal Reserve was founded. This is delivered with an unmistakeable air of concern by a very credible source – Robert Hemphill, Credit Manager of the Federal Reserve Bank of Georgia: – "If all bank loans were repaid, no one could have a bank deposit, and there would not be a dollar of coin or currency in circulation. This is a staggering thought. We are completely dependent on commercial Banks. Someone has to borrow every dollar we have in circulation, cash, or credit. If banks create ample synthetic money, we are prosperous; if not, we starve. We are absolutely without a permanent monetary system. When one gets a complete grasp of the picture, the tragic absurdity of our hopeless situation is almost incredible – but there it is." (21)

The Federal Reserve Bank of New York explains in a brochure: "Currency cannot be redeemed or exchanged for Treasury gold or any other asset used as backing … so the question of just what assets back Federal Reserve notes has little but bookkeeping significance." (22) If we look at this with a sense of irony, which we must, we might conclude that fancy pieces of paper have replaced solid gold bars as surety for our entire money supply, and creative accountancy is used to prop-up the system.

Continue to next page...

In percentage terms, the Bank of England provides us with an idea of how the money in circulation in the UK is broken down. In coinage and paper currency, it indicates that there is 3% – comprising 4.5 billion banknotes worth about £80 billion. A figure of 18% is said to be held as 'reserves', although its web-page does not indicate what these are, or how they were created. The largest segment of 79% is said to be 'bank deposits' – which are probably records of account stored in computer chips. But it is interesting to note that the BOE does say that money cannot be created at will, as the process is governed by the amount of 'reserves'.

However, money created at will, and money created at the behest of the government, may be regarded as two separate matters. When the government needs to raise money to cover budgetary deficits, we now know that it issues treasury bonds for sale to the public – but this is not inflationary. However, the sale of the remaining notes to central banks is inflationary, as they are used to create still more money. Since all modern money is fiat, there are no real limits to the amount that can be created – so the quantum will continue to be whatever governments and custodians of the system deem to be expedient.

A lingering problem: A significant drawback with the current financial system is that the vast majority of people understand far too little of it. The following extracts reflect the extent of the quandary:

In its issue on 24th September 1971, the Wall Street Journal reported that: "A pro-International Monetary Fund seminar of eminent economists could not agree on what money is, or how banks create it." The July 20th, 1975, issue of the New York Times published an article entitled 'Money Supply – A Growing Muddle', and it floated the specific question: "What is Money Nowadays?" The Wall Street Journal of 29th August 1975 commented: "The men and women involved in the arcane exercise of watching the money supply aren't exactly sure what the money supply consists of." (23)

At the time of these articles, the haze that shrouded the monetary process had become more opaque as a result of the abandonment of the gold exchange standard in the US. This occurred a few years before two of the editorials were published, and almost at the same time as the first. This heralded the abstract concept of fiat money, and ever since, the winds of change have not been strong enough to disperse the unwelcome haze – even for experts.

So, if the monetary system is capable of foxing the so-called experts, and some of its own, we can't expect it to be very much different for the majority of the general public. Here is a priceless example: "Some time ago Mr A. F. Davis mailed a $10 Fed note to the US Treasury Department. In his letter of transmittal, he called attention to the transcription on the bill, which said it was redeemable in 'lawful money', so he then requested that such money be sent to him. In the reply, the Treasury merely sent two $5 bills from a different printing series – bearing a similar promise to pay." (24) Bizarrely, there was not a hint of an explanation from the Treasury.

But this lack of transparency simply maintains the status quo, thereby hindering a great deal of our effort to understand and mitigate the problems that currently exist. In terms of priority, the destructive phenomenon we are about to discuss would certainly be high on the agenda.

The Boom-and-Bust Phenomenon: This is a most unwelcome feature of the economic rollercoaster and, in its merry-go-round of ups and downs, the present inevitably bumps into the past. But, in just a blink, the next ride is underway and another stealthy boom invades the markets.

At recurring ten-to-twelve-year intervals, this event has had devastating effects on local and global economies, yet it still seems to roll over modern-day affairs with consummate ease. Earlier, we floated a couple of ideas about its invisible beginnings – how it burgeons, and then grows rapidly out of control. One view was that this destructive scenario is largely driven by the random forces of human nature, which are both complex and difficult to subdue. However, the other point of view was that economic bubbles are non-organic, as they emanate from financial engineering within the system itself. As we are about to see, the last proposition is closer to the mark, but the former certainly acts as an accelerator to the boom-and-bust process.

'Financial engineering' refers to the arbitrary creation of fiat money, which is possible in the absence of the gold exchange standard or any other benchmark system. The boom-and-bust scenario is subsequently caused by the expansion and contraction of the fiat money supply, which occurs when too much money is produced and loaned during the boom phase, followed by decreases into the contraction phase.

So let's take a closer look at how this works.

As we gleaned from the 'Paris Flood', the creation of a torrent of new money out of thin air caused the boom, which then stoked inflationary fires. The French economy collapsed during the 18th century as a result of this process, when hordes of French citizens tried to redeem their banknotes for coins, but there were too few coins to cover the face value of the paper. However, the real key is this. "When the quantity of money expands without a corresponding increase in the supply of goods, the effect is a reduction in purchasing power of every monetary unit. The relative value of the overall money supply goes down, and this is the classic mechanism for a large increase in inflation." (25)

So let's take a look at a simplified example. If the money supply was suddenly doubled with no corresponding increase in housing stock, potential buyers would have the ability to bid existing prices up to double or beyond, thereby creating a massive boom – as the law of supply and demand would prevail.

But we must also bear in mind that, since the fiat money supply is an arbitrary process, with nothing behind it except debt, its quantity can go down as well as up. This starts a period of contraction which often leads to the 'bust' phase. The contraction occurs when people start to redeem their debts and refuse to borrow new money – possibly because of fear, higher interest rates, or a bleak financial or political landscape. Just as money is created when the Fed purchases bonds or other debt instruments, it is extinguished when those item are sold, as the money is given back to the system. At this point, prices start to level off, then decline.

It is the interchange between periods of expansion and contraction of the money supply that causes the economic rollercoaster effect, but this is not always a joyful ride as we have to endure its recurrent booms, busts, and depressions. We said earlier that the random forces of human nature impact this process, as there is an increased willingness to invest, speculate, gamble, or spend during the boom phase. Gary Richardson and Tim Sablic of the Federal Reserve Bank of Richmond aptly described the public's sentiment when an opportunity is in the offing:

'The siren of speculation has all too often lured otherwise sensible people into financial foolishness', and they reported that this helped to cause no less than eight banking panics between 1863 and 1913, as well as several threats to the national payments system. (26)

But it is the general lack of awareness of how the money game is really played that allows inflation to silently grind away, and thereby reduce the value of our savings. Describing the imbalance between the production of money and goods, and a lack of purchasing power, George Washington lamented: "A waggon load of money will scarcely purchase a waggon load of provisions." (27)

In contrast, the Byzantine Empire flourished as a centre of world commerce for eight hundred years without falling into bankruptcy nor, for that matter, even into debt as a result of a stable, gold-coin-backed monetary system. But let us fast-forward several centuries: "By 1990 in the US, an annual income of $10,000 was required to buy what took only $1,000 in 1914 after around 1,000% inflation had taken its toll." (28)

We will now end our journey by reiterating a very intriguing piece of information: *"If global debts were extinguished, there would not be a coin or paper note of currency in circulation anywhere in the world."*

If this happened in our dreams, we wouldn't be worrying about inflation and the boom-and-bust phenomenon – we would find ourselves haggling and trading fungibles.

The Debt Extinguisher

Postscript

It is now 6th June, 2022.

The world has witnessed extraordinary events during the past three years, and global economies have experienced unprecedented difficulties. As a result, it has been necessary for governments to provide financial support in different forms, for individuals, families, small businesses, corporate entities, and local and regional administrations.

In order to facilitate government assistance, new currency has been created in what is believed to be record quantities. In spite of this, many businesses have failed and inflation is now 'raging'. In the midst of this complex set of events, there has been an enormous new boom in real estate values, and now a crash within the wider economy is said to be looming.

In the UK, the Headline on the front of the *Daily Express* on 6th May 2022 was: *"Hold on to Your Hats! Recession Looms."*

If we remind ourselves of some of the earlier subject matter, we are able to understand why this is unsurprising.

As we gleaned from the 'Paris Flood', the creation of a torrent of new money caused a temporary boom, which then stoked inflationary fires. The French economy collapsed during the 18th century as a result of this process. A similar torrent of new money has been created during the past three years and, once again, inflationary fires have been well and truly fuelled.

The real key to the problem is this. "When the quantity of money expands without a corresponding increase in the supply of goods, the effect is a reduction in purchasing power of every monetary unit. The relative value of the overall money supply goes down, and this is the classic mechanism for a large-scale increase in inflation."

When we consider the dire after effects of the 'Paris Flood' back in the 18th century, perhaps Winston Churchill summed it up in a nutshell: *"The farther backward you can look, the farther forward you are able to see."*

Yes, hold on to your hats!

'Paris Flood': Metaphor used in connection with – the 'flooding of the French economy' during the early 18th century by the creation of excessive amounts of new money (Chapter 3 – John Law).

Glossary

Acronym: A phrase formed from the initial letters of other words (used abundantly in this book).

Advisory Service: A service in which a professional provides advice about investment.

Analysts: Professionals who work for large brokerage firms and merchant banks analysing (often) charts and fundamentals to report on national economies, individual companies and various financial markets.

Arbitrage: This is a non-speculative transfer of funds from one market to another to take advantage of small differentials in price in a commodity, stock or currency pair.

Asset Backed Securities: These are created by buying and bundling loans (for example, mortgages) and creating securities backed by those assets. (See within context of Chapter 9 definition).

Back Test: A back test uses historical data to see how well a particular trading strategy would have played out.

Bear: Someone who believes prices will decline.

Bespoke Tranche Opportunity – these new derivatives were really Credit Default Obligations (CDOs) that had simply been rebranded, according to Bloomberg News in 2015.

Bid and Ask: This is also known as 'the bid and offer'. The bid is the highest bid to buy a particular stock (or security), and the ask is the lowest price on offer to sell that stock (or security). The difference in price is the spread (see 'spread' later in glossary).

Bilateral Intervention: Currency intervention refers to the practice of a country's monetary authorities buying or selling their own currency in the foreign exchange markets with a view to guiding its value.

Black Box: This is a computer programme that has been designed to assimilate certain data in the financial markets, so that trading decisions can be made.

Bull: Someone who believes prices will rise.

Basis Point: This is often abbreviated to (BPS) and refers to a common unit of measure for interest rates in, for example, mortgages as well as other percentages in finance. One basis point is equal to 1/100 of 1%, or 0.01% or 0.0001 and is used to denote the percentage change in a financial instrument.

Boom and Bust Cycle: This is the process of economic expansion and contraction that repeatedly occurs in a capitalist economy, and seems to be an integral part of the business cycle.

Bubble: The process of continuous expansion of prices when the masses follow a new trend in the financial (or other) markets.

Chart: A graph that depicts the price movement of a given market. For example, daily price bars or candlesticks could be used to denote the Open, Close, High and Low during the session.

Commodity: Raw material which is traded on the commodity market, such as oil, gold, silver, grain, coffee, coco, wool or pork bellies.

Congestion: A price pattern characterised by extended sideways movement.

Consolidation: (See Congestion).

Correction: This occurs when prices contract to sensible levels after exceeding realistic values.

Credit Default Swap: (See within context of chapter 9 definition).

Credit Derivatives: For example – bonds made up of bundles of mortgages or loans.

Currency Lot Sizes: The standard size for lots is 100,000 units of currency. Mini lots could be 10,000 or 1,000.

Currency Mortgage: A mortgage or loan in a foreign currency. These were popular in the eighties and early nineties in the UK. Instead of pounds, mortgages were available (for example) in Japanese yen, where interest rates might have been lower than those available in the pound.

Day Trade: A trade that is liquidated on the same day it is initiated.

Debenture: A document (debenture deed) held by a lender setting out the terms of a loan and may be charged as a fixed charge on a specific property (or properties).

Deflationary Measures: Deflationary measures are ones that are intended or likely to cause deflation. Deflation is caused by a decrease in the consumer price index (CPI).

Delinquent Mortgage: A mortgage which is in arrears or default. (See within context of Chapter 9 definition).

Derivative: Financial instrument that is valued according to the expected price movement of an underlying asset, for example – a Commodity, Currency or Share. (See within context of Chapter 9 definition).

Doubling down: This is when traders attempt to recover money from bad trades. The strategy is based on doubling up on their position when, for example, a stock price falls.

Down Trend: A general tendency for declining prices in a given market.

Draw Down: The equity reduction in a trading account (losses).

Due Diligence: This is a thorough appraisal of a particular business, which is carried out by an interested buyer. This would involve a full review of its assets and liabilities, as well as its future potential.

Economic Cycle: This is the fluctuations in the economy between periods of expansion and contraction.

Equity: The total monetary value of an account.

Equities: These are freely traded stocks and shares in publicly quoted companies. The holders of these shares are entitled to the growth in the company through an annual dividend payment.

Fade: To trade in the opposite direction of a particular market signal or price move.

FA: This is an abbreviation for Fundamental Analysis – which uses economic data, such as inflation rates, interest rates, economic growth rates and current political factors, for the purpose of forecasting prices. For individual companies, the Fundamental Analyst will look at its accounts, its order book and other important data for the same purpose.

Financial Instrument: These are assets that can be traded (e.g., stocks). (See within context of Chapter 9 definition)

Foreign Currency Mortgage: A foreign currency mortgage is a mortgage which is repayable in a currency other than the currency of the country in which the borrower is resident.

FTSE 100: Financial Times Share Index, monitoring the movement of the leading 100 publicly quoted shares by market capitalisation.

Fundamental Analysis (FA): Analysis of financial market instruments based on their underlying economics, by use of accountancy information for company valuations. In essence, FA measures the intrinsic value of companies.

Game Plan: In finance, this is a well thought out and disciplined trading strategy.

Gap: A price zone in which no trades occur. For example, if a market that has previously traded at a high of £5 and then opens at £5.40 on the following day, the price zone between £5 and £5.40 is a gap.

Get Rich Quick Scheme: Often an ill-conceived proposition designed to mislead the public and relieve them of their money.

High Probability Strategy: A trading strategy that has well above average prospects for success.

Intra-Day: A term used to describe a situation where trades start and end in the same day.

Intrinsic Value: The difference between the market value of an underlying security (in a traded option for example) and the exercise price.

Investment Trust: Company formed to invest the collected funds of shareholders by the acquisition of shares in other companies.

IPO: This is an abbreviation for Initial Public Offer. This is the process of floating a company and offering its shares to the public.

Joint Stock Company: These originated in the 17th century and are now rare. A joint-stock company is a business entity in which shares of the company's stock can be bought and sold by shareholders. Each shareholder owns company stock in proportion, evidenced by their shares (certificates of ownership). Shareholders are able to transfer their shares to others without any effects to the continued existence of the company.

Liquidity: The degree to which a given market is liquid. This means there is a sufficiently large number of trades daily so that most reasonably sized buy and sell orders can be executed without significantly moving prices. It allows the trader relative ease of entry and exit.

Long: A position established with a buy order, which profits in a rising market. (See within context of Chapter 9 definition).

Loss Leader: This is a pricing strategy where a product is sold at a price below its market cost to stimulate other sales of more profitable goods or services.

MA Crossover: The crossover of two moving averages (for example, 8 and 20) which may indicate an opportunity to buy or sell the market.

Margin: This is the amount of money borrowed from a brokerage firm or a bank to purchase an investment. It is the difference between the total value of the securities held in an investor's account and the loan amount from the broker.

Margin Call: A margin call occurs when the value of an investor's margin account falls below the broker's required amount. The investor is required to deposit additional money.

Open Outcry: This is a method of communicating between professionals on a stock or futures exchange trading floor.

Open Position: A live position in the financial markets.

Option: The right to buy or sell a fixed quantity of a commodity, currency or security at a particular date, and at a particular price (known as the exercise price). Unlike a futures contract, the purchaser of an option is not obliged to buy or sell at the exercise price and will only do so if it is profitable.

Option Volume: (See volume).

Over the Counter Stocks: (OTC) is the process of trading securities for companies that are not listed on an exchange. They are traded 'over the counter' by a dealer network.

'Paris Flood': Metaphor used in connection with – the 'flooding of the French economy' during the early 18th century by the creation of excessive amounts of new money.

PEG Factor/Strategy: The PEG strategy is widely regarded as a means of finding undervalued stocks. It is calculated by dividing the Price Earnings Ratio (PER) by the Earnings Per Share (EPS) growth rate.

Pip: This is an abbreviation for 'price interest point' or 'percentage in point'. A pip represents a tiny change in price between a particular currency pair, such as GBP/USD (the pound and the US dollar) and is 1/100 of 1%. For example, GBP/USD may be quoted as 1.327(6)4. The pip in this case is highlighted in brackets on the fourth digit after the decimal point (6). The fifth digit after the decimal point (4) is the tick (later defined in this glossary), and 10 ticks are equal to one pip. This means that if the 5th digit in this example (4 ticks) changes to 10 ticks then the (6) pips would increase to (7).

Point: Points are used in various contexts in financial matters and represent increments of price change (up or down) in percentage terms. Foreign exchange is different as the convention is to measure price movements (up or down) in pips, as we can see immediately above. To use a simple example, if the price of a particular stock moves from $10 to $11, then it is said to have moved one point, as a point is equal to one. In a futures contract, a point is represented by a price change of 1/100 of 1%.

Pre-Exhaustion Flurry: The last flurry of buying after a sustained upward trend in the price of a security, which is followed by a downturn.

Prohibition Era: The era between 1910 and 1933 when alcohol was banned in the USA.

Promissory Note: A negotiable instrument that contains a promise to pay a certain sum of money to a named person, to that person's order, at a specified time in the future. It must be signed by the maker and delivered to the payee or bearer.

Proprietary Trading: This occurs when the trader uses the firm's own money to trade the financial markets.

Proxy: A person acting in place of another. For example, a member of a company can nominate another person (who does not need to be a member) to cast a vote.

Putative Bottom: A hypothetical (or what is believed to be a) bottom in the market.

Rediscount Rate: The rediscount rate is also called the discount rate, or bank rate, and is the interest rate charged by central banks for loans of reserve funds to commercial banks and other financial institutions.

Rally: A rise in the price of a security (often after price has declined).

Resistance: This is a price area at which a rising market is expected to encounter increasing selling pressure, which is sufficient to stall or reverse the advance.

Revolving Door Scam: Another way of describing the 'robbing Peter to pay Paul' scam.

Scalper: A trader who seeks to profit from very small price fluctuations.

Securitised Mortgage: For homeowners, the securitization of mortgages means that their mortgage loan does not belong to a single lender. The loan is part of a pool owned by investors. A mortgage service company is responsible for collecting mortgage payments and sending them along to the pool. (See within context of Chapter 9 definition).

Short: A position that is taken by selling the market, which profits from declining prices. (See within context of Chapter 9 definition).

Short Straddle: See straddle in options and short position.

SMA: A Simple Moving Average is the average price during the most recently fixed number of days. For example, a 5-period moving average would take into account the last 5 days data and add the closing prices together, then divide by 5. A moving average line would be plotted from the points derived from a number of similar calculations.

Spike: A rapid rise and contraction in price in the financial markets.

Split Strike Conversion: This is also known as 'the collar' or the 'reverse conversion' and typically works over a much longer time period. It is a bullish strategy which involves buying stocks, then buying near the money put options, and selling out of the money call options.

Spread: The spread is the difference between the bid and offer prices (see bid and offer).

Stock Jobber: A market maker on the London Stock Exchange prior to the big-bang.

Stop Loss: This is also known as a stop order. A trader places a 'stop loss/order' to mitigate his loss if his long or short trade moves against him by a pre-set amount.

Straddle (Options): This is a neutral trade that involves simultaneously buying a call and put at the same strike price and with the same expiration date. It requires the underlying asset to move in an explosive nature (preferably upwards) to make the trade profitable.

Strategy: A carefully conceived plan which is used by the trader to trade a financial market for profit.

Support: This is a price area at which a falling market is expected to encounter increased buying support, which is sufficient to stall or reverse the decline.

Switching: See arbitrage.

TA: This is an abbreviation for Technical Analysis – which is the study of market action, primarily through the use of charts, for the purpose of forecasting future price trends.

Tick: The smallest increment of price movement, up or down, in a market.

Ticked: (See tick)

Trend: The tendency of prices to move in a given general direction.

Vaudeville: Entertainment featuring musical, comedy art usually on stage.

Volume: The total number of shares or contacts traded during a given period.

Bibliography Research Material, and Background Reading

'All That Glitters – The Fall of Bearings' (by) John Gapper & Nicholas Denton. Published in 1996 by Penguin Group. Index Code: ATG/96.

'The Embarrassment of Riches' (by) Simon Schama. First published in Great Britain by William Colins and Sons in 1987. Index Code: TEOR/87

'A Very English Deceit' (by) Malcolm Balen. Published in 2002 by Fourth Estate. Index Code: AVED/02.

'Banking and the World' (by) Jeffry A. Frieden. Published in 1989 by Hutchinson Radius. Index Code: BATW/89.

'Bernie Madoff – The Wizard of Lies' (by) Diana B. Henriques. Published in 2011 by Times Books. Index Code: TWOL/11.

'Betrayal – The Life and Lies of Bernie Madoff' (by) Andrew Kirtzman. Published in 2009 by Harper Collins. Index Code: B/2009.

'Business Dictionary' (by) Michael Greener. First Published in 1970.

'Confessions of an Economic Hitman' (by) John Perkins. Published by Berrett-Koehler in 200. Index Code: CEHM/04.

'Dictionary of Finance and Banking' (Oxford) (by) Market House Books in 1993.

'Extraordinary Popular Delusions, The Money Mania' (by) Charles Mackay. Published by Cosmo Classics in 2008. Index Code: EPD/MM/08.

'Financial Times': 01/10/87. Index Code: FT/01/10/87.

'Financial Times': 25/08/87. Index Code: FT/25/08/87.

'Financial Times': 01/10/87. Index Code: FT/01/10/87. *'Financial Times':* 17/10/87. Index Code: FT/17/10.87. *'Financial Times':* 19/10/87. Index Code: FT/19/10/87.

'Financial Times': 20/10/87. Index Code: FT/20/10/87.

'Flash Boys' (by) Michael Lewis. Published by W. W. Norton in 2014; Allen Lane 2014 and Penguin Books in 2015. Index Code: FB/15.

Fool's Gold' (by) Gillian Tett. Published by Little, Brown in 2009 and Abacus in 2010. Index Code: FG/10.

'Going For Broke' (by) Judith Rawsley. Published by Harper Collins in 1996. Index Code: GFB/96.

'Liar's Poker' (by) Michael Lewis. First Published by Hodder Stroughton in 1989 and by Hodder Stroughton in paperback in 2016.

'Madoff – The Man Who Stole $65 Billion' (by) Erin Arvedlund. Published by Penguin Books in 2009 – Erin Arvedlund Copyright. Index Code: TMWSB/09.

'Madoff With the Money' (by) Jerry Oppenheimer. Published by John Wiley and Sons in 2009. Index Code: MWTM/09.

'Mastering the Trade' (by) John F. Carter. Published by McGraw-Hill Trader's Hedge in 2006. Index Code: MTT/06.

'Money Land' (by) Oliver Bullough. Published by Profile Books 2018. Index Code: ML/18.

'Options Made Easy' (by) Guy Cohen. Published by Pearson Education in 2013. Index Code: OME/13.

'Ponzi' (by Donald Dunn. Published by McGraw-Hill in 1975. Index Code: P/75.

'Ponzi's Scheme' (by) Mitchell Zuckoff. Published by Random House Paperback Edition in 2006. Index Code: PS/06.

'Rogue Trader' (by) Nick Leeson. Published by Little Brown and Company in 1996. Index Code: RT/96.

www.swanlowpark.co.uk (FTSE100) from 1985 to 1990. Index Code: Swan/90.

'Technical Analysis of the Financial Markets' (by) John J. Murphy. Published by the New York Institute of Finance in 1999. Index Code: TAFM/99.

'The Almighty Dollar' (by) Dharshini David. Published by Elliott and Thompson in 2018. Index Code: TAD/18.

'The Big Short' (by) Michael Lewis. First published in US by W. W. Norton and Company in 2010; then by Allen Lane in the UK in 2010. Later published by Penguin Books, with a new afterword, in 2011. Index Code: TBS/11.

'The Creature from Jekyll Island' (by) G. Edward Griffin. There are 42 reprints between 1994 and 2018. There are five editions between 1994 and 2010.

There is a Japanese edition in 2005; a German edition in 2006; and a Chinese edition in 2017. It was first published by American Media in 1994. Index Code: TCFJI/94.

'The Euro' (by) Joseph E. Stiglitz. Published by Penguin Books in 2016. Index Code: TE/2016.

'The Great Crash of 1929' (by) John Kenneth Galbraith. First published in USA in 1954. It was first published in the UK by Hamish Hamilton in 1955. With a new forward, it was published by Penguin Books in 2009. Index Code: TGC29/09.

'The King, the Crook, and the Gambler – A Very English Deceit' (by) Malcolm Balen.

Published by Fourth Estate in 2002. Index Code: KCG/02.

268

'The Netherlands' (Updated by) Vicky Hampton, Phil Lee, Suzanne Morton-Taylor, Emma Thompson, and Jeroen Van Marie (of) Roughguides.com. Index Code: TNETH.

'The Tulip Folly' (articles published by) Lorraine Boisseneault in 2017.

'Too Good to be True' (by) Erin Arvedlund. Published by Penguin Group in 2009. Index Code: TGBT/09.

'Tulipmania' (by) Anne Goldgar. Published by the University of Chicago Press in2007. Index Code: T/07.

Notes and References Defined Within the Context of the Chapters

Introduction

(Glossary) Unlike this very generous outcome, speculation in games of chance or 'get-rich-quick schemes' (*) tend to be very unforgiving, as you can lose your hard-earned stake or worse.

(Glossary) In the long run, high probability strategies (*) tend to produce fairly reliable results for disciplined speculators.

(Glossary) At various stages during the boom-and-bust cycles (*) later depicted, irrational, counterproductive emotions were generated on a grand scale when traditional values and beliefs were trampled in the rush to 'get rich quick'.

(Glossary) With so many moving parts, bubbles are regarded by those in authority as intractable events that make an unwelcome appearance during the economic cycle (*).

Chapter 1

(Glossary) This turned out to be a pre-exhaustion flurry (*), signalling that the price of tulip bulbs was about to tumble.

(Glossary) In contrast to most of the events described in this book, it is also important to recognise the fact that certain booms are not financially destructive as, in time, they are absorbed by the economic cycle (*).

(1)   It has even been reported that the collapse of Tulip Mania precipitated a devastating stock market crash (search-engine analytics/24).

(2)   'Constantinople now had eighty shops selling flower bulbs, which were supplied by three hundred growers' (T/0731).

(3)   It seems however that by 1725, enthusiasm for this goddess of all flowers had reached epic proportions when the decision had to be taken to cap prices and it is reported that one notable specimen had been given the ominous name of the 'bankrupter'(T/0732).

(4)   The Dutch had started to receive shipments of tulip bulbs from Asia in the 16th century and it wasn't long before similar sentiments permeated this part of northern Europe (T/0720).

(5)   In the first half of the 17th century, in fact, around two thirds of the population owned, on average, between five and eleven paintings of some kind (T/0769). At this time, still life paintings featuring tulips and shells were very popular, as well as portraits of certain tulips in full bloom (T/0786).

(6)   Rarity defined a standard of beauty that led to the high prices that were often paid (T/07129).

(7)   Some tulip bulbs could change hands several times before they flowered (T/07129), creating a price hike with each link in the chain. From its source, it has been reported that one bulb fetched f600 and tripled in price in just three weeks (T/072).

(8)   The records show that Cornelius Guldewagen of Harlem was involved in a very large transaction for no less than 1,300 tulip bulbs in early 1637 (T/07113).

(9)   Some therefore believed that there were ways in which man could use his craft in order to influence the process of nature (T/07115).

(10)   It would be wrong to suggest that the whole of Dutch society was involved in tulip mania but most of those involved were connected to each other in some way – and the province of Holland was the centre of influence (T/077).

(11)   As a result, there were very many disagreements between tulip buyers and sellers, some of whom took their claims to court to seek redress, both before and after the end of tulip mania (T/07138).

(12)   In January and early February 1637 some tulips bulbs saw a much larger increase in price than normal (T/07201).

(13)   There were bankruptcies, but 'Tulip Mania did not destroy the wealthy cosmopolitan economy of the time, or even the livelihoods of most participants' (T/077).

(14) One particular source indicates that the demise of Tulip Mania precipitated a crash in stock prices, but this is not mentioned in any other of the material that has been researched, and neither have any references to banking problems been found (T/0723).

Chapter 2

(Glossary) At the turn of the 18th century, there had been a rapid increase in the formation of new 'joint stock companies' (*) and this became a prelude to the most remarkable period of speculation England had ever seen.

(1) Law was appointed Controller General of French Finances by the duke, and believing that the wealth of any nation was dependent on trade, reminiscent of the South Sea Company, he had become the instigator of big, bold plans. As well as setting up the Mississippi Scheme, he was responsible for establishing Banque General, which was regarded as the first central bank of France. (search-engine analytics).

(2) Toward the end of the first decade of the 18th century, England's national debt was estimated to be somewhere between 9 to 10 million pounds, a great deal of which had been incurred in order to support the efforts of the army and navy during the country's long-standing hostilities with France and Spain (KCG0215).

(3) Sticks were notched on two sides and then split down the middle – the depositor retaining one strip and the treasury the other (AVD/0214).

(4) The Chancellor found that the Exchequer had the paltry sum of 5,000 pounds in its kitty when he took office, and England was literally at the fiscal brink with the national debt now confirmed by his Investigation Committee at nine million pounds (KCG0214).

(5) But, cunningly, this was Blunt's precursor to a more grandiose lottery, in which the prizes were bigger still, and this was to be placed on offer with tickets costing 100 pounds (2/11wk).

(6) By a stroke of good fortune, or the very heavy purchase of tickets, a vast proportion of the winners came from the wealthier reaches of society, (AVD/0229) however, the two national lotteries are said to have raised 3.5 million, and were held for several years thereafter.

(Glossary) In the meantime, the 'stock-jobbers' (*) and 'monied men' continued to conduct their affairs in the tea-rooms, small offices and dens in and around Exchange Alley, as this had been a tradition throughout the last decade of the seventeenth century, and still formed a significant part of everyday life.

(7) On 2nd May 1711, Harley therefore announced the new company's formation, and said that it would not only be engaged in trade in the south seas, but its aim was also to take-over the floating portion of the national debt of £9 million (AVD/0230).

(Glossary) In many cases, the creditors would actually be exchanging debentures (*) for shares with an artificial value, backed by a project that would have to negotiate very perilous waters before it could fulfil its promises.

(8) Harley was therefore desperate to negotiate peace with France and Spain, but his pleas to the House were fiercely resisted by Robert Walpole and the Whigs, in full knowledge that the South Sea enterprise might founder without it – and the Whig dominated Bank of England would thereby maintain its primacy (AVD/02/47).

(9) Having located discrepancies in the army's accounts, both the duke of Marlborough and Walpole were now charged with corruption and sent to the tower (AVED/0230).

(10) Early in January 1712, the directors pressed Harley for a huge flotilla, attended by 4,000 soldiers, to carry goods and merchandise into the south seas (AVED/03234).

(11) Harley, now the Earl of Oxford, was a notable absentee at board meetings thereafter and, on 25th July 1714 Queen Anne was forced to sack Harley. Just seven days later, Queen Anne passed away and the Hanoverian, George 1st, became King of Great Britain (AVED/023).

(12) In March of 2013, a peace deal was finally struck in Utrecht, and it was magnanimously agreed that England could supply the colonies with slaves for a period of thirty years (AVED/0234).

(13) After debating these proposals for a considerable time three acts of Parliament were passed (EPD/MM/08/47/8).

(14) Accordingly, there was a marked appreciation in the value of its shares, however, the increase in revenue that was so vital to underpin such a rapid spurt was commensurately weak (EPD/MM/08/48).

(15) This news was received by members of the public almost as though a pathway to riches had thrown open its fettered gates, and the company's shares rose from 130 to 300 pounds in anticipation that a bill would now be passed in its favour (EPD/MM/08/50).

(16) Unsurprisingly, shortly after the passing of this bill, the shares in the South Sea Company pulled back quite sharply from 310 to 290, more than likely in a bout of timely profit taking by the intuitive few, including the directors (52CMC).

(Glossary) Keen to maintain a state of ignorance, South Sea Company board members were never going to allow the corporation's stock price to retreat to its intrinsic value (*); amongst other things, this would expose their sinister, fraudulent game.

(17) With the South Sea Company leading the pack, this period of chicanery took another sinister turn – companies were now being set up to fail (EPD/MM/08/54).

(18) Recognising that these deceptions had now become a threat to the state, the King published a proclamation on the 11th June 1720 which declared that all unlawful projects should be classed as public nuisances and prosecuted accordingly (EPD/MM/08/57).

(19) Emotions were now running very high indeed, and both the duke of Portland and Mr Hungerford stepped into the proceedings with carefully chosen words of appeasement (EPD/MM/08/66).

(20) One speaker was Mr Broderick, who said, "They have secured themselves with the losses of the gullible, and thousands of families will now be reduced to beggary." (EPD/MM/08/67).

(21) Significantly, he went on to say, "I founded my judgement of the whole affair upon the unquestionable maxim that 10 million, which is more than our running cash, could never extend 200 million beyond which our paper credit extended."(EPD/MM/08/68).

(22) Following his speech, a particularly vehement member stepped forward, Lord Molesworthy, who made it plain that he was seeking the

death penalty for the directors of the South Sea Company and suggested that they should be thrown into the Thames in sacks (EPD/MM/08/73).

(23) Lord Stanhope said, "Every farthing possessed by the criminals, whether directors or not directors, ought to be confiscated to make good public losses." (EPD/MM/08/75). What a hypocrite he turned out to be. By now, the South Sea Company's treasurer, Mr Knight, had left the country with documents containing all the dark secrets of this organisation's fraudulent acts against both the state and its people (EPD/MM/08/77).

(24) After all, around 1.5 million in sterling had been won and lost and ((EPD/MM/08/64) it was estimated that attempts had been made, through the creation of bubbles, patents and fraud, to rake in a figure upward of 300 million pounds (EPD/MM/08/54).

(25) During this period of 18th century speculation, someone who was reasonably well-off would have earned a few hundred pounds a year. Further down the social ladder, a domestic servant would have earned around ten pounds a year, and most artisans would have made, just a few shillings a day. On the other hand, anyone living at this time with £100,000 would have enjoyed similar status to that of a multi-millionaire today (search-engine analytics).

Chapter 3

(1) It was Bloomsbury in London during 1694 and, probably through infatuation, or maybe love and honour, both men had quarrelled over a certain Elizabeth Villiers (AVED/02/16).

(2) Some historians believe that Law was a knave and a madman, whilst others suggest that he was an innovative but wayward genius (EPD//MM/08/29).

(3) Yet again, this evoked very strong suspicion about the pamphlet's origins and, following quite lengthy discussions, Parliament concluded that the contents of the document entitled 'Land-Bank' would not be suitable for Scotland (EPD//MM/08/4).

(4) As early as 13th century, Venetian traveller, Marco polo, is said to have reported the use of rudimentary promissory notes written on

parchment, following his visit to China between 1271 to 1275 (4) (155cfji).

(5) At the same time, he attracted the wrath of the magistrates in Venice and Genoa, where he was expelled on the grounds that he was a bad influence on the local youth (EPD//MM/08/5).

(6) With this in mind, he roamed through Flanders, Holland, Germany, Hungary, Italy and France for well over a decade, studying the local customs, absorbing new developments, and exchanging ideas within influential circles (EPD//MM/08/4).

(Glossary) Interest from loans should never exceed the value of the entire lands of the state. He had therefore realised that the face-value of 'promissory notes' (*) needed to be underwritten by some other asset – and that this asset should be one of recognised value.

(7) At this time, France's national debt stood at no less than 3000 million livres, against which there was a revenue of only 145 million, and 142 million of this was earmarked for the government's coffers (search-engine analytics).

(8) Hundreds of ministry men were sent to the Bastille and one very rich banker, Samuel Bernard, received the death sentence (EPD//MM/08/9).

(9) Only 80 million went toward the payment of real debts, and around 100 million found its way into the pockets of the courtiers (EPD//MM/08/9).

(10) In fact, the duke is said to have been so anxious, that he signed certain documents presented by Law without proper examination and, in haste, delegated matters that he should have attended to personally (EPD//MM/08/9).

(11) However, after hearing Law's proposals, a royal edict was published on 5th May 1716, in which Law was thereby authorised to establish a bank by the name of Law and Co (EPD//MM/08/10).

(12) The capital of the Bank was fixed at six million livres, and made-up of twelve thousand shares of 500 livres each, with billets d'état for the remainder – the latter being 'state issued public securities' (EPD//MM/08/10).

(13) Against the backdrop of this much improved economic scene, other branches of Law's bank were therefore established in Lyons, Rochelle, Tours, Amiens and Orleans (EPD//MM/08/11).

(14) In spite of the current lethargy of the South Sea Company a French corporation was formed at Law's behest in August 1717, which would have the privilege of exclusive trading rights in Louisiana, up to the western bank of the great Mississippi (EPD//MM/08/11/12).

(15) The French Chancellor, D'Arguessau, was also aware of the imbalance, and immediately started a quest for Law's head (EPD//MM/08/13).

(16) At the beginning of 1719 an edict was published which granted the Mississippi Company the exclusive right to trade in the East Indies, China and the South Seas (EPD//MM/08/14).

(17) Desperate for respite, he moved to the Place Vendome but was still pestered, and local residents became very angry at Law for this upheaval (EPD//MM/08/16).

(18) However, people were completely taken aback when the Count d' Horn, who was the younger brother of Prince d' Horn, resorted to murder (EPD//MM/08/21).

(19) Deciding to err on the side of caution, the servant reported to his master that the shares were trading at 8,000 livres (EPD//MM/08/19).

(20) Indeed, as the Indian and Mississippi stocks rose, more 'billets de banque' were printed to keep pace (EPD//MM/08/28).

(21) Upon Law's refusal, the prince withdrew three huge waggon loads of coins (specie) after inundating the bank's cashiers with paper notes (EPD//MM/08/29).

(22) A Council of State meeting was held at the beginning of May 1720 in which Law, D'Argenson and all ministers were present (EPD//MM/08/33).

(23) On a night of protest, the Hotel de Ville was illuminated by a number of large bonfires at its façade, and cheering crowds used piles of banknotes to fuel the blaze (EPD//MM/08/35).

(1) Major oil-fields were being tapped in Kansas, Illinois, Louisiana, Oklahoma and Texas, and John D. Rockefeller's Standard Oil Trust dominated the world's petroleum markets (search-engine analytics).

(2) The country's major cities were in the process of being electrified, which soon enabled the use of 1900 telephones and, only a couple of years later, the Ford Motor Company was founded in 1903 (search-engine analytics).

(3) He reportedly told a relative in the early days that he wanted to make so much money that he would be as rich and famous as America's wealthiest families – the Carnegies and the Rockefellers (P/75/XIV).

(4) The undisputed master of this scam had been William Franklin Miller who, around 1899, set-up for business as the Franklyn Syndicate in Brooklyn, and then opened an office in Boston. (PS/06/106).

(5) After raking in a million dollars, he was exposed by the New York Herald and sentenced to ten years in Sing Sing (PS/06/106).

(6) However, C. D. Sheldon, alias Wilson, alias Hoyt, alias O. D. Washburn soon followed him with another 'Peter to Paul' scam in Canada. Fortunately, this imitation of Miller's scheme was soon brought to a halt (PS/06/107).

(7) Then there was the law; the trusty vanguard of financial probity. It was well known in some parts of 1920s America, that certain criminals had bought their pardon, simply because they had connections, and were able to pay enough money (P/75/3). In a prominent case, Dan Coakley, Ponzi's eventual high-profile lawyer, and the District Attorney for Massachusetts, Joseph Pelletier, were found to have joined forces to operate a lewd extortion racket known as 'the badger game' (P/75/296).

(8) On 24th July 1920, a huge chauffeur driven limousine known, back in the day, as Locomobile purred slowly through the Boston Streets and gently negotiated its way through the surging throngs of adoring Ponzi fans (Search-Engine Analytics).

(9) The air close to the harbour was pungently seasoned with odours of fish, livestock, fruit and leather goods, but these were all customary smells in this part of town (P/75/3).

(10) Securities Exchange Company issued written receipts for the cash it received and these clearly stated that investors' capital and interest would be repaid in either forty-five days, or ninety days, thereby reflecting the arrangements that had been made (PS/8/107).

(11) However, news of this astonishing 50–100% return had spread throughout the different walks of Bostonian society like wild-fire and, ironically, the flames had been fanned by sceptical news coverage from the Boston Post (PS/8/186).

(12) At this time, all the scheduled repayments to investors had been met by the Securities Exchange Company, yet, Ponzi's scheme had also caught the eye of Banking Commissioner, Joseph C. Allen (PS/8/11), as well as the belligerent Post (P/75/175).

(13) As the door of Ponzi's vehicle opened, the tip of his trade-mark malacca walking-stick touched down, and out he stepped (PS/8/12).

(14) Ponzi had always been keen to promote the image of a successful and wealthy immigrant, during his first four years in Boston, he worked as grocery clerk, a road drummer, a factory hand and a dishwasher (PS/8/25).

(15) Unsurprisingly, Banco Zarossi collapsed under the weight of a huge scandal when it was discovered that Zarossi, like William Miller and C. D. Sheldon before him, had embarked on the very same old 'robbing Peter to pay Paul' scam (PS/8/ (2) (26/7).

(16) On 29th August 1908, he paid a visit to the offices of one of the Bank's clients, Canadian Warehousing Company (PS/8/28).

(17) Montreal Detective, John McCall, who had been alerted by suspicious staff at the Bank, confronted Ponzi at his boarding house (PS/8/29).

(18) Ponzi's cellmate was swindler, Louis Cassulo, who, a decade later, was in the thick of things at the Securities Exchange on that warm day in July 1920 (PS/8/139).

(19) He was a convicted forger, ex-convict and strongly suspected of having fleeced depositors at Banco Zarossi. (P/75/46) Against this milieu, the normally ebullient Ponzi was feeling down on his luck so, just seventeen days after regaining his freedom, he decided to take a southbound train towards the Canadian American border.

(20) Following reckless speculation, this crooked paradigm of American prosperity was said to have been responsible for a national financial panic in 1907 (P/75/49).

(21) Fearful of even the slightest implication – and then a spell on the chain-gang – Ponzi soon made his way to the Appalachian mining town of Blocton (P/75/51).

(22) Her left arm, shoulder and breast were so severely burnt that Dr Thomas informed Ponzi that her position was desperate, as gangrene could set in at any time (P/75/53).

(23) From here, Ponzi moved to the cattle and cotton town of Wichita Falls, Texas, which was 'owned' by Joe Kemp and Frank Kell (P/75/56).

(24) During this very same year, Ponzi met his beloved Rose Maria Gnecco, and they were married on 4th February 1918 (P/75/78).

(25) Shortly after the collapse, he was served with a warrant which charged him with stealing 5,387 pounds of cheese valued at 45 cents a pound (P/75/86).

(26) Inspired by his truly eventful journey on American soil, he set up – 'Charles Ponzi Export & Import' (P/75/87).

(27) After discovering that postal marketing would cost a nickel per circular for domestic companies, and eight cents for international firms, Ponzi worked out that his production and distribution costs for the magazine would be $35,000, and his income would be $80,000. This would yield a nifty profit for each edition, as well as promote his export and import business – but Ponzi soon ran out of money (P/75/87).

(28) A letter writer from Spain had requested a copy of the 'Trader's Guide' and enclosed with his correspondence was a 'Postal Reply Coupon' (P/75/89).

(29) The Universal Postal Union had been founded in 1874 and, following a meeting of sixty-two nations in Rome in 1906, it was decided that Postal Reply Coupons would make it easier to send mail across national borders (P/75/93).

(30) After consulting with Robert de Masellis, a foreign exchange expert at Fidelity Trust Company, Ponzi discovered that, in certain other European countries, the exchange rates against the American dollar offered even bigger opportunities (P/75/95). At this time, the Austrian

krone had fallen from the equivalent of 20 cents to just a penny (P/75/96).

Chapter 5

(1) Ponzi was still in the dark about the redemption of both Postal Reply Coupons and stamps in return for cash, as well as the availability of coupons in very large quantities, so he had made the fateful decision to contact postal officials back in March of that same year (P/75/120).

(2) He was able to recognise his vulnerable position straight away, in spite of the fact that he was in the right, so he appointed a Securities Exchange client and lawyer, Frank Leveroni, to open settlement talks (P/75/161).

(3) On 4th July 1920, Ponzi appeared on the front page of the Post for the first time, and the headline read "Boston Man Sued For $1 Million" (P/75/159).

(4) Of course, with the staggering interest rates of 50–100% in forty-five to in ninety-days, there was still a constant stream of investors, so it is hardly surprising that in a period of just nine months Ponzi was said to be raking in $1 million a month by July 1920, which would soon be $1 million a week (PS/8/10).

(5) Indeed, Ponzi's financial alchemy was increasing day on day. With his bank accounts bulging, and with no possibility of cashing in Postal Reply Coupons or stamps, he decided he should diversify (PS/8/233). He is said to have invested in businesses that he felt sure would be profitable, such as real estate, unsecured loans to friends, associates and business people but, at the top of his list, Ponzi was determined to gain control of one or more banks (145).

(6) Then, he bought a small tenement house in the west end for the modest sum of $6,000 (PS/8/143). However, when Ponzi eventually turned his attention to banks (PS/8/145).

(7) Ponzi breezed into Hanover Trust as though he owned the place but, in the eyes of some of the staff, the reality of the matter wasn't too far from the truth (PS/8/147).

(8) On 15th July 1920, Hanover Trust completed the sale of a large proportion of its stock to Ponzi for $187,500, effectively giving him control (PS/8/147).

(9) Between them, they decided to appoint a foreign exchange expert, Mr Abbott, from another Boston bank((PS/8/170).

(10) So, on July 23rd, Ponzi hired the publicity professional, William McMasters, a former employee of the Boston Post, to step into his corner (PS/8/174).

(11) However, articles on Sunday 25th and Monday 26th July certainly had a different tone, highlighting the comments of Clarence Walker Barron who had scoffed at Ponzi's scheme (PS/8/238).

(12) "**PUBLIC NOTICE:** *I have made a personal agreement with District Attorney Pelletier to cease receiving funds from the public for investment with the Securities Exchange Co ...*" (PS/8/200).

(13) Thus, Ponzi decided that he would rob a bank to get the assets he needed and, as a member of the executive committee of Hanover Trust, he knew it had at least $5 million 'in liquid' ((PS/8/198).

(14) In order to support his cause, Ponzi now decided to appoint the corrupt but charming lawyer, Dan Coakley, who had 'connections' in high places ((PS/8/202).

(15) Ponzi was even challenged by one reporter on how he cashed the International Reply Coupons, but said that it was a secret he simply would not tell – nor could he tell ((PS/8/216).

(16) By Friday 30th July, still more problems surfaced. Information provided by Thomas G. Patten, the New York Postmaster, was heralded by – 'Extra Coupon Plan Exploded: Postmaster Says Not Enough in the Whole World to Make Fortune Ponzi Claims' ((PS/8/218).

(17) The Post now had what it wanted and, on Monday 2nd August 1920, it declared in its headline: 'PONZI IS HOPELESSLY INSOLVENT' ((PS/8/238).

(18) Ponzi's last hope now was auditor, Edwin Pride, who had been appointed by Boston Federal Prosecutor, Dan Coakley, to audit Ponzi's scheme ((PS/8/236).

(19) However, Barron published a story indicating that the Postal Union had only printed, worldwide, around $200,000 of coupons annually for the three years up to the end of June 1919 (PS/8/238).

(20) Ponzi managed to barter Daniels down from $100,000 to $50,000, and the matter was settled after they both attended the courthouse that day and Daniels withdrew the suit (PS/8/245).

(21) Indeed, wild stories abounded, whilst the authorities floundered, and 'The Boston American' declared soon after that Ponzi had become the most talked about man in the whole of America and Canada (PS/8/238).

(22) Ponzi didn't know that the Post's Montreal correspondent, Herbert Baldwin, had been given his current picture, and was touting it around and asking leading questions (PS/8/256).

(23) Without further ado, Allen ordered Hanover Trust to stop paying cheques drawn on all of Ponzi's accounts and, following mild resistance from Hanover Trust, its principal, Chmielinski, agreed ((PS/8/259). The newsboys now cried "Ponzi Stopped" ((PS/8/263).

(24) His beloved Rose revealed on 12th August that she knew about his prison record when she married him, and she still loved him anyway ((PS/8/278).

(25) The Post's headline now read: "Ponzi Arrested. Admits Now he Can't Pay $3,000,000 Short" (PS/8/284).

(26) However, he ended up spending three months thereafter Allen turned the screws until federal charges could be brought (PS/8/286).

(27) At this time, it was unheard of that someone could face a federal and state court on the same facts so Ponzi refused to cut a deal (PS/8/286).

(28) With Ponzi having thrown the towel in, Allen's anticipated repercussions became reality. Some local banks now collapsed within days, in the proverbial 'pack of cards' scenario (PS/8/295).

(29) Ponzi's scheme had attracted well over 20,000 clients, and they eventually received, after the Securities Exchange's failure, 37.5% of their original investment, but this was paid as late as 1930 (PS/8/298).

(30) He faced further charges for selling soft pardons to known criminal and the authorities were determined to throw the book at him (PS/8/297).

(31) In an abbreviation of his own name, he set up 'Charpon Land Syndicate' offering investors 200% in 60 days based on his fantastically over-estimated ability to sell ten million lots of property around Jacksonville (PS/8/305).

(32) He was described as being the 'most accomplished confidence man since Charles Ponzi' after employees and investors lost billions of dollars when the business collapsed (P/75/1).

(33) "I had given them the best show in their territory since the landing of the Pilgrims. It was easily worth fifteen million bucks to watch me put the thing over (Search-Engine Analytics)."

Chapter 6

(1) After the demoralising austerity suffered during the war years, most westernised nations wholeheartedly embraced the chance of a fresh start (Search-Engine Analytics).

(2) On the back of the cultural surge of the twenties, ex-banker and Vice President to Calvin Coolidge, Charles Gates Dawes, introduced the Dawes' Plan (Search-Engine Analytics).

(3) However, these remedial steps were successful, and inflation was contained at around 0.4% throughout the remainder of the twenties. Farmers were particularly affected during this decade because the fiscal intervention left their production costs very high and forced their sales values down, thereby reducing margins to almost unworkable proportions (Search-Engine Analytics).

(4) But now, these parvenus would be up against seasoned professionals in the finance world 40.

(5) By the late summer of 1928, in fact, the volume of shares traded had increased so dramatically, that this phase of the boom was often referred to as 'stock market fever'. As a result, the Times Industrial Average rose by 35% after new record volumes of shares had been traded by June that year 45 (Search-Engine Analytics).

(6) This rapid increase in the number of market participants caused an escalation in the demand for brokers' loans – or margin 45.

(Glossary) However, if their value dropped to a level which wiped out the broker's margin, and then depleted the client's deposit, a margin call (*) would be made.

(7)   It was against this background, in fact, that investment trusts rapidly gained in popularity (Search-Engine Analytics).

(Glossary) Such was the prestige of certain 1920s investment trusts (*), like the Blue Ridge and Shenandoah Corporations, that the value of their own stock was sometimes much greater than the value of their underlying assets.

(Glossary) In reality, all that some people really wanted during the 1920s was an open position (*) in what they regarded as a winning market.

(8)   But this may be considered a weak excuse for some of the top professionals who were unwittingly caught up in the dire events that eventually unfolded 26.

(9)   Both the industrial and factory production indexes began to decline and, in the aftermath of the war, it seems that America had gained too much economic and industrial ground far too quickly 111.

(10)   America's house building sector also experienced problems during the 1920s and this industry was a hugely important cog in the economy 111.

(11)   With many Americans still in a buoyant mood, there were certainly fears from those in authority that any negative commentary, or direct warning of danger, might be seen as an attempt to undermine stock market confidence 206.

(12)   At this time, banks were borrowing money from the Federal Reserve at a rate of 5%, and re-loaning it to the call market at 12%. This was splendidly described as the best arbitrage game in town (Search-Engine Analytics).

(13)   As a result of the humongous scale of this boom, it has often been assumed that almost every adult in the nation was engaged in speculation, but this notion would be quite misleading 207.

(14)   It was common for values to be 'talked-up' by influential and articulate personalities of the time 63.

(Glossary) Over the next month however the market declined sharply, losing 17% of its value on the first correction (*).

(15) In the six years prior to 1929, the world had seen the Dow Jones industrial average increase fivefold in value, and prices peaked at 381.17 on September 3rd 1929. Over the next month however the market declined sharply, losing 17% of its value on the first correction (*). Following a brief recovery, the downturn quickly resumed, and accelerated into 'Black Thursday's mass sell-off' (Search-Engine Analytics).

(16) They chose Richard Whitney, Vice President of the Exchange, to employ the financial resources at their disposal to place bids for large blocks of shares in certain blue-chip companies, at prices well above the current market (Search-Engine Analytics).

(17) When the markets re-opened on 'Black Monday' – 28th October, 1929 – the frantic sell-off recommenced producing a record loss in the Dow of 13%. The following day, over 16 million shares were traded, a record that was not broken until 1968, which was nearly forty years later (Search-Engine Analytics).

(Glossary) Sadly, this did not prove to be the end of the decline. Following a putative bottom (*) in the markets in November, they attempted to rally over subsequent months, and reached 294.07 on April 30th, 1930.

(18) The markets then embarked on a steep decline which culminated in 1932 when the Dow closed at a low of 41.22 on 8th July. This concluded a financially shattering period in the US stock market, which had experienced a total loss in value from its peak, of 89%. This was the lowest the market had been since the eighteen hundreds but, fortunately, the Dow has never seen these price levels since (Search-Engine Analytics).

(19) This was an ironic twist as many of these same enterprises had been extremely willing to lend money during the boom – yet they were suddenly experiencing frightful liquidity problems (Search-Engine Analytics).

(Glossary) Between 1982 and 1985, derivatives (*) became the new-fangled 'tools of the trade', and these instruments were so called because their value derived from the price movement of an underlying asset, which might be a particular stock, commodity or currency.

(Glossary) The LSE now became a private limited company, which introduced an automated price quotation system to replace the 'open-outcry' (*) method.

(1) As for Barings, it was reported that two thirds of the Bank's profits had come from securities dealing, so their forecasts for 1987 were positive (GFB/96/65).

(2) Throughout the 16th, there were large falls on the DJIA in America, as there were lingering concerns from the previous day about an Iranian missile strike on two oil tankers, one close to Kuwait's Mina Al Ahmadi port (Search-Engine Analytics).

(3) Baring securities under Heath, had used a put option to hedge against a possible fall in the Japanese markets, and made £20 million in the process (GFB/96/85).

(4) This famous old institution had competed for primacy alongside other family-controlled merchant banks such as the highly esteemed Rothschilds, Kleinwort Benson, Hambros and Schroeder (RT/96/2).

(5) According to reports, Nicholas William Leeson had singlehandedly brought about the collapse of Barings Bank and, on Saturday 2nd December 1995, he was sentenced to six and a half years in Tanah Merah Prison in Singapore ((RT/96/1).

(6) The man himself claimed that his unauthorised trading began when he tried to recover a loss of £20,000, incurred by a colleague in Singapore during the spring of 1992 (RT/96/7).

(7) However, during an interview with David Frost in Hochst Prison in Frankfurt, Leeson claimed that by mid 1993, he was almost back at break-even (GFB/96/167).

(8) How he survived for so long remains a mystery. On the eastern trading exchanges, such as SIMEX and Osaka, futures contracts (def.) lasted three months (ATG/96/14).

(9) After all, it transpired that their man in Singapore was responsible for taking the largest losing bet in the history of the Japanese stock market (GFB/96/3), with an exposure to £3 billion's worth of Japanese shares (GFB/96/23).

(10) Leeson himself, in fact, placed the figure at nearly four times this amount (GFB/96).

(Glossary) Within a very short space of time for such an inexperienced dealer, he became their 'star trader', principally by use of arbitrage techniques, also known as 'switching' (*).

(11) By the close of business that day, the Nikkei closed at 17,885 and Leeson is said to have been long 68,039 Nikkei 225 futures contracts, short 26,000 Japanese Government Bonds, and had a mixture of Euro yen and Nikkei option positions open – and no one knew when this market would hit the bottom and start to rally (RT/96/4).

(12) The Barings family originated from the Netherlands and, after a spell in Germany, Johan Baring eventually found his way to London in 1717 (GFB/96/3).

(13) This 1762 enterprise, in fact, provided the bedrock upon which the Barings family were able to expand their operations into other areas and, by 1763, this included banking (GFB/96/3).

(14) In 1848, the Times reported that Barings held such great balances in American money, that their influence in New York was enormous, perhaps equivalent to that in Europe (FT).

(15) It was vital to uphold the enviable reputation of the British banking industry so the Bank of England, as well as Barings' competitors in the City, rallied to support this distinguished old institution. The cost was £17.1 million, which would be around £450 million in today's money (FT).

(16) It was 4:00 pm on Thursday 23rd February, 1995. The Senior Settlements Director from Barings in London, Tony Gamby, visited the office of the Bank's CEO, Peter Norris (ATG/96/17).

(17) When the pit trading session closed, Tony Railton and Simon Jones, Operations Manager for South East Asia, finally managed to sit Leeson

down, but he seemed to be agitated and soon left the meeting (GFB/96/14).

(18) One of the executives, Mary Walz, had already heard the news from Singapore earlier in the day, when she was informed that SIMEX had made a £45 million margin call (ATG/96/19).

(19) Tony Hawes, the Barings' Group Treasurer, had started to unravel the convoluted mess that the rogue trader had left behind, and he was mortified (ATG/96/22).

(20) Inexplicably, it transpired that not a single one of Leeson's losing bets had been hedged and this was a rapidly declining market as a result of the earthquake in Japan (ATG/96/23).

(Glossary) Tony Hawes reported from Singapore that he had discovered that Leeson had been selling options on behalf of Barings in the 88888 account, and there were thousands of them. A vast number of these were 'short straddles' (*).

(21) The BOE was under the control of the Treasury and its senior civil servant, Sir Terry Burns, who had been put in the picture earlier about Barings by Pennant-Rea (ATG/96/38).

(22) It started at 10:00 am and amongst those present was the distinguished looking Andrew Buxton, the Chairman of Barclays, which was then the country's largest bank (ATG/96/47).

(23) A few months after Leeson had been caught, his illegal trading activity was trumped by Toshihide Iguchi in September 1995, who was accused by Daiwa Bank of hiding $1.1 billion in trading losses over a period of, no less than, eleven years (GFB/96).

Chapter 8

(1) A prelude to this was said to be the release of the 'Mosaic Web Browser' in 1993, which made access to the world-wide web possible (1/11pttb).

(2) By 11th September 2001, and for the first time in 26 years, not a single IPO was brought to the market (Search-Engine Analytics).

(3)	By the late summer of 2002, in fact, the NASDAQ had returned to the same 1,250 mark as in 1995 and in October, it reached its low of 1,114.10 (FT).

(4)	The FTSE100 followed a similar path during this era. Just before Christmas in 1995, this index of the UK's top companies had reached 3,658.30 (FT).

(Glossary) Although this 'loss-leader' (*) process could be useful in the short-term, far too many dot-com companies were unable to turn the corner, and move into profitability.

(5)	It is reported that one venture capitalist, Fred Wilson, lost 90% of his net worth when the dot-com bubble burst after being heavily involved in the funding of new companies (wk/4/11).

(6)	Members of the public were still aggressive investors at its very climax and, by the end of 2002, over 100 million people are said to have lost as much as $5 trillion in the stock market (4/6/bm).

(7)	The market capitalisation of a fibre optics company, '360 Networks', reached 13 billion dollars, but it filed for bankruptcy a few months later (Wpa/5/11).

(Glossary) In fact, it had been a preliminary learning exercise to help me get a handle on foreign currency mortgages (*), which had become the 'new news' in the domestic and commercial property markets in the UK.

(Glossary) Alongside these, I kept the trading fund in a sterling account, and drew money from this to purchase other currencies, in lots (*), when there was a buying opportunity.

(Glossary) Currency fluctuations involving the pound had to remain within 6% on either side of the bilateral intervention rate (*), otherwise the local account manager was likely to intercede, as well as there being the possibility of central bank intervention.

(Glossary) Of course, I took the easy way out and continued in the property markets but, at the same time, found a broker who would provide me with an advisory service (*) until I could find my own way around.

(Glossary) From this point, it wasn't long before I developed an exploratory game plan (*), so I put this to the test by conducting paper exercises for a while and looking back at the performance of stocks that would have matched my criteria.

Glossary) I also wanted to be in a position where I could, at least, stop my loss (*) at a certain point if the trade went the wrong way and thereby retain most of my capital.

(Glossary) Now we can move onto other key parts of a company's profile, which often come under the heading – fundamentals (*).

(Glossary) In our quest to locate undervalued stocks, we are now going to learn about the PEG factor (*), and this is where 'the rubber meets the road'. The PEG is simply the Price Earnings Growth.

(Glossary) Anyone who had adopted the PEG (*) strategy during the dot-com boom, would have been unlikely to buy a single share in one of the upstarts.

(Glossary) If you had a stock with a prospective 0.5 PEG factor on your watchlist, you could set up a moving average (MA) cross-over (*) system to optimise the timing of your buy.

Chapter 9

(1) When the dust settled from the collapse, it was eventually estimated that around $3 trillion in asset value had evaporated including, amongst other things – pension money, real estate values, investments and savings 288 Fool's Gold.

(2) In fact, as early as 2004, the FBI warned of a growing epidemic of mortgage fraud, but the need to be more circumspect was largely disregarded by most mortgage providers. search engine analytics.

(Glossary) CDOs became so popular, in fact, that it wasn't long before institutional traders were considered to be outsiders within their own industry if they didn't trade these credit derivatives (*).

(Glossary) With such unfettered enthusiasm in both financial and consumer credit circles, it was only a matter of time before the asset backed securities (*) markets over extended, and then rolled over.

(Glossary) A very large number of these delinquent mortgages (*), in fact, were found to be – 'sub-prime'.

(3) On the other hand, over 400 banks and credit institutions did not survive this financial apocalypse, including the well-known sub-prime mortgage lender, New Century Financial, Countrywide, Lehman Brothers and Bear Stearns. search engine analytics.

(4) It has been reported that nine of America's largest banks eventually had no choice but to sell shares to the Government. After their initial refusal, a 'take it or leave it deal' was tabled in October 2008, which they reluctantly accepted 285 Fool's Gold.

(5) On 30th September 2008, the German, Belgian and Luxemburg governments poured money into Dexia, which, prior to going into the boom, had been one of the financial powerhouses of Europe 281 F/G.

(6) The Irish Government found that it had no choice but to Guarantee the deposits of all its banks, and Iceland went one step further by nationalising its entire banking system 281 F/G.

(7) During the early part of its formation in the late 1990s, banks were hell bent on finding innovative ways to circumvent irritating obstacles, such as the rules imposed by the 1988 Basel Accord, which was overseen by the 'Basel Committee on Banking Supervision' (BCBS) search engine analytics.

(8) The very earliest whispers of distress and fatigue, in fact, emanated from IKB in Germany when it demurely reported a liquidity problem. search engine analytics.

(9) One of the contrarians was Michael Burry who formed Scion Capital back in 2001 search engine analytics.

(10) In order to follow through with his bet, Burry had estimated that Scion would have to commit around \$80 to \$90 million in capital, but he believed that the returns could be somewhere up to 20 – 1 search engine analytics.

(11) "It has been in the interests of money mandarins to convince the public that these issues are too complicated for novices. Through the use of technical jargon, and by hiding reality inside a maze of bewildering procedures, they have caused an understanding of the nature of money to fade from public consciousness. It is generally regarded as beyond the understanding of mere mortal" (P135 CFJI/11).

(12) Alarm bells were well and truly activated when they found that certain CDOs with 'AAA' ratings were made up almost entirely of sub-prime mortgages search engine analytics.

(13) This had exposed a potentially dire situation because, as we have already seen, if delinquent mortgages in the mix reached just 7/8%, the CDO was finished (128/9 Fool's Gold).

(Glossary) To enable them to profit from the inevitable crash, they took a short position (*) in the CDO market, and some took the same position against the stock of certain banks, mortgage lenders and large house builders.

(Glossary) With heads in the sand, many of Wall Street's big players were still buying and keeping the markets high, as they had never considered that a short selling programme (*) of this scale could be initiated without them knowing about it – but how wrong they were.

(Glossary) In reality, a Swap was a kind of insurance policy used to insure against defaults on certain financial instruments (*) – and defaults were now inevitable in the mortgage and bond markets, as they were not just overheating, they were white hot.

(Glossary) The Swap provided a perfect way to be positioned, quietly, on the opposite side of the trade to almost all of those on Wall Street who still had long positions (*) in the mortgage bond markets.

(14) However, Michael Burry departed from Scion Capital straight after, leaving a legacy of 489.34% returns for investors (net of expenses) between November 2000 and June 2008 search engine analytics.

(15) According to the Wall Street Journal on 17th September 2018, John Paulson's hedge fund firm, Paulson and Company, was said to have made $20 billion on their short position between 2007 and 2009, driven by bets against sub-prime mortgage products Wall Street Journal.

(16) To prevent its collapse, the Federal Reserve loaned this global giant $85 billion, and took a 79.9% stake. 279 Fool's Gold.

(17) By September 2008, the International Monetary Fund estimated that the total losses from this catastrophe could possibly reach $1,000 billion 268 Fool's Gold.

(18) Only one trader, Kareem Serageldin of Credit Suisse, was prosecuted. He was sent to prison for 30 months in 2012 search engine analytics.

(19)   In the face of all of this, it is worth noting that JP Morgan emerged as the largest Bank in the world with a market capitalisation in 2009 of $170 billion, and amongst its celebrated advisors were personalities like Al Gore and Tony Blair (291 Fool's Gold).

Chapter10

(1)   To put the scale of Madoff's scam into a meaningful perspective, it has been pointed out by one commentator that his $65 billion loss exceeded, at the time, the combined fortunes of 'Bill Gates, Tiger Woods and Roman Abramovich' (1). search engine analytics.

(2)   The Bank of Credit and Commerce's collapse in 1991, due to its alleged 'extraordinary affairs', gave rise to claims of wildly fluctuating amounts, but it certainly seems that they were also in the tens of billions (2). search engine analytics.

(3)   The term 'hedge fund' had been coined back in 1949 by Alfred Jones (154). search engine analytics.

(4)   He was facing eleven criminal counts, including securities fraud, mail fraud, wire fraud, money laundering, making false statements and perjury. TGTBT/09/1

(5)   Three of Madoff's victims had made statements in front of Judge Chin. George Nierenberg, a filmmaker whose family had lost everything asked why conspiracy charges had not been brought by the Government, which would have thereby opened up an investigation on other suspects such as Madoff's wife, Ruth, sons Andrew and Mark and his brother, Peter. TGTBT/09/3

(6)   As the evidence unfolded, a vast number of investors also discovered that they had been introduced to the same accountancy firm– Sosnik, Bell and Company – who were mentioned over 900 times in a 162-page legal document. TGTBT/09/64

(7)   Financial analyst, Harry Markopolos, had persistently said that Madoff's 'split strike conversion' strategy could not produce the returns claimed by Madoff. TGTBT/09/8

(8)   David Friehling, Madoff's long-standing accountant, was eventually indicted. search engine analytics.

(9)   Then it was Madoff's turn. He said, "When I began my Ponzi Scheme, I believed that I would end it shortly, and I would be able to extricate myself and my clients from this scheme. When I didn't, I always knew that this day would one day come." TGTBT/09/3

(Glossary) The evidence would later reveal that incoming money was placed in a Chase account numbered: 140081703, and that Madoff's illegal scheme had started after just one year's bad results, when Madoff started doubling down (*) to recover the losses. search engine analytics.

(10)   Elie Wiesel, who had survived Hitler's death camps and was a Nobel Peace Prize laureate, was truly appalled at Madoff's fraud. MWTM/09/18

(11)   Bernie was always pressed by his parents to concentrate his mind on ways to make money. MWTM/09/22

(12)   Academically, Bernie was anything but brilliant and, when the collapse of BLMIS became world news, one ex-school chum said that someone else had to be involved as the Madoff could never have gone it alone. MWT/09/40

(13)   One of Bernie's class-mates in the sophomore year at Far Rockaway High School, Jay Portnoy, recalled that the English class had been given a reading assignment, which required the students to read a book of their choice and deliver an oral book-summary to the class. MWTM/09/21

(14)   The first Scout law Bernie promised to uphold was – "A Scout tells the truth." MWTM/09/32

(15)   Ralph Madoff's materialistic credo soon clicked into gear when the fifteen-year-old Bernie let on that two of his schoolmates were making good money between semesters by installing sprinkler systems for new home owners in the suburbs of Nassau County. MWTM/09/43

(16)   Interestingly, on their marriage license, Ralph's occupation was listed as 'Credit' and Sylvia's as 'None' B/2009/274

(17)   Olin's mother had heard whispers that the Madoffs were running some sort of share dealing operation from their home across the street. MWTM/09/28

(18) In fact, Ralph Madoff was immersed in financial difficulties and serious tax problems, and these issues had been long-standing. MWTM/09/28

(19) Bernie didn't feel that this was much of a reception party, so he quickly joined a fraternity known as Sigma Alpha Mu. MWTM/09/47

(20) His room-mate, Marty Schrager, couldn't help but remember a very cute 16-year-old accompanying Bernie during this weekend, and this was Ruth Alpern who would become Bernie's wife in November, 1959. MWTM/09/51

(Glossary) They were so called simply because of the colour of the paper upon which the companies were listed, and their shares were known as 'over the counter stocks' (*).

(Glossary) BLMIS, and just a handful of other brokers, provided services in this niche market, where a firm's brokerage income was usually supplemented by a proprietary trading account (*).

(21) Carl Shapiro was certainly a man of substance, and one of the first clients of BLMIS in the 1960s. TMWSB/09/31

(Glossary) This appealed to Shapiro because he had realised that he could make money by arbitraging (*) the market with quick 'in and out' transactions on price differentials.

(22) By 1969, in fact, the National Association of Securities Dealers made it a rule that all securities sold to clients had to be delivered within five days. TMWSB/09/32

(23) In 1971, the NASDAQ introduced a computerised communications web which was capable of competing against the NYSE and the AMEX, thereby providing cutting edge facilities for a network of broker dealers. TMWSB/09/33

(24) Contrary to popular belief, the Madoffs did not invent the NASDAQ but BLMIS was one of the five broker dealer firms that set it off in the early 1970s. It was Gordon Macklin. TMWSB/09/33

(25) During 1975, the Securities Exchange Commission was now pressed by Congress to introduce a National Market System (NMS) which would improve the efficiency of the market place. TGBT/09/43

(26) This had been established back in 1885 and was hopelessly out of date, but Madoff believed that it had the potential to compete with the NYSE and AMEX. TGBT/09/41

(27) Meanwhile, over at the NASDAQ, the shares of over 3,000 companies were listed on its exchange by 1981 as compared to 2,500 quoted on NYSE and AMEX. TMWSB/09/36

(28) First, Madoff Securities International Limited was opened in London in 1983, and its sole purpose was propriety trading. Next, they hired the formidable Neil Yelsey from Solomon Brothers in 1986, who was an expert in the field of statistical arbitrage. TGBT/09/74

(29) He designed a computer software programme by the name of 'Madoff Integrated Support System' which was built by TCAM Systems Group. TGBT/09/42

(30) By agreement with the other Cincinnati members in 1995, it was decided to move the black-box (*) to Chicago, which was the home of the Chicago Board of Options Exchange. TGBT/09/41

(31) Professor Leon Metzer, who delivered lectures on alternative investment management firms at Columbia and Yale Universities, would eventually say in his congressional testimony that hedge fund registration would not have prevented Madoff's setting up this kind of pyramid scheme network. TGBT/09/96

Chapter 11

(1) In 1992, however, the SEC decided to close their operation down, thereby severing a very productive relationship for all concerned. TGBT/09/56

(2) In 1985, Maurice 'Sonny' Cohn and Alvin Delaire had decided to leave the trading floor at AMEX and, furnished with a large number of contacts, became fund raisers for Madoff. In February that same year, Cohn formed Cohmad Securities with Madoff, and their new enterprise eventually shared office space with BLMIS. TGBT/09/50

(3) Whenever the roller coaster of inflows and out flows of cash swung downward, many of his primary fund raisers would be incentivised to bring in more investment, and some were paid as much as $500,000 a month. TGBT/09/170

(4) This part of the operation was so secretive that the entrance to its offices was cleverly obscured within a dark mahogany wooden wall. search engine analytics.

(5) Under them were Jo Ann Cupri who processed client requests, Eric Reardon who was the first point of contact for clients, and Eric Lipkin who handled the payroll for all the employees TMWSB/09/175.

(6) Instead, he relied on just one IBM AS/400 to silently run his multi-billion-dollar fraud, which only he himself had access to – and this was probably a critical factor in the investigations that were to follow. search engine analytics.

(7) Robert M. Jaffe managed Cohmad's Boston office from 1989, and was said to have earned roughly $100 million in fees and performance related payments during just over a decade. TWOL/11/71.

(8) It was discovered, in fact, that Cohmad had paid out, from the year 2000, no less than $67 million for professional services, and 85% of Cohmad's total investment income had derived from fund raisers. TMWSB/09/69

(Glossary) However, it was later revealed that proxies (*) were in place and it was really Bernie who had the biggest stake.

(9) One fund that charged excessive fees was run by a French aristocrat, and was called Access International Advisors. TMWSB/09/84

(10) The two Italians who ran these funds also collected a huge 5% entrance fee, as well as an annual 1.5% management fee. TMWSB/09/84

(11) The Fairfield Greenwich Group was established in 1983 but, like many asset management firms, it really came into the picture in the mid-nineties. TMWSB/09/83

(12) Incentivised by the fact that Madoff did not take a slice of the fee income, these particular feeder funds would eventually rake in annual payments of $135 million and, by 2004, Fairfield had placed 85% of its assets with Madoff. TMWSB/09/125

(13) Edgar de Picciotto had formed the Geneva based bank, Union Bancaire Privee in 1969. As a result of an extraordinary expansion programme, it had a global presence by the early seventies and, today, this powerhouse has $140.3 billion in assets under its management (Wick).

(Glossary) When he was later asked about the bank's due diligence (*), Picciotto explained that he himself had dealt with this.

(14) This elderly Jewish grandma had first met Madoff in 1990 and, that same year, opened the Eurovaleur Fund which was managed by the well-known Felix Zulauf. TMWSB/09/130

(15) Having borrowed this legacy, Kohn went on to obtain a full banking license for Medici in 2003 by courtesy of the Austrian authorities. Cohn claimed that her returns during the previous decade had averaged 12.01%, but she conveniently failed to explain that the whole of this amount had been invented. TMWSB/09/134

(16) The marketing of hedge funds became big business and eventually extended to the brokerage divisions of a number of Wall Street banks, including the likes Barclays, Bank of America, Bear Sterns and Goldman Sachs. TGBT/09/88

(17) Then, in 1998, news broke that 'Long Term Capital Management' was on the brink of collapse, after taking highly leveraged bets to the tune of $120 billion. TGBT/09/79

(18) The top performing funds around the world included the likes of Renaissance Technologies on Long Island, Citadel in Chicago, Farallon in San Francisco, Julian Roberts' Tiger, Lon Cooperman's Omega, and Highfields in Boston. search engine analytics.

(19) After doing some digging at Fairfield Greenwich in 1998, Ken Nakayama of Deutsche Bank began to wonder how Madoff was really making the returns he claimed. TGBT/09/126.

(Glossary) Madoff's 'split strike conversion strategy', also known as 'reverse conversion', had just about reached its heyday during the middle of the nineties, when option volume (*) peaked, and started to decline.

(20) Picard would later conclude that hedge funds were not about technical indicators, investment strategies or expert advisors (90). Picard's main concern with Madoff was the shabby pieces of paper upon which account information was recorded, as the returns simply did not correlate with market action. TGBT/09/92.

(21) Three years later the big investment bank and insurance conglomerate, Oppenheimer, bought Tremont at $19 a share, not knowing that it was Madoff's phony profits that were behind its remarkable and consistent rise in stature. TGBT/09/100.

(22) It worked and by 11th September 2001, not a single IPO (*) was brought into the marketplace. search engine analytics.

(23) Many of the smaller broker dealers also realised that their ability to make easy money had been negated at the stroke of a legislative pen when, on 9th April 2001, the decimalisation of stock prices was introduced. TMWSB/09/74.

(Glossary) In the preceding system, prices usually ticked (*) in increments of 12.5 cents, with a spread (*) of 25 cents, however, the new system ticked in increments of just one cent with a spread of around two cents. This left broker-dealers very little room to make their usual 'easy money' on the spreads (*), so even though most loathed the new system, they had to keep in stride with the times in order to survive.

(Glossary) Financial instruments known as derivatives (*), and in particular, 'credit default swaps' (*) now began to establish their presence in the marketplace, particularly when the dot.com bear market ended in 2004.

(24) As presented, it would have meant that Madoff's trades accounted for an impossible 82% of all the volume in the S&P 100 Options Index. TMWSB/09/126.

(25) By 2004, hedge funds had become very popular investment vehicles for pension funds, and this is hardly surprising as the likes of Fairfield Sentry had somehow been churning out 12–15% returns, year after year, even in bad markets. TMWSB/09/107.

(Glossary) The explosive action continued into 2006, when some hedge funds did initial public offerings – or IPOs (*).

(26) By now, two trillion dollars had found its way into hedge funds. TWOL/11/156.

(27) They had placed $250 million with the Sentry fund, and they knew that this firm relied on Madoff for its results. TGBT/09/192.

(28) In the most devastating financial crisis ever known, stock markets eventually went down by 47%, and around 75 hedge funds had to be liquidated, whilst others suspended client withdrawals. Sandra Manzke at Tremont Capital now claimed that she was 'disgusted with hedge funds' and declared that she had lost her $280 million fortune with Madoff. TGBT/09/163.

(Glossary) As part of the ploy to pull this off for so long, Madoff had asked a couple of his 17th floor employees to back-test (*) for profitable stock price trends in blue chip companies, so that he could fabricate phony trading records for his clients.

(29) The industry professionals knew that electronic trading on the scale alleged by Madoff, should have left visible footprints, but the likes of Deutsche Bank, Salomon Smith Barney, Goldman-Sachs, Merrill-Lynch and others on the street reported that they couldn't remember seeing any signs of his trades. TGBT/09/93.

(30) The President of Cohmad Securities, Marcia Cohn, would later be sued by the SEC for having ignored many suspicious practices which clearly indicated that Madoff was engaged in fraud. search engine analytics.

Chapter 12

(1) Interestingly, America's new central bank was modelled on the Bank of England, which had been formed well over two centuries earlier. search engine analytics.

(2) But this sequence of problems didn't yield when still more recessions disrupted economic stability in 1975 and 1981. search engine analytics.

(3) "It is fascinating that we cannot find more agreement amongst ourselves on this vital issue. We seem to differ so much on definitions and on, really, an unbiased, frank, honest, correct understanding of how our monetary system really does function." CFJI/Pref.1

(4)   Inferences may have been drawn in the past from the discovery of artefacts such as tally sticks, which suggest that prehistoric accounting records were kept for different modes of trade in the early commodities markets. search engine analytics.

(5)   Croesus introduced a monetary system based on the circulation of gold and silver coins, which later proliferated throughout the whole of ancient Greece. search engine analytics/Encyclopaedia

(6)   Byzantium was renamed Constantinople in 330 AD by its Emperor, Constantine the Great, who introduced a gold coin called the 'solidus' and one in silver named the 'miliarense'. search engine analytics/ Encyclopaedia

(7)   Frederick 2nd (1194–1250), who was also the Holy Roman Emperor from 1152, started to mint gold coins during his Crusades and recovered Jerusalem in 1228. Notably, this was achieved by a negotiated treaty instead of war. search engine analytics/ Encyclopaedia

(8)   The categories of money that emerged, may be defined as follows: CFJI/137/8

(9)   During the 13th century, travellers, pilgrims, wealthy merchants, and moneyed men were able to leave their stashes of coin at a Templar church in one city, and carry 'a letter of credit' to a different Templar refuge, where they could exchange the letter for their money. search engine analytics/Encyclopaedia

(10)   "The first exhilarating effect of this flood of new money was the flush of apparent prosperity, but that was soon followed by raging inflation." CFJI/161

(11)   Newton's account is said to have paved the way for a much-needed benchmark system for monetary control – and this was 'the gold exchange standard'. Royal Mint Archives.

(12)   This established gold as the only standard permissible for redeeming paper money, as the other metals used for this purpose had devalued the exchange mechanism. CFJI/21.

(13)   A very prominent member of the forum was Paul M. Warburg, a partner in Kuhn, Loeb, and Company, who was also the delegate for the Rothschild banking dynasty in England and France. CFJI/6.

(14) "At the point at which the Federal Reserve Act was passed, the number of non-national banks had increased to 71%, holding well-over 54% of the deposits – and the Jekyll Islanders wanted to reverse this trend." CFJI/12.

(15) During the two decades that followed its inception, the Federal Reserve did very little to stem the problems within the financial system, and it presided over the crashes of 1921 and 1929, as well as the Great Depression of 1929–1939. search engine analytics.

(16) This offered a great deal of protection against manipulation, whereas a paper monetary standard meant that currency could be created at will. CFJI/87.

(17) 'But only a couple of months after the presidential mandate, a joint resolution of Congress repealed the 'gold clause' and, for a time at least, the much-needed benchmark monetary system managed to survive in the United States. Investopedia.

(18) In spite of this, the IMF was soon utilised by its custodians as a means through which gold could be eliminated from world finance. CFJI/85

(19) "In the absence of the gold standard, there is no way to protect savings from confiscation through inflation." CFJI/148

(20) "Treasury notes are redeemed with the proceeds of identical notes, which are sold to the public when existing ones become due." Walter Wriston/Citicorp Bank.

(21) "If all bank loans were repaid, no one could have a bank deposit, and there would not be a dollar of coin or currency in circulation. This is a staggering thought. We are completely dependent on commercial Banks. Someone has to borrow every dollar we have in circulation, cash, or credit. If banks create ample synthetic money, we are prosperous; if not, we starve. We are absolutely without a permanent monetary system. When one gets a complete grasp of the picture, the tragic absurdity of our hopeless situation is almost incredible – but there it is." Robert Hemphill/Federal Reserve Bank of Georgia/courtesy G. Edward Griffin.

(22) "Currency cannot be redeemed or exchanged for Treasury gold or any other asset used as backing … so the question of just what assets back Federal Reserve notes has little but bookkeeping significance." CFJI/186

(23) "A pro-International Monetary Fund seminar of eminent economists could not agree on what money is, or how banks create it." The July 20th, 1975, issue of the New York Times published an article entitled 'Money Supply – A Growing Muddle', and it floated the specific question: "What is Money Nowadays?" The Wall Street Journal of 29th August 1975 commented: "The men and women involved in the arcane exercise of watching the money supply aren't exactly sure what the money supply consists of." Wall Street Journal/New York Times.

(24) "Some time ago Mr A. F. Davis mailed a $10 Fed note to the US Treasury Department. In his letter of transmittal, he called attention to the transcription on the bill, which said it was redeemable in 'lawful money', so he then requested that such money be sent to him. In the reply, the Treasury merely sent two $5 bills from a different printing series – bearing a similar promise to pay." CFJI/136.

(25) "When the quantity of money expands without a corresponding increase in the supply of goods, the effect is a reduction in purchasing power of every monetary unit. The relative value of the overall money supply goes down, and this is the classic mechanism for a large increase in inflation." CFJI/142.

(26) 'The siren of speculation has all too often lured otherwise sensible people into financial foolishness', and they reported that this helped to cause no less than eight banking panics between 1863 and 1913, as well as several threats to the national payments system. search engine analytics.

(27) George Washington lamented: "A waggon load of money will scarcely purchase a waggon load of provisions." CFJI/27

(28) "By 1990 in the US, an annual income of $10,000 was required to buy what took only $1,000 in 1914 after around 1,000% inflation had taken its toll." CFJI/20